THE HIDDEN REMNANT

THE
HIDDEN
REMNANT

by Gerald Sykes

HARPER & BROTHERS,

NEW YORK

THE HIDDEN REMNANT

Copyright © 1962 by Gerald Sykes

Printed in the United States of America

FIRST EDITION
M-L
Library of Congress catalog card number: 62–7302

To the institutions which helped this book:

The Bollingen Foundation
The British Broadcasting Corporation
Harper & Brothers
The MacDowell Colony
The New School
The Salzburg Seminar
Yaddo

Contents

Foreword

If the story of Adam and Eve were as simple as it seems, no one would remember it today. It would have been explained—and forgotten. If the fruit they ate meant only what we were told as children to believe it means, the Genesis myth would also have been eaten—by time. Fortunately for its survival, and for our depleted modern symbolic treasury, it has both a juvenile and a mature appeal. It presents the serpent, for the many, as the villain, and it also presents him, for the few, as the hero. When we are young we all long for Eden, and many of us never get over a hopeful expectancy of unearned bliss. But in time a few of us are reconciled to losing it—and may even prefer the adventure of losing it. From antiquity to the present these few have inverted the childish fable and seen the serpent as a symbol of consciousness, a needed Lucifer in darkness. Aware of the need to rely on their own minds, they consciously disobey the first law, ancient and modern, the law which commands acceptance of traditional destiny. They reject authority. In its place they set up their own judgment.

It is a momentous act, far more perilous than it seems, for example, to the carefree, job-assured young college graduate of today who saunters blithely and unwarned into the minefields of knowledge. As we shall see, it is a revolutionary act that must be completed unless it is to destroy the revolutionist. It is an act that is meant to lead to ripeness but usually leads to ruin. In our prosperous society, however, the ruin can be concealed by stock portfolios or favorable newspaper clippings or organizational or matrimonial security. It may come out only during the third cocktail before lunch or the meeting with one's analyst. Nevertheless this ruin is a prime fact of modern American experience, copiously documented by our literature and our clinics, and a source of great reassurance to our foreign enemies, who are aware that psychological decay goes hand in hand with economic disaster. In 1925 this ruin took the prescient form of a poem called *The Hollow Men* and ending, "This is the way the world ends / Not with a bang but a whimper."* In 1961 this ruin took the form of a cover story in *Time* devoted to widespread contemporary evidence of "Guilt & Anxiety." Both the muse and the market place have become alarmed, in the usual order, and each clamors for a reassuring faith.

When a society confers a large number of diplomas that are used as talismans against suffering and thought—unsuccessfully, of course —there is a general retreat to past faiths (of prediploma days) that once worked and may work again. A half-educated mass, no longer young, no longer favored by its cult of youth, finds that it has advanced too far into the unknown. An instinct for self-preservation asserts itself blindly and unintelligently; the members of the mass "regress," as we now say, and if examined closely, they give every evidence of panic. They *demand* faith, secular or religious, in a way that never won it. They *demand* protection against their enemies. In moments of honesty they confess that they have lost the capacity to love and learn and celebrate. In other words, they are helpless. Privately they wish they had never eaten the fruit of the forbidden tree. Publicly they exploit as greedily as possible whatever limited knowledge they have plucked from it.

The half-educated naturally abound in a society that has taken as giant a cultural step as ours. Enlightened, well-wishing, hopeful, prosperous, school-trusting America was stricken inevitably by mass anxiety and mass regression—this, of course, at the very moment when a rival land, only embarked on the first stages of a technological revolution, and therefore not subject as yet to some of its new cares, might well surpass and destroy it. For us, the chief price of technology, though there have been many others, is the hidden collapse of millions of well-meaning citizens whose only fault has been to improve their condition without realizing what this meant. Such people are entitled to the understanding that their panic prevents them from giving others, but they do not often get it. Instead, they are dismissed as hapless parvenus or laboratory beasts. Such people are a much more important social problem than any of the oppressed minorities who are now eagerly joining their ranks and compounding their confusion.

* The Notes beginning on p. 231 provide more detailed information about works referred to in this book.

Here, however, we are concerned with the self-reliant few who have been able to leave Eden without regrets. Only a handful of revolutionists who have known how to complete their private revolution will ever be able to lead those who failed to—that is, the vast majority of our educated class today. A considerable portion of this book will explore the reasons why these successful revolutionists are so few in number, what conditions have brought them into existence, and above all what is demanded of them for their continued existence. It is a complex demand, made by a complex time, and its description, collected from some of our most adventurous minds, throws a new light on the predicament of the self-reliant few.

In this book they are called the Remnant. The word was first used by Isaiah, who speaks of "a very small remnant" without whom Israel would have been destroyed. Plato also speaks of "a very small remnant" that honestly seeks wisdom. The word has been revived in relatively recent times, as if in response to a growing need, by Matthew Arnold in a lecture given, significantly, in New York, and by William Butler Yeats in his journals. Here the word is used in the sense of being required by a more acute and a more general cultural crisis than those rather protected men had to face. The Remnant today is confronted by facts as nakedly brutal, and many times as mystifying, as any to be found in Isaiah. The Remnant can no longer be restricted to any single class of prophets or priests—nor to their modern equivalents among artists, scientists, scholars, or professional men. Statesmen and businessmen may qualify, for example, despite their greater exposure to the truth-inhibiting populace; and women are barred no longer from the unseen tabernacle. (Whoever would restrict the Remnant to his own kind would merely reveal his own shakiness.) On the other hand, this sort of polite, democratic inclusiveness means little, since the demands being made upon the Remnant are such that it may fail to come sufficiently into being. All walks of life are called, but few of any kind can be chosen. The requirements are so severe and so many-sided.

These requirements are defined and illustrated in the course of the ensuing "lay analysis" of modern psychology, which might also be called a consumer's research report on psychoanalysis. The depth of the Remnant's problems led me inescapably to the depth psychologists, some previous acquaintance with whom also helped to shape my conception of the Remnant. The question I have asked them is: "What do you still have to say to our most resourceful and our most

determined minds?" For in the course of this work I have made a
discovery: Many of the less important finds of the psychologists are
already in the clinics, while their more important finds are of a
quality that can be understood and used only by the very intelligent.
(The half-educated they merely confuse further or fill with ignorant
hubris.) Yet their best work has failed to reach our best minds, all
too often, because a well-known "professional deformity" has put
it into too narrow a context. In spite of their extraordinary verbal
skills, Freud, Jung, Adler, and their colleagues have not spoken the
language of their best potential readers.

Valuable ideas, sometimes literally life-saving ideas, have therefore
failed to get through to the audience meant to receive them—at
the very moment when psychology is being downgraded by that
audience, through unawareness of its real contribution. There has
been a breakdown of communication on a disastrous scale, and no
attempt at *la haute vulgarisation* will help it. On the contrary, all
vulgar modes of thought are especially dubious here. The interpreter
must address himself to our best minds.

The historic example of the old Remnant, and the possibility of
a new one—these are the interpreter's allies. Once psychology is laid
before truly intelligent eyes, such as a Remnant can be expected to
possess, it is both stripped of its pretensions and given its rightful
due. For example, no modern theories of the mind, however "revolutionary," are quite as original as they are popularly thought to be.
Psychology owes many debts to antiquity—and to the more recent
past as well. Sometimes its discoveries are mere restatements of the
formerly obvious—for instance, some sexual observations—that had
been obscured by Victorian genteelisms. A knowledge of its world-
wide genealogy is part of the awareness needed to transform a rather
raw and ungainly science into the wise art of living it was meant
to be. On the other hand, academic insistence on these earlier
sources must not be permitted to rob it of its dynamic capacity to
lead one to a radical encounter with oneself (which needs the shock
of revelation) or to throw a brilliantly new light on the mythologies
of the past. It may not have told us anything unfamiliar about the
nature of good and evil, but its elucidation of the mechanics of
regression and the difficulties of integration is marvelously fresh and
tonic—to those who can take advantage of it. It has gone further
into the feminine part of man and the masculine part of woman
than we have ever gone before. It has told us with new authority

when human beings are like one another, and when they are not. And how they can change, and how they cannot.

But this is getting ahead of a story that is surely as dramatic, as intimate, as misunderstood, as significant as any of our times. A story that I have tried to tell as much for others as for Americans, though it seems more specifically addressed to my fellow countrymen. It attempts to describe a situation that is so intricately involved with science, politics, philosophy, art, literature, education, and religion that to ignore it, as it has become increasingly fashionable to do, or to see it with a specialist's squint, would be distinctly more pleasant—for everyone except the reader. When that reader is the best possible reader, he is entitled to a boldness commensurate to a pioneering task. He will be lenient when it falls short of its objective. He will understand why no attempt has been made at completeness, which would have been impossible as well as tedious; why the aim here, instead, is at centrality, at portraiture, at present-day relevance. Quite legitimately he wants to see the forest, not the trees, especially when it is *this* primordial forest, *these* long-sunless trees. Psychology needs pruning. My clippers have been provided by the Remnant.

This story acquires more meaning and more beauty when it is addressed, not to man's averageness but to his highest capabilities. The Remnant gives psychology a new and much-needed norm. In this picture of the forbidden tree the focus is not on those who should never go near it but on those who can climb it, eat the prohibited fruit, and yet come down in a state of grace. They are *not* crippled or disfigured or hollowed by it. On the contrary, it enables them to carry their burdens, and those of others, with skill. It is, however, a rare accomplishment, and if too few bring it off, then our whole experiment in mass education will fail.

The Remnant is democracy's overlooked hope.

I

The Certainty
of Miseducation

1

Faust Is a Boy

The task that confronts the Remnant is best introduced by a single segment of it which is certainly on everyone's mind today. The whole world knows that we Americans have the highest living standard, and that we owe it to our superlative capacity to extract tangible benefits from what were once only the unrealized dreams of Europe's pure science. We are practical. We make science work. Others may have provided the blueprints for it, but we *built* the most famous plumbing in the world. While others thought out the theories of nuclear physics, we *built* the first atomic bomb.

The American scientist is therefore in a favored position. We all want more power, and he is the key to it. There cannot be an increase of military strength or economic abundance or physical comfort without his co-operation. He is so irreplaceable that he has been granted an old secret wish, which has been to get rid of the dark "Faustian image" that once encumbered his magical trade. By a public relations maneuver unknown to his predecessors he has replaced the image of Faust with a symbol of boyish innocence. He doesn't really mean any harm; there is nothing sinister about him; he is just a good fellow like everybody else. An image of innocence has been constructed out of modest salaries, the reek of acids, anti-narcissistic steadiness, white smocks, gardening hobbies, a preference for pipes and baseball and hearty laughter. Science is impersonal; it deals only in facts. There is no need to look at a scientist closely, as you might have to at an artist. The scientist doesn't count; only his work does.

And yet the new image has not proved universally convincing. An eminent philosopher speaks of the "disastrous oversights of the

2

scientist," while a historian finds a prime motive of scientists to be
"fear of facing life." A journalist studies the men who created the
atomic bomb and gives a picture of narrowly overspecialized mental
brilliance which leads to unprecedented destruction for the world,
the threat of total destruction, and a slow awakening among the
scientists to their own responsibility for it. Their previous ignorance
of their own mental processes, and of their role in history, calls for
interpretation. And so we hear an eminent psychologist saying:

> No one will maintain that the atomic physicists are a pack of criminals
> because it is to their efforts that we owe that peculiar flower of human
> ingenuity, the hydrogen bomb. The vast amount of intellectual work that
> went into the development of nuclear physics was put forth by men who de-
> voted themselves to their task with the greatest exertions and self-sacrifice
> and whose moral achievement could just as easily have earned them the
> merit of inventing something useful and beneficial to humanity. But even
> though the first step along the road to a momentous invention may be
> the outcome of a conscious decision, here, as everywhere, the spontane-
> ous idea—the hunch or intuition—plays an important part. So it is not
> the conscious effort alone that is responsible for the result; somehow or
> other the unconscious, with its barely discernible goals and intentions,
> has its finger in the pie. If it puts a weapon in your hand, it is aiming at
> some kind of violence.

I must confess here to a personal prejudice: I prefer the kind of
scientist willing to listen to the psychologist, willing to examine
himself for any unconscious tendencies toward violence. It is *not*
reassuring to encounter so much power united to so much self-
ignorance. I agree that "we are faced with the problem of the moral
backwardness which has failed to keep pace with our scientific,
technical and social accomplishments."

But I do not think that many scientists will accept this kind of
discipline. Old habits will prevail, I fear, habits of passing on such
problems to others "qualified to deal with them," of hopeful belief
that our present legal control of the individual is enough to prevent
disaster. Scientists will not often impose any new moral burdens on
themselves, but they *will* seek to impose them on politicians and on
the public. They have already done so. And after all, in the circumstances, isn't it all that can be reasonably expected of them? The
bomb is now a fact. Whatever the complex motivations that produced it, the problem is how to control it. Only politicians can do
that.

The would-be boyish mind is speaking again. Responsibility is being ducked. And late at night, to put himself to sleep, the scientist can always turn to Roderick Seidenberg's *Post-Historic Man*. Once upon a time man lived only by his instincts, like an animal, and so there was no history. Then his mind began to interfere with his sleep, and as a result he perceived a discrepancy between instinct and intelligence, with the result that religion, art, history, and criticism came into being. They, however, were only a temporary instrument of his real gift, which is for *organization*. (He is really an ant, not a man.) We have now entered a new age in which all "human" values, which still mean so much to our culture lovers, are doomed by the momentum that our gift for *organization* has obtained, and in time the new order of communism *and* capitalism will take over completely, and the discoveries of the mystics, poets, and myth-makers will disappear and be forgotten. It will take quite a while, however, and in the meantime the more "creative" part of our population will suffer unendurably in a losing battle with the pismires, who are crawling all over him. Good night, sleep well!

It is rather a routine lullaby by now, and scientists do sleep after hearing it, all except a few. Those few have been registering some objections lately. They find a suspicious element of *enjoyment* in a refrain of despair that was first sung by Spengler. Can the singer *prefer* the predicted extinction of the individual, which would mean less strain on himself? Is he ready for anything rather than self-realization? The intoxications of prospective suicide are many.

Germany has provided some fairly memorable instances of this reckless state of mind, under conditions that may be in the process of being approximated here in America. These conditions were: overprivileged status for the scientist; reference of all difficult moral problems to the state; almost complete urbanization of the scientist; contempt for anything short of maximum efficiency; contempt for any language that exceeds technical limitations; above all, a preference for knowledge acquired outside a context of being. Knowledge without humiliations, knowledge that compensates for hidden emotional failures—such is the real Faustian arrogance that brings on serious psychiatric disorder. It produces and is produced by "green" people, in the sense that they are like unseasoned wood; people who have made too much of a cultural leap from rough pursuits to pursuits that require balance and art; people who might easily collapse if their external security, on which they heavily depend, were put in jeopardy. Or as we have been calling them, half-educated people who want the pleasures of the apple without the sternness of its lessons.

The innocent mask can conceal all this from the scientist himself. That is the American twist to the medieval plot; Faust is really a boy at heart. He wants to do good. He wants to be patted on the back—loved. His deal with Mephistopheles didn't really take place, because Mephistopheles (evil) doesn't exist.

Remarkable shrewdness accompanies this curious self-delusion: sly "appeal to the maternal instinct," as a psychologist has called it, through helplessness; detestation of equal encounter with women, who can knock any intellectual conviction askew; preference for the kind of woman willing to be a good sport; frequent sexual impotence; smart patter about homosexuality; astonishing ability, in the midst of intricate mathematical calculations, to turn on the adolescent charm. It is a syndrome that has become distinctly familiar. Outside a privileged circle, its appeal is on the wane. Its ability to produce valuable ideas has sharply dropped. Its present esteem therefore seems due for curtailment, but only after a very grave disaster to which it will have generously contributed.

Perhaps this example, which touches briefly on a certain blindness in some of our most gifted and important human beings, will indicate why a Remnant must question its own unconscious mental processes in a way that these scientists never do. Perhaps also a new use for the psychologists has been indicated—for those willing to do most of the work.

2

The Price of Technology

One trait is outstanding in the scientist (or any other person) who *will not* examine his unconscious motivations. Such a person refuses to be vulnerable. He cannot lay himself open to a genuine "examination of conscience," because he is afraid of what he might find; it might wound his self-esteem, or demand the revolution he is refusing. Naturally, behind his armor his anxieties proliferate, while less and less of the outside world gets through to him.

Vulnerability, and we shall soon be seeing why, is a predominant trait of the Remnant. It is indeed the beginning of wisdom and of knowledge with grace. A member of the Remnant *listens*. He is ready to see with "the innocent eye." He is open to new experience. If he is a man of action, he is ready for thought. If he is a man of thought, he is ready for action. All this means that he is willing to be wounded, or to be temporarily ineffective and insecure. He faces his own evil. He is willing to kill off an old portion of himself, the instant he notices his attachment to it. He accepts the pain of continual self-transcendence. He accepts his own skin, his own mind, his own place in a historic order. (This does not mean that his social position may not change; almost invariably, because of his talents, it does, bringing a greater need for self-conquest.) He hunts out obscure ancestral legacies of mind, as prime obstacles to consciousness. And he realizes that his vulnerability means estrangement from his group, a harder struggle for recognizable self-fulfillment, considerably delayed recognition, and, sometimes, no recognition at all. (Who, except one subordinate and the audience, recognizes the high consciousness achieved by an obscure Danish prince in

Shakespeare's best-known play?) Vulnerability must be its own reward.

This, together with the striking fact that there is no vulnerability in the boy Fausts, should be enough to serve as a preliminary definition of the kind of behavior required of the Remnant. There will be more definitions, exact and also exacting, but there are some kinds of understanding that definition may actually impede for a time, and it is such understanding that I want to mark now as more important than precision. Precision is always important, but human needs change rapidly; within a generation we have already passed beyond the time when a poet said provocatively, "The spirit killeth, the letter giveth life." The reign of the letter has been necessary and good, to correct the earlier excesses of the spirit, and it still decrees the main ingredients of an honest style, but it too has bred excesses. We can now hide behind it as well as a more venerable shield. Usually it goes by the name of a scholarly "discipline." When it takes the name of a science it can be the new obscurantism, almost as bad as the old. So we must come out from behind it and decline its tough-minded consolations, if we would find that vulnerability to experience in which alone lies awareness and, finally, strength.

A few people grow their muscles where their injuries were. Only through the admission of disaster can they become free. If it is true, as another poet said at about the same time, that ours "is essentially a tragic age, so we refuse to take it tragically," then plainly the first step toward health would be to seek out all the reasons for a refusal that is also a refusal of our greatest dignity and our greatest strength.

The psychologists are better qualified than any others of our time to aid us in this study. Through daily immersion in disaster, usually unfaced, unused disaster, they have come to be our best counselors in the important distinction between those tragedies to which we are entitled and those tragedies to which we are not entitled. If they do not always merit the word "scientific," they do merit the word "experienced." Occasionally they can be called wise. As we shall see, they are as interesting in themselves as in their ideas, which is one reason why there is considerably more stress here on the human genesis of their ideas than the reader will find anywhere else. A more significant reason is that here they are described with one kind of measurement in mind: how much clarity can they bring to the most discriminating readers of our day? This book seeks to pre-

sent what it considers the most exciting intellectual drama of our
day in a manner that will hold and satisfy our most exacting
audience.

It therefore begins with no routine examination of the origins of
modern psychology. Those will come along in due time, but now
the story must be seen concretely from the point of view of a highly
critical audience, which means that its relevance comes first. A
routine examination of origins, in the style of a university thesis,
might gratify a pedantic or a filial impulse but no more. Certainly
it would not rescue psychology from the jargon that puts another
barrier between it and its best readers. A better start, I believe, one
that would help to make the story real from the beginning, would
proceed from something that can be observed everywhere today.
That something is the effect of a lucrative and liberating technology
upon the behavior of even our most independent citizens. All
readers of these words enjoy mechanical advantages that none of
their ancestors enjoyed before them. Even if our inventiveness had
never gone further than the steam engine, our common habits and
thoughts would have been transformed more vividly than any previous contrivance had been able to effect. As it is, we have undergone one technical revolution after another; our untiring ingenuity
is such that we now sometimes doubt our ability, because of the
boy Fausts, to survive it; and meanwhile, a decidedly minor portion
of our scientific energy has gone into studying the strain that these
achievements have brought along with them. Modern psychology
is an improvised collective response to a slowly recognized collective
danger.

However irregular this approach, it is historically the truest one.
For the hard-pressed Remnant it is also the most useful one. It will
not take long to explain my meaning, which is addressed above all
to those people who have begun to recognize the human cost of our
great industrial advances and would like to know what the psychologists have done to help us meet it.

The mere mention of "psychology" still raises objections. Some
people have only to hear the word to respond with an impatient
question that has grown bolder of late, as psychology's original prestige has diminished: "Why bother about it?" The question originates in an ancient fear: "Don't eat the fruit of the forbidden tree,
it can only get you into trouble!" Such people long for less critical
centuries when psychology was implicit, so deeply rooted in religion,

folklore or way of life that to isolate it, to make a special study of it, would have been not only irreverent and dangerous but unnecessary.

Others have better-informed objections. Once they read everything they could get their hands on about psychology, but now it no longer arouses the interest that it did when it was still new and startling. Even when they despise a journalistic attitude toward other subjects, such people have taken a city editor's view of this one—and passed on to more timely intellectual events, now that Freud, Jung, and Adler are no longer news. Their question has become: "Why bother about it any more?"

Still others have had some disillusioning encounter with practitioners of psychology. Their question is: "When is it going to get better people?"

The answer to all three questions, I believe, is that no one asks them, no one takes either a traditional or a journalistic or a disillusioned attitude toward psychology unless he assents to his own moral destruction. The psychologists have raised fundamental questions—many more than they are generally credited with—that demand constant consideration. If practitioners do not put these questions well, then we must do their work for them. Even our ablest artists and thinkers, as we shall see, have evaded some of these questions. We know less about ourselves than about any other portion of society, and our lack of self-knowledge is now our most acute social problem. But psychology is also a necessary bridge to that personal metaphysics that each individual, even if he has a traditional faith, must continuously reforge for himself, unless he is to be defeated by forces that have been released by our otherwise benevolent technology. We are confronted by a specter that cannot be banished by waving a sacred text or a newspaper or an unworthy practitioner's bill at it. And this because we live today.

We Americans are citizens of the country that has been most fully exposed to the effect of technology on man. We dwell in an Eden that rings with the music of the pneumatic drill and is decorated with oil derricks. In the account book of history this single fact may outweigh all others. Older nations, especially those in Western Europe, have inherited ancestral bulkheads against mechanization—habit, ceremony, eccentricity, laziness, prudence—that the United States has lacked, not only because of our more recent origins but because of our eagerness to be instruments of progress, our fervent belief in modernity. That belief, together with our great natural advantages, has led to our emergence as a great world power in a very short time. Now some of us are adding up the price, in our own lives, of our astonishing economic and military advance. Are we as fortunate as we seem?

If there is any subject on which the Remnant can speak with some authority, it is this one. More than any exploited workers or any persecuted minority, they have paid the price of our prosperity. They have had to live with the specter that everyone else waves away. They have been waved away too. They have known what it is to live under the dead hand of the future, the unexamined confidence that education will someday do away with this and all our other problems. And, except when they have been rewarded in one way or another for keeping quiet, thereby severing their connection with the Remnant, they have had few of the benefits of our new national wealth. On the contrary, with its genius for functional typecasting it has tried to reduce them to the level of décor, entertainment or idea men.

Few subjects are more apropos, even in Western Europe, protected, superior Western Europe, where the old humanities still prevail—and are departing fast. The so-called Americanization of Europe—really its "technicization"—symbolized by le hot dog veritable and the ubiquity of jazz (that search for ecstasy as a relief from efficiency) has been beating night and day against those traditional bulkheads. It may be a hidden source of anti-Americanism. Europeans are beginning to realize that they are really in the same boat with us, not only economically and militarily but intellectually. It is a bitter pill for them to swallow: that we have preceded them in some nonmaterial aspects of the modern experience.

The minority of Americans who have paid the real price of our technical splurge have been rewarded with a new kind of understanding. This understanding might be compared to an antibody that immunizes against a common disease. More than anyone else they appreciate the additional mental disinfectants that the psychologists (usually Europeans) have given them. Involved in a life-and-death struggle of Zhivagoan proportions, though not yet threatened with the bodily extermination that Pasternak's hero feared, they cannot afford the affectation of boredom with which so many European intellectuals have turned away from the psychologists.

Much publicity has been given the psychiatric help required by

Americans. Not long ago a fund-raising poster in the New York subways shouted, "One Out of Every Ten Americans Is Emotionally Disturbed," with the implication that this disturbance has reached the point of insanity. Other statistics have been equally dramatic. Abundant evidence has come from mental hospitals that intense psychiatric need follows swiftly upon intense industrialization. If this is true, then history is already crying "Next!" with an unpleasant leer to other peoples in other parts of the world, and we have merely pioneered—or guinea-pigged—an endurance test of mechanization's effect upon man. Apparently Freud had this strain upon our instincts in mind when he said: "America is the most grandiose experiment the world has seen, but I am afraid it is not going to be a success."

Not many Americans share his pessimism—or could afford to in public, even if they felt it. Our protestant minority, however, knows what he meant, and much of its best literature is a variation or an anticipation of the same theme. Now this minority begins to see that the rest of the world, according to its separate customs and sometimes while full of anti-American scorn, may be about to imitate us, internally as well as externally. If any single fact emerges from the world's front pages, it is that we Americans are simply the vanguard of an experiment that all mankind must now pass through, since all mankind has plainly declared for the same kind of material advantages that we have. The rest of the world possesses, or soon will possess, the power to obtain them, whatever the cost in "decadence." Future complications are nothing to the citizen of a backward country, compared with an empty stomach or a child dying of cholera. And advanced countries will not be content until they have just as many automobiles, refrigerators, antibiotics, nuclear submarines as we do.

In such circumstances the old humanities, or what is left of them, are bound to be put to flight, until much consciousness and much experience can organize new ones. Gabriel Marcel has already written a book on *The Decline of Wisdom*. Wisdom is now, he says, regarded as an obstacle to progress. If ever there is a vigorous revival of wisdom, it will probably begin in the United States, if only because American progress was first and more headlong. Such a revival will be primarily a handiwork of a conscious minority, yet to make its presence felt but already deceived by neither ecclesiastical nor political nor aesthetic substitutes for personally achieved clarity. This minority will have lived with the gadget long enough to know that it is a passion that must be gratified, that it has to become universal before it can be humanized, that meanwhile there must be an antispiritual interregnum during which all tributes to the spirit are courtesy titles. The apathy that hangs everywhere today over the world of ideas is not an accident. Who will listen to ideas when he is rushing to the supermarket, the doctor's magic needle, the television clearance sale, the nuclear policy debate? If ever a hard road lay before a group of people, it lies before the minority that cannot live without ideas.

When they are made aware of the specific aid that has been given them by our psychologists, as one of modernity's few compensations to a Remnant, their intelligence will not permit them to reject it. The psychologists' contribution comes to them, it is true, usually unlabeled as such; more often it wears medical tags and seems meant for the padded cell or the severe case which can barely go out in public; and yet this contribution is also available for nonclinical purposes. It is one of the intentions of this book to make it still more available, to remove the medical tags and replace them with more humane ones.

What have the psychologists to say to the Remnant? It is a question that needs some clarification before it can be considered.

First of all, who are the psychologists? They are men who call themselves scientists because they make a claim to objectivity about the most subjective of subjects. They seek laws that will apply to everyone. It is a heroic claim. No sooner do we begin to regard them as scientists, however, than we find that they are men trying to understand the nature of man, men subject to the same limitations as other men, men influenced bewilderingly by differing backgrounds, temperaments, times. It is therefore unprofitable to debate, as so many have done, whether or not their contributions are scientific in a strict sense of the word. It is more to the point to discover and try to understand the symbols—each torn as much from their own flesh and blood as from their patients'—that they have given us in their quest of elusive universals. For whether or not they found laws, they did find symbols, magnificent symbols that our most alert minds began to employ almost as soon as they were in print.

The psychologists raided ancient mythologies, chiefly the Greek, to erect a new Olympus in our minds. In their search for the unconscious "projections" that created the original pantheon, they set up a new pantheon. It, too, must be decoded now by those who would create a viable new mythology, a truth that the most critical mind can accept and use.

Because of the medical problems with which they are associated, little is really known of the symbols that the psychologists originated, the insights they have provided into love, marriage, religion, ethics, politics, art, education. Far too often we believe we already know their new language. This is a self-deception. The new language requires a leisureliness of absorption, an absorption through more than the mind, that present-day conditions make all but impossible. As yet there are no masters of the comparative psychology that we need—or the new art of living it might lead to. The Remnant will have to produce them.

Put in this broader perspective, the psychologists are happily shorn of their overstatements. A recurrent note of paternal omniscience, such as has been detected in their writings, meant self-indulgence or the humoring of patients, or the introduction of huckster methods where they had no place. The same is true of the bitter factional disputes of various schools, so often marked by the mutual tolerance of rug dealers. Once psychology is seen as a collective response to a collective danger, the petty wrangle over screen credits is forgotten, while we settle down to a close study of the film itself, which has much to tell us of ourselves and our neighbors. The psychologists are then put properly to work.

When we see them thus, calmly and without partisanship—a heroic demand, as we shall see, to make on ourselves—we may be inclined to regard them less as lawgivers or healers than as a new kind of difficult and obscure poet, writing a new kind of group legend that requires continual reinterpretation. The marrow to which they penetrate will never fully be *explained* to a free imagination, but it can be conveyed by inspired, empirical images. The psychologists frequently give us such images. Only the half-educated will not rejoice. None of us knows nearly well enough what he wants to know about himself, if only for reasons of competition. Some people actually enjoy self-knowledge, however bitter, for its own sake. For practical reasons of keeping the ship of state afloat it is also advisable. Sociologists point out daily that our society has reduced to a minimum the verbal agreed-upons that make civilized relations possible, and that each year they seem to grow fewer. They describe a situation which they say in other places and times has been followed by the destruction of millions of human beings. Some of them say that our own situation is still worse, potentially, and that our institutions have failed to understand or correct it. Unless, therefore, we acquiesce in our own destruction, it would seem sensible to draw upon the symbols given us by highly gifted men who addressed themselves specifically to our problems. A few years ago we were confidently intent on the rebuilding of society; now, chastened by the events of our day, a few of us appear to be resigned to the more painful and more modest task of rebuilding ourselves. Such people will know that if order of a lasting kind is ever to be constructed again (it will certainly not just happen) its base must be the self-confrontation of individuals, and individuals who in all likelihood rejected at least some of the order they found at their birth.

This suggests the nature of the Remnant's private "revolution." No task could be more arduous. This must be the real reason why our artists and intellectuals, no less culpably than the boy Fausts, in the main have so noticeably lost heart, why they conduct symposiums on their own "failure of nerve," why they frequently take refuge in institutions that they formerly despised or, quite simply, in honors and money. They have seen how difficult their lonely task is, and they have recoiled from it. They now acquiesce in their own destruction, and their best efforts are bent toward making it as painless as possible. To this end they have perfected the art of ridiculing anyone who would do otherwise, because the mere existence of such a person seems an assault upon themselves.

It is impossible not to sympathize with them, even in their less lovable moments: they have been the victims of so much miseducation. A miseducation, almost wholly unconscious, that has certainly not been confined to our schools—or even to our homes. Its public effect has been suggested by the question, the subtitle of a lecture given recently in several European universities: "Is the American Way of Life Russia's Secret Weapon?"

This miseducation has become such a Gordian knot that many intellectuals see no untying of it before 1984. Despair has become their fraternity pin, their badge of tough-minded honesty. They more than anyone else have assisted the downgrading of the psychologists. By the standards of the psychologists, however, their despair is neither honest nor tough-minded; it is childish self-indulgence. So deep is their dependence on external authority that they would prefer annihilation to taking arms against their internal enemies. They cannot see themselves as soft because they keep so busy. They cannot believe that scholarship, in which they increasingly excel, may be used as an amulet against terror—to dispel dangers by magically *naming* them. They do not perceive the difference between despair and a courageous acceptance of tragedy.

The psychologists have delivered no one from tragedy, in a legitimate use of that word, but they *have* redrawn its boundary lines. It must also be conceded that they were brought up on nineteenth-century optimism, and the longer they lived into our own time the more they doubted their own methods. Even so, when they are considered as a unit, creating a reverberant dialectic of oppositions among themselves, and when they are confronted with their best critics, they give us, as we shall see, a more practical introduction to the strategies of minority survival, ancient and modern, than we can get anywhere else.

3
Serpent Wisdom
for Modern Doves

Since vulnerability is their first requirement, it follows that the Remnant is relatively defenseless. The slightest break with the mores means a chink in one's armor, and a full-scale, conscious break means a full-scale, unprotected flank in a war with pitiless enemies. The first form that this war takes today is political. The individual must relate himself to the group which made him possible. It is therefore appropriate that the Remnant should take stock early of its political position, the hazards thereof, as well as the weapons, sometimes unexpected, which have been put at its disposal.

To attribute an innocent eye to the Remnant is not to suggest an innocent, childlike heart. They must indeed "become as little children," as one of their great leaders counseled, if they are to see clearly and enjoy life as it should be enjoyed; but this can only be achieved after a realistic and prolonged struggle, during which their craftiness is more in evidence. One of the rarest accomplishments is to keep innocence and cunning in oneself, side by side, and in balance, so that one is enabled by the latter to express the former. Usually the innocent want only to be innocent, in complete unawareness of their own evil, and the cunning want only to be cunning, though they appreciate the advantages of an innocent mask. These wiles produce a major political problem.

The psychologists have been of real help here, but their help has generally gone unappreciated because most people's concept of the unconscious is textbookish. If a former football star, broadcasting the description of a game in which a new star is being born, with still greater luster than his own, says when the new star limps to the sidelines, "I do hope his injuries are not minor," the half-educated will howl knowingly. It is a slip of the tongue; the unconscious has popped out; their textbooks have helped them once more to spot the psychopathology of everyday life. The Remnant will also laugh, but hardly with so much satisfaction. It is such a minor manifestation of the unconscious, and there are so many others, such as the inordinate glee of the half-educated, of greater importance. An understanding of the unconscious, on more significant levels, will help in one's survival.

The dark side of modernity first became apparent to everyone through political disasters. After 1914 and 1939 even the most thick-skinned optimist could no longer regard our century as an advance in wisdom or happiness. There were other dates almost equally painful. A dangerous primitivism had appeared in an age of progress. It had been possible to overlook the psychic maladjustments and malnutritions that more quietly coincided with the large-scale industrialization; they were private, they did not get into the news-papers. But wars and dictatorships did. In fact they crowded everything else off the front page. A disillusionment that had begun with a few poets and thinkers became general. The man in the street felt it. Unemployment, blitzkriegs, blockbusters, gas chambers, forced confessions, and hydrogen bombs contributed to the realiza-tion that man's new skills were not leading him to the paradise on earth that he had expected, that he would still prefer to expect.

This is now the most obvious problem of our times. We know that our continuance as a species depends upon greater clarity about it. Yet although this dependence points directly at our psychologists, few readers know that they have written about politics. Even the Remnant is usually ignorant of their books on this subject, and it stands to lose most through this kind of laziness. More fear is ex-pressed each day for the continued existence of the class which it represents. This is a favorite theme of present-day literature. The usual prognosis is bad.

What have the psychologists said about politics? Once again it is unwise to be restricted to a single school. As a unit, creating a valuable crossfire of personal disagreements, these men have most to say. Each of them suffers from professional deformity, but their over-all merit is that their specialty teaches them to look at politics in a new way. "Sound" political training today is usually economic. The more "rational" we are, the more we tend to make the same mistake that the wealthy German industrialist Thyssen made in Hitler's early days. Thyssen contributed a great deal of money to Hitler, at a time when he needed it most, in the belief that he was *buying* him. He thought he could control Hitler. He was mistaken, and he paid for his mistake with his life. If he had understood the psychological forces at work in Hitler and the German people, he would not have made his mistake. Some of the blackest pages in modern history might not have been written.

None of our psychologists would have made Thyssen's mistake. Each of them would have been intent upon a hidden factor that escaped his attention. For instance, in Freud's book *Civilization and Its Discontents*, which among other things applies his insights to communism, not for a moment does he take communism at its face value. Though he wrote the book long before communism had had a chance to disillusion some of its well-wishers, as it did in 1936 at the Moscow Trials, he was quite unimpressed with its claim to be working for a better future and for the brotherhood of man. Instead, he saw it as disregarding a fundamental aggressiveness in man which *must* be satisfied. He said that this aggressiveness takes its most murderous forms when it is nominally, as in communism or Christianity, at the service of a noble doctrine like the brotherhood of man. It is most evil when it preaches the most good. His book, written in 1929, reads like a preview of the Moscow Trials. The enormous self-deception that made possible those trials, with their conscience-free tortures, lies, murders, had all been analyzed before they ever took place. Khrushchev's famous denunciation of Stalin was anticipated by thirty years. This kind of insight is still not encouraged in the Soviet Union. In our country, on the other hand, as we shall see, it has often led disillusioned ex-communists to rush to psychoanalysis with equal fanaticism. It has rarely been used as it should be used.

If Thyssen had read the analysis of the German people that was published in 1936 by Jung in Switzerland, he might have realized what he was getting into. Jung produced an essay entitled *Wotan* in that year which called the Nazis and Hitler by name and said they were a clear indication of national possession by an archaic fury. "We are always convinced," Jung wrote, "that the modern world is a reasonable world . . . I venture the heretical suggestion that the abysmal depth and character of old Wotan explain more of National Socialism than all . . . reasonable factors put together." Through his experiences with German patients who had come to him in Switzerland for psychotherapy Jung said he had reached the conclusion that a great many German people were being possessed by a seemingly defunct German god and were therefore ripe for violence and destruction.

Alfred Adler approached political problems from still another position. Adler's best-known contribution, the concept of the "inferiority complex," has often been used journalistically to explain Hitler, the envious corporal who had also failed as a painter. But for Adler the inferiority complex was inherent in the human condition. "To be a human being," he wrote in *Social Interest*, "means possession of a feeling of inferiority that is constantly pressing on towards its own conquest." So it was not only Hitler who was in danger of overcompensating for a private sense of failure, it is all of us. "All failures," Adler wrote, "are failures because they are lacking in fellow-feeling and social interest. . . . The meaning they give to life is a private meaning. . . . Their goal of success is a goal of mere fictitious personal superiority, and their triumphs have meaning only to themselves." If such a criterion were generally inculcated, and accompanied by a keen, realistic indoctrination in how such failures can pretend to be interested in others, we should all have much less to fear from demagogues. The enlightened public required by democracy would be here. The Remnant would not be called upon to guide democracy toward the intelligence it needs.

The reason an enlightened public is not here, says Erich Fromm, is that the public does not want to be enlightened. In *Escape from Freedom*, written in the United States after the Nazis had compelled him to leave Germany, Fromm analyzed the general fear of enlightenment that made the Nazis possible. He found a widespread fear of freedom that is of course an invitation to dictatorship—and not only among Germans but in modern man. Since the Middle Ages, he says, there has been a steady increase in individualism, with a growing mastery of nature and a growing power to reason. This has also meant, however, a growing sense of isolation and insecurity among people. In our day they have reacted to their fear of private responsibility with a return to herd brutality. This thesis of a compensatory interregnum of ignorance and violence, after much enlightenment and progress, has made a profound im-

pression on those persons who stand to suffer, and indeed have
already suffered, the most from it.

Another American psychologist, this one born in the United
States, William Sheldon, in a variation on these repeated emphases
on unconscious factors, relates recent historical disasters to the
human body. The body, he says, *is* the unconscious. Our twentieth-
century wars he traces to our improved medical methods. Instead
of letting inferior human stock be weeded out by nature or the
Tarpeian Rock, we carefully preserve it. The result is a world population that has quadrupled in little over a century and that desires,
as an inevitable consequence, nothing more than its own violent
destruction. We *had* a pleasant poker game; now there are too many
players and not enough cards to go around; so we want, unconsciously, to have the whole thing stopped. (This helps us to understand the Boy Fausts.) Our earth groans with an oversupply of
"poor protoplasm poorly put together." That is why we have more
delinquency, more nihilism, more wars. Fascism, he says in his book
The Varieties of Temperament, meant the rise of a more aggressive
body-type that, with the decline of Christianity, ousted a gentler
body-type who had ruled over us when we still lived in the shadow
of the Cross. Men with aggressive body structures (and aggressive
minds) always gravitate toward power, unless they are psychologically outwitted by gentler bodies (and gentler minds). The relevance of this to our Remnant is obvious.

Each of these psychologists has his shortcomings, but none of
them would be fooled by the kind of reasoning that causes either
excessive illusions about politics or excessive disillusionment with it
such as characterizes most educated people today. As a unit they
suggest a new science which might be called psychopolitics, the
study of unconscious factors in statecraft. Psychopolitics is in its
infancy, but already it offers a new kind of serpent wisdom to those
whose occupational detachment makes them harmless as doves.

One example will suffice, for the time being, of how it might be
put to use. At this moment a great many foreign critics are saying,
some anxiously, some exultantly: "Why does the U.S.A., which such
a short time ago behaved like a young nation, now behave like an
old and tired one?" Or, as a caustic Frenchman has put it, "The
Americans are the only people who have passed from barbarism to
decadence without ever having been mature."

When confronted with this familiar charge of premature fatigue and decadence, which has been repeated in so many anti-American broadcasts, psychopolitics has an immediate suggestion: genuine truthfulness. What is demanded of persons is also demanded of nations: we must, as we say in our excellent idiom, "come clean." Is there any truth in it? Ruthless analysis will find, as we shall see, that there *is* truth in it. Ruthless analysis will also make a discovery that throws the whole problem into a new perspective. *All* our most serious national ills come from having embarked upon a revolution which is far more than merely political, or even merely social—and from failing to carry it through. We are committed to a task so great and unpredictable, and in many ways so inhuman, that we must rethink its whole conception even while its momentum carries us forward into one surprise (now usually unpleasant) after another. And only those who can complete their own private revolutions can provide effective leadership in such a vast program of reappraisal and redirection. They alone have the required experience. They alone can attain the required perspective.

Psychopolitics will show them that Americans are really far from being as conservative, politically or otherwise, as their actions often indicate. Their sometimes reactionary behavior is part of a natural rhythm of progress and regress. The revolution in which they are caught up is the least dramatizable of revolutions, because it is so advanced and as yet, in a sense, so unhistoric. It is a giant step for which no adequate ideological descriptives exist. It asks more of the boy Fausts and the half-educated than they can perform. It makes no impression on other nations because they have not yet gone through it. It seems to them a local disease. They cannot even imagine it. And we do not know how to tell them about it.

It spares no one. We are all conditioned by it, but perhaps now a few can redefine and reshape it. And reproclaim it. This is a task in which, as we shall see, the resources of psychopolitics are untapped.

4

The Source
of Contemporary Power

One of the first concerns of psychopolitics is mass hysteria. The fact that German mass hysteria became bloodier in our time than any other mass hysteria does not mean that other peoples have not been equally irrational and capable of equally repugnant crimes. This fear is uppermost in any honest mind, which early discovers its own susceptibility to emotional pressure and its own capacity for destruction. We are not afraid of our new weapons; we are afraid of what the human mind, which we know first through our own mind, might do with them. We also know that masses are more easily hypnotized than individuals, that mental infection spreads through fear of loneliness.

Today, when the subject of mass hysteria is raised, the next two words are usually "mass media." We are not in the midst of a shooting war, but we are in the midst of a culture war. The chief battlegrounds of this war are: "Is television bad for children?" "Is canned entertainment making our people too passive?" "Does this passivity lead to neurosis?" "Do we as a people expect too much to be given to us?" The "inner-directed" fight on one side, the "other-directed" on another, and we have yet to hear from the "autonomous," who should know the answers, according to David Riesman, when his "population curve" delivers them to us with a minimum of effort on anyone's part. If, as seems quite unlikely, that happy day ever arrives.

It is more important to think about the mass media than it is to think about Big Brother. Big Brother is already here in our midst, and he works in an advertising agency. If he is to be combatted effectively, we must understand what he has already done to us. The problems of dictatorship are anything but remote.

Not all demagogy is political. Terrifying headlines on page one have made us forget a more insidious manipulation of the mass mind that goes on every day from page two to page two hundred. The misuse of propaganda is not confined to states or parties or power-crazy individuals. Before warring nations competed for the sympathy of neutral nations in 1914, before Bolsheviki and Fascisti made spectacular bids for popular support a few years later, before Nazis outdid them at Nuremberg, before contemporary would-be dictators copied them all, the art of commercial advertising was already a formidable new cultural phenomenon—and undoubtedly contributed many ideas to its bloodier imitators. The adman may not have known that he crashed the Sportspalast, but he did. For that matter, he and his many metamorphoses slowly infiltrated the editorial sections of newspapers and magazines, as well as comic strips, movies, radio programs, television shows, industrial design, the theatre, books, painting, education, psychology, government, philosophy and religion to such an extent that it is now customary to recognize his hand almost everywhere and to raise no eyebrows at all. We are all aware of the fact that in our time no great wealth or power can be attained or retained without a subtle and dynamic understanding of the mind of the common man. That is why the common man receives so much flattery at the same time that laboratories demonstrate, as we shall see, his doubtful educability.

Thoughtful people have known for a long time that the advertising business was a natural and necessary development of technology, that it quite logically reached its most luxuriant growth in the most advanced technology (their own), that its moral influence greatly exceeded its economic function, that it has left a mark upon our people that has been widely discussed and widely condemned abroad. "Anyone who takes the trouble to study the techniques" of picture magazines, writes the sociologist Herbert Marshall McLuhan, ". . . will easily find a dominant pattern composed of sex and technology. Hovering around this pair will usually be found images of hectic speed, mayhem, violence, and sudden death." On the jacket of his book, *The Mechanical Bride*, women's legs in silk stockings are neatly fitted into the cogs of a wheel that causes another wheel to move, as a symbol of the eroticism that McLuhan says is needed to keep the gears of industry turning.

McLuhan's thinking is typical of the kind that the Remnant is beginning to require. He has a sensitive appreciation of modern poetry and painting and of the latest developments in architecture, biology and anthropolgy, yet he has been able to examine Madison Avenue at close hand and to learn some important lessons from it. He has explored the sales subtleties of the copywriter, the curious relationship of the front-page layout of *The New York Times* to Picasso, the conscious mythology of certain cartoons, the shrewd transcendentalism of *The Reader's Digest*, the various perversions of the Bill of Rights, the prefabrication of a movie hero, the vast difference between soap opera and horse opera, the nuances of the new washing machine matriarchy, and a thousand other strange proliferations (with pictures) of a folk culture that, to judge by the magnitude and lustiness of its output, is many times more vigorous than that reflected in Percy's *Reliques*. In a day and a place where "the revolt of the masses" is an accomplished fact, where popular vulgarity is champion by knockout, a trained observer has gone into the most energetic market place of our era, from which similar sensibilities usually recoil in horror, and he has emerged with the embryo of an important idea.

His idea is that we have much to learn from "the modern artist, deluged with the art styles of all times and all places (thanks to archaeology and anthropology) [who] was obliged for mere self-preservation to seek not *a* style but to penetrate to the essence of the art function and process itself." He says that "the outlines of world order are already quite visible to the student of the whirling flood released by industrial technique. And they are to be discerned in the very way the flood operates. Poe's sailor in 'The Maelstrom' saved himself by co-operating with the action of the flood itself." He counsels us to "ignore all the national and local time-trappings of comfort, fashion, prosperity, and utility in order to seize upon the master forms of human responsibility and community. In art this brought about the transformation of the artist from bohemian 'victim' to culture 'hero.' In politics it calls for a proportionate extension of arduous vision."

The commercial demagogy that McLuhan exposes—and tries to utilize—is a natural consequence of large-scale industrialization, which brings, along with its blessings, psychological maladies that other nations besides ourselves are now plainly catching. One has merely to walk the streets of London, Paris, Rome or Berlin, or listen to the broadcasts of Moscow or Peiping, or read the newspapers of Tokyo, Calcutta or Cairo, to see that this epidemic is international. The United States, as the first nation to be exposed fully to these maladies, is also the first to take minority measures to find a cure for them. The United States is the real vanguard of an experience that all mankind must now pass through; it has had the disease worst and first, and now it is slowly producing remedies against it. Such remedies begin naturally with our most sensitive and imaginative people.

This means, among other things, that the Soviet Union cannot hope much longer to get anyone to believe that under socialism technology will not have essentially the same effect as it has had upon us. Time lag has fostered the dissemination of this rather racist untruth, together with the retention of nineteenth-century slogans, nineteenth-century art, nineteenth-century women's fashions designed to suggest that in Russia an old-fashioned wholesomeness has vanquished a degeneracy to be observed nearly everywhere else. It is a Victorian-dress revival of a messianic "chosen people" myth which expertly joins the reactivated emotional power of newly secularized Christianity to rational plans for a better material life for everyone. These plans, however, do not permit dissent, even about the details of their fulfillment. Criticism must accommodate itself to the functional demands of large-scale political surgery which justifies itself with a complete and omniscient plan for the future reconstruction of man and society. Naturally the Soviet leadership persists in ignoring modern Western psychology, whose theory of the unconscious would—and explicitly does—undermine its dialectic. Just now, in contrast to other phases they have known, the Russians do not want truth, they want strength—and are acquiring it through a butter-knife manipulation of the mass mind that infuriates our admen; it is even more dishonest than their own methods, and it may prove more effective. It does not have to woo the customer, and it rests upon a *mystique* which, however antiquated, seems to appeal to more powerful human impulses than the itch for possession. Our admen had almost forgotten that any such impulses still exist.

By and large, therefore, in spite of all the blood on their hands, the Russians are winning the propaganda war, at least where mechanization still stirs the savage breast. We can only hope to reach those who have been disabused of the illusions it creates, those fellow decadents who realize that anti-Americanism means usually, not the moral fervor or cultural superiority it simulates, but a fairly psychopathic fear of the adjustments that older peoples are going to have to make when they embrace, and are embraced by, the "Americanization" they now desire. After a very short run as Lochinvar we have turned into a horrifying Exhibit A in the case of Culture v. Robotization. Another grim irony: only a highly conscious minority can save us now. They alone have the experience to see the real story of what has happened, and the wit to tell it so that the rest of the world will understand. Even so they will have a hard time; they step on too many toes. And their story is too sure to be re-enacted in the rest of the world. If it passes from analysis into art, it will be tragic art—with few anywhere who do not refuse to take it tragically.

Nevertheless it offers a great role to the Remnant, mobilizing its best talents and rescuing its art from clannishness and its behavior from irresponsibility. The new tyranny of mass emotions, the tyranny of the least common denominator, which can so easily finish off what remains of the democracy it invokes as its justification, provides the Remnant with a social function. It is an austere function, sure to be unpopular, but it may save us as a people. Only a few can descend into the mind of Demos, that perilous source of contemporary power, and emerge from it uncorrupted and reinvigorated. (It is significant that William Faulkner wrote what is generally considered his best novel, *Light in August*, after a stretch in Hollywood.) One thing is certain: even if one's professional style calls for popularly unintelligible mathematics or popularly unintelligible poetry, one can no longer stand aloof from the problems of the populace. To stand aloof has already become far more perilous than to seek to master these problems, as far as that is possible. Like Pirandello's Henry IV, who tried to live as if this were the eleventh century, the secessionist is sure to awake some day and discover that he is "all grey inside, that everything has fallen to pieces, that everything is finished, and he is just arriving, hungry as a wolf, at a banquet which has already been cleared away."

If the Remnant can even slightly perform the Augean labor of cleansing Madison Avenue, next to which the ancient mythical feat of Hercules seems a trifle, it will be not only because its members have turned from victims into heroes but because they have made a modern study of the myth-making process. Only by a clear understanding of the psychology of myth can they free themselves from "national and local time-trappings of comfort, fashion, prosperity, and utility." If our great new cultural weapons are ever to be used well, these few must cut through the topical to the timeless. And here the psychologists can suggest a way.

The redirection of Madison Avenue's power needs the guidance of the new pantheon which waits unused in our minds.

5

The Uproar in Acheron

It is all very well to speak of getting help from the psychologists, but when we actually turn to them, down there in the Acheron that Freud laid claim to in the motto of *The Interpretation of Dreams*, we realize why a trip through the underworld has traditionally required a guide. The distorted, unruly shades that made Dante's descent into the Inferno so harrowing are not without their parallels among the living. Demonic arrogance can be found in present-day clinics. Too large a number of our practitioners provide disturbing examples of the half-educated, presuming to speak above their intellectual and moral station, while others are quite as dangerous in their own way as the boy Fausts. The wealth of a magnificent treasury is not being used as it should be used.

It is astonishing how quickly this young science has stiffened into system. Freud writes of the "system that psychoanalysis was careful not to become," but Freudianism as we know it today contains a systematic and official explanation of every kind of human behavior and presents its explanation in a tone that is fully as dogmatic as that of any church or political party. In a recent centennial volume to honor Freud, Alfred Kazin attributes this trend to contemporary reluctance about "carrying your thoughts beyond the point at which everybody already agrees with you. Nowadays everybody is something of a Freudian, and to many Freudians the truth is in their keeping, the system is complete. But what mattered most to Freud was relentlessly carrying on the revolution of human thought." As much might be said of other schools, which have shown signs that they might be equally rigid if equally successful.

Once the Remnant has appreciated how much it can be helped by the psychologists, it will want to cut through this rigidity. It will become impatient with system, which so often is a bureaucratic defense mechanism of the specialist, and seek to penetrate to useable ideas. It will want these ideas not only for urgent problems of science, government and economics, such as have been sketched in the preceding chapters, but also for equally important problems of love, art, religion, philosophy and education.

The path to these useable ideas is through the personalities of the men who created them. When these ideas are abstracted too quickly, they wilt and die. Seen in their original human context, however, as well as in the context of the present need for them, they have astonishing life.

Unfortunately, shrewd abstraction offers quicker results to lazy minds. Hence there is a sharp difference between popular and unpopular approaches to psychology. Even when they know they can never get it, most people want a precise and authoritative guide among the ambiguities of the inner life. That is why system is so popular—and so arrogant. People demand ready-made, easy-to-understand explanations of their behavior. The lust for power of certain practitioners provides them with these easy answers—and the desired note of authority. A few, however, refuse to give this kind of subservience. A few are sufficiently self-reliant (and realistic) to realize that the new science must have (and no doubt always will have) many dubious coastlines. Exactitude is too much to expect. To believe that the personal equation can ever be removed from psychology is like asking personal guidance from an I.B.M. The frequent hoots of the psychologists at one another—shaky behavior such as one encounters in almost no other science—mean that in their domain there is no certitude. A few actually like it better that way. But not the populace. The populace wants authority. And may get it some day, in politics as well as in science, with even less real voice in the selection of its leaders than it has now.

Fortunately, there has been a growing movement towards comparative psychology. (I do not mean the academic animal studies which that term denotes professionally, but a careful and open-minded comparison of what the most pertinent psychologists have to say to us about our different concerns.) Some years ago it was comparative religion that pointed the way to liberation from ancestral prejudices, and now when we quarrel as pugnaciously over Freud v. Jung as we once did over transubstantiation, we need a similar sense of parallel experience, of common humanity, to deprovincialize us again.

Theoretically, more and more psychologists are agreed on this, and, in their practice, use increasingly eclectic methods, because true healing means being as supple as nature herself. Doctrinal rigidity may be a sop to the practitioner's laziness, but it does not help the patient. And so more books are trying to capsule the different schools.

But a truly useable comparative psychology, such as this book is meant to be, is obliged to venture beyond the close confines of one science. Unless it did so, it would soon become meaningless, except to a few timid students. The quick, intuitive minds of the Remnant would be bored by its prudence—and impatient for a frank discussion of debatable issues, in all their uncontrollable complexity. Let me illustrate this by showing how a brief introductory survey of one of the more notorious aspects of modern psychology—sex—leads naturally and inescapably into questions of history, industry, literature, art, music, politics, sociology, and what the younger generation is thinking about today. And the minds of some readers will undoubtedly range much further than that.

It was the sexual discoveries of modern psychology, as everyone knows, that first brought it to general attention. Some publishers still attribute the usually good sale of books on psychology to the fascinations of sex. This is a superficial interpretation, as we shall see, but it has a heavy-handed, sales-graph persuasiveness. The arrival of our century coincided with the desire of a great many people, who had been recently delivered from many manual tasks and social tabus to become better informed, perhaps more energetic, certainly more outspoken about their erotic activities. This preoccupation may have been a by-product of intensive industrialization, a fearful pursuit of instinctual gratifications that were plainly menaced by the factory whistle (never before so much impotence), or it may have been simply a prerogative of new-found leisure, or a frantic compensation for lost religious faith. Whatever the explanation, it is certainly one of the most widely discussed phenomena of our times— or it was when it seemed newer.

The sexual revolution, which is probably as important an event in contemporary history as any political change of power, struck with its most dramatic impact in those places where puritan morals were most unconsciously entrenched, where Queen Victoria continued to reign from her tomb. It was by and large a metropolis-directed, anti-provincial youth movement which mobilized bright, or sometimes merely lazy, children against stuffy, or sometimes merely inarticulate, parents. It seems to have sprung up more spontaneously than medieval crusaders were ever mobilized against infidels. Ironically, the name most frequently associated with it is that of Sigmund Freud, who, of all people, was one of the farthest from it in personal habits. But this is only one of the many misunderstandings that we encounter in a story that has become encrusted with them because it arouses so much emotion.

The sexual revolution seems to have originated, as far as that word can be used, in England, where factory smoke first smudged man's ancient rapport with his instincts. William Blake was its earliest poet. He could "damn braces, bless relaxes" and ask if "the vig'rous joys of youth" were "ashamed of the light"; he could seek to recreate an uncontaminated Eden of his own, with his naked self as Adam and his naked wife as Eve, in his own back yard, because he had already seen the "marks of weakness, marks of woe," in "England's green and pleasant land." In our own country Walt Whitman carried on this resistance movement in the name of "the body electric"—or in the more scholarly phrase of his admirer William James, "the religion of healthy-mindedness." In both Blake and Whitman the faith of the puritans was replaced by the faith of the anti-puritans, as the shadow of the steel girder darkened across their garden. They had seen the trend of the puritan mind, which lent itself all too readily to a cult of efficiency and an equation of prosperity with virtue, and they reacted with quick poetic insight, the Cockney testily, the Long Islander with a bland optimism that is now one of the chief drags on his influence.

In time this anti-puritan movement, which in our country recruited such writers as Theodore Dreiser and Sherwood Anderson, and was augmented often by European immigrants of talent, had to face the counterattack of tradition, of those American classicists with aristocratic affiliations or sympathies—e.g., Henry James and T. S. Eliot—who put anti-romantic pressure on our egalitarians and our sex rebels to make their peace with tradition and good manners. This battle is still in progress on the pages of our literary reviews. A chief item of the news of the last two decades is that many talented writers of immigrant stock have switched their allegiance from the "democrats" to the "aristocrats," or as one of them—Philip Rahv— has phrased it, from the "redskins" to the "palefaces." A well-worn, if rather incredible, path ran from Stalin to Trotsky to Henry James.

"Causes" became suspect, they inspired too much tired journalism, while the work of art became the one thing worth serious consideration.

So drastic and rapid a change of allegiance, which resembles certain kinds of religious "conversions" where the *only* truth is discovered immediately after another truth, equally sure, has just exploded, will be found, as we go along, to be characteristic of an aggressive psychophysical type. Fortunately, we have much data on this type who predominates in our day. This kind of human being is more often found in the business world than in the arts, but he is now making his presence felt in the latter, and in other arts as well as literature. Later we shall see him among those painters who switched almost overnight from "socially conscious" murals in post offices, full of pistons and oil cans and grim proletarian faces, to image-free abstractions that looked like linoleum. He also appears among composers who once ransacked Methodist hymnals for the right kind of American folk tunes to put in their program music and who now write nothing but sonatas and quartets in the most severe neoclassical style.

All this may seem remote from the sexual revolution. It is not. The energy released by our new mechanical skills has to seek an outlet, whether political, religious, aesthetic or, as seems to be true in the vast majority of cases, in aimless pleasure of the dial-twiddling type. Rarely any longer does this energy remain fixed on a sexual object to the exclusion of everything else; such concentration of purpose came more readily in Krafft-Ebing's day. Thanks to our labor-saving, leisure-creating devices, we are now subject to so many daily pressures that seldom, unless we move in very exalted circles, do we have time for purely erotic obsessions. When they do appear, as in the hero of Vladimir Nabokov's *Lolita*, they wear a velvet jacket and seem to voice an anachronistic cry for a life of single-track passion, however weird or tedious, as opposed to motelized regularity.

And yet, although the conspicuous sexual rebel is obsolescent, he continues to exist as a type, and sometimes, to judge by the Kinsey Report, in the most solid professions. He is that person who cannot find anything in the present-day world that honestly kindles his enthusiasm but sex. In a world gone grey with market reports, time studies, tax regulations and path lab analyses he finds sex to be the one green thing.

Usually, to be this kind of sexual rebel today is to date oneself. The younger generation, as a rule, extinguishes its own sexual rebellion in early marriage and exhausting responsibilities, and goes on from there to what it deems more serious questions. Puritanism can wear a bikini. Sexual liberation is rarely a cause with young people any more, though it may be a major activity. On the contrary, they seem to have made more of a cause of religion, though as yet in no rigorous or impressive way. Perhaps they have had so much specialized information thrown at them and have seen so clearly the interior dismemberment to which it leads in their parents and teachers, that now they no longer want the pieces of a puzzle but some glimpse of a picture into which the pieces will fit. That, at least, is what I think I see in their rather confused answers to the inquiries that are frequently conducted among them by editors and teachers.

In their answers they often seem prematurely middle-aged about theology, monogamy and experimentation of any kind. In fact, that is the standard complaint of the editors and the teachers, who perhaps regard themselves as having been more dashing in their own youth than they really were. Another complaint is made against the younger generation's "silence," which suggests that the editors and teachers have overlooked the strain that this silence conceals, the strain of inheriting a world full of question marks and almost no certitudes at all. They should, of course, get over their "quest for certitude," which is indeed immature and not courageous at all, and they should welcome with open arms their oversize portion of doubt and anxiety, which can stimulate the imagination to prodigies of creative conquest; but to counsel them thus, as so many of our educators do, is the kind of sermon which conceals incapacity. The silent generation will have something to say when it finds its tongue. It will say: "Why didn't you tell me the real story?"

The real story is not simple. The apparent digressions of the present chapter will suggest the discursive manner in which it must be pulled together before it can be told. The sexual revolution, no less than the Industrial Revolution, is only part of the story. No single-minded theory will be of much help. If the story were simple to gather or simple to understand, the Remnant would be a smart, prosperous club off Fifth Avenue with a large waiting list. Actually its members have to get along without that kind of prestige, and their task is harder than it was "by the rivers of Babylon," when they hanged their harps upon the willows and wept.

6
Science and Emotion

The dispassionate calm of scientists is traditional. I too believed in it—until I began to look at scientists scientifically. As a novelist and literary critic, I had taken an amateur's interest in psychology, written a few articles about it, and finally signed a contract with a publisher to do a book about it. Thereafter I met psychologists by the dozen and made the discovery that they were every bit as emotional as anybody else.

They are especially emotional on one subject—"that thing about Freud and Jung," as one of my literary friends had called it while prudently warning me against my project. Not since boyhood quarrels in Kentucky about the relative merits of Lee and Grant had I encountered such polemical intensity. To some people Freud was personally responsible for most teen-age delinquency; to others Jung was so vague and mystical as to be absolutely unreadable. To some Freud stood for an outdated positivism that now impeded any clear thinking about our real problem; to others Jung was anti-Semitic and pro-Nazi.

After years of research I have come to the conclusion that there is no truth in any of these accusations. I believe they are all rationalizations, and rationalizations to which many others who are not professional psychologists are also addicted. I believe that Freud and Jung stand for opposing sides of the human mind, that their dialogue is central enough to invite comparison with characters in Greek tragedy, and that when we denounce one or the other we merely reveal our incapacity to confront an unknown portion of ourselves. None of these accusations would stand up after close scrutiny of the lives and work of the men in question; all of these accusations have been publicly exploded long ago. Yet they persist. Why? Because people want scapegoats for their own intellectual laziness and their own spiritual cowardice.

But there is more to it than that. Psychology establishes such an intimate and powerful hold upon its students that once allegiance has been given any school—and each of us must begin with a single school, the one to which we are naturally drawn—a complete change of intellectual habits is required before we can even become aware of other schools. And then our first reaction is bound to be one of pain and distaste. The progress from psychology to comparative psychology—a progress that many people are going to have to make, unless there is to be a return to the rancor of the religious wars, with modern demagogic complications—is always hard.

A brief preliminary examination of the lives and works of Freud and Jung will show why this is so. Fortunately, they are so eloquent, they embody so dramatically two opposite sides of the mind, and of contemporary experience, that they turn dry elucidation into good theater. Together they form one of psychology's most far-reaching debates—and an excellent introduction to problems that sooner or later each of us must face.

The name of Freud is usually associated with what has been called the sexual revolution. Actually, as we have seen, that event began long before he did his work. Historically, it can be traced to the Industrial Revolution. It began in fact as a protest against the anti-human tendencies of that event and its poetic forefathers were, as I have indicated, Blake and Whitman.

This lyric movement has since had to face the counter-attack of tradition, and is intellectually on the defensive today, but it still continues as a protest. The typical sexual rebel believes in sex with religious fervor. His rebellion seems to vary according to his sense of a lost spiritual heritage, and when he feels himself utterly dis-owned of a tradition that he can accept—cut off, so to speak, with a library card—he can become a satyr. Orgasm is his substitute for feeling. This is a development that Whitman could not have fore-seen. The effect of industrialism upon love has been so drastic as to make a great many people demand physical gratification in lieu of every other amorous reward. It has generated an unprecedented mass fear of impotence. In a world of steel and asphalt sex takes over certain aspects of the divine.

There has probably been more moralizing on this than on any

other phase of twentieth-century life. Most of this moralizing has been beside the point because it has failed to take into account just these historical crosscurrents. We could not want a better example of why a sound understanding of psychology must precede a sound understanding of morals.

Freud's ideas on this complex and highly controversial subject are often misunderstood. In effect he wrote that sex is impersonal, nature blindly concerned with her own propagation, and that if we attach the wrong emotions to our part of the process, if we remain ignorant of the unconscious forces that are the principal determinants of our behavior, we become ill both in mind and in body. Health requires that we be aware of these unconscious forces, which originate in early childhood, so that we can sublimate them in socially acceptable tasks.

It is a stern doctrine, but it has been confused with moral laxity because it calls for close examination of a subject that is generally regarded as unsavory. If it means a release from inhibitions, it also imposes—after a trying experimental period which is the real reason why traditional moralists fear it—still stricter standards in their place. If it takes a deterministic attitude toward previous morality, it goes on to demand another which is much more difficult to observe.

Sex seems to have been the road Freud had not taken, the life he had not lived. As a family man his life was extremely correct. One biographer states flatly that he never had any sexual experience outside marriage. This is unprovable but significant. It suggests that the man whose name more than any other is linked with broad sexual knowledge had little of it through personal experience.

No spinster, certainly, was ever more aware of every erotic nuance. Sex was his poetry. Together with his extraordinary talents, this was what made him so persuasive. But he was also aided by the fact that he was Jewish. As in the case of Marx, his scientific achievements were part of the expansion of a gifted, ancient, persecuted people which had only recently emerged from the ghetto. This people had an extraordinary insight into the evils of a decadent Christianity, an insight, born of a vigorous intellectual tradition and a long experience of injustice, that lent itself especially to reductive analysis. Marx had reduced the evils of the political economy to the profit motive and predicted that under socialism the state would wither away. Freud reduced the evils of the inner life to misunderstanding of the erotic instinct and predicted that after psychoanalysis the mind would become healthy. Each put his finger on a weak spot in an enemy position that he was supremely qualified, not only through his private talents but through his background, to expose to the world.

It has now become apparent that both these great insights suffered from oversimplification. Men's disillusionment with Marxism came earlier and on a larger scale. This has led often to a denial of its values. Freudianism had no Russia to work on, and by its nature it is less on parade, but disillusionment with it continues and may diminish its perceptions for those who need them most. It is nevertheless a very powerful movement, especially among those urbanized people who have felt the attack of industrialism upon their instincts. It is particularly strong among city dwellers in the United States today, and for just this reason. Our city dwellers have usually become aware of their psychological problems through sexual and economic frustrations. A treatment, therefore, which may release them from erotic and aggressive inhibitions has the dramatic appeal of a psychic appendectomy promising not only health but happiness and prosperity as well. It is the sort of down-to-earth treatment that makes sense in a busy market place.

So Freud's therapy is definitely related to the Industrial Revolution. This will become clearer when it is compared to the therapy of Jung, who came forward a little later to call attention to those aspects of the inner life that had been relatively unaffected—or affected in another way—by technology. In response to the needs of a suffering and confused humanity, our period has produced not only the specifically *contemporary* psychology of Freud but the relatively *timeless* psychology of Jung. The two unite in a dialogue admirably suited to comparison. *Not*, however, to controversy. I hope it will be clear why a partisan attitude in this debate is especially barren.

Offhand the timeless quality of Jung's psychology would seem fatal to it. Certainly it does not appear to equip it for survival in an age which daily grows more industrial, more political, more warlike. His psychology is somewhat like a Platonic academy in the midst of a radioactive battlefield. It differs also from our socially useful academies in its open doubt of the intellect, at least the intellect as characteristically employed today. Far from admiring the typical mentality of our urban culture, Jung mistrusts it.

Jung was a Swiss, and his psychology reflects the desire of his people—and of others like them—to live an orderly, traditional life in an era of violent change. In contrast to most Jews—who are born inescapably into turmoil—most Swiss try to stay out of it. Jung cannot be "explained" by his Swissness, any more than Freud can be "explained" by his Jewishness, but in each, beneath the accomplishments of a truly international mind, resides an impersonal element, identifiable with his people, which helps greatly in the exposition of modern psychology, because it polarizes modern social experience.

Jung's silent invocations are rural and classic, rather than urban and modern. Thus his work would seem to be as anachronistic, as unreal, as cultish as his opponents have described it, if there were not always classic problems among the most contemporary and if a truly modern consciousness did not also have to contend with them. It is Jung's anachronism, in fact, his seeming irrelevance, that constitutes finally his greatest strength—at least for those who, as youth deserts them, begin to realize that not all their problems turn on childhood influences or the encroachment of civilization upon instinct; that there are other problems equally pressing and as old as the hills.

But to understand the origin of Jung's ideas it is necessary, as it was with Freud, to know a few facts about his life. He was born in 1875 in Switzerland, the son of a Protestant clergyman, and for our time had a life of privileged tranquillity. He was a paleontologist and classical scholar as well as a psychologist, traveled widely throughout the world, and lived, until his death in 1961, on the shores of Lake Zurich.

From these bare facts emerge four important considerations:

First, Jung was born into a period, later than Freud's, when natural science felt somewhat less confidence in its powers to explain all or almost all of life. Jung was therefore encouraged to devote some of his scientific energy to philosophical problems that Freud had expressly excluded from the purview of psychoanalysis.

Second, Jung had a temperament that was expansive rather than reductive and that led him in time to rebel against what he called Freud's "nothing but" analysis. Gifted with a robust constitution and a robust attitude toward nature—until shortly before his death he vacationed periodically in a remote, electricity-less, servant-less house that he built himself—he did not make a poetry of the biological, but of the divine.

Third, he became scientifically as much interested in religion as

Freud had been in Eros, and discovered within himself a similar pioneering genius in its study.

Fourth, although he was born into less conflict with society than Freud, their roles have been reversed since the positivism championed by Freud has become a new orthodoxy. Now it is Jung who is at greater variance with the intellectual mores of his day.

Freud believed that the mind of man could be explained, if one persisted long enough, in terms of his *immediate environment*. Jung believed that one can only begin to understand it by going back to all of the many factors which entered into its making, which lead in every case to the *remote past*. It can be demonstrated, he says, that we are commonly possessed by archetypes as old as the race itself. Such a perspective will dismay the quick, pragmatic, modern temper, which can only feel equal to its problems by jettisoning most of the past, but such a perspective, Jung says, is the only way to truth and health. Once Christianity was overturned, modern man had to face all the internal demons that the Church had kept at bay for him. The way to rebuild our lives is to relax the will, stop being merely contemporary, and seek harmony with nature. Our troubles are erotic, especially when we are young, but they are many other things as well, and the first step in dealing with them is to see them in historical scale. Only in so doing will we find a durable sense of purpose, and we need a sense of purpose quite as much as we need biological fulfillment.

The roots of character are not all here and now, and even the most elaborate autobiographical search will not uncover more than a few of them. Society is as sick as Freud says it is, but we need not be— if we are willing and able to become what we innately are.

Such a restatement of their positions is fair to neither Freud nor Jung. But even these glimpses will indicate the nature and sources of their conflict. And if we try to understand it, we see that it is as human, as foreordained, as meaningful as the conflict between two heroic characters in a Greek tragedy. These men are not only historic personages, they are also parts of ourselves and they enact a play that goes on daily in our own minds. We all have to live in the vigorously contemporary world of Freud, and we all have to live in the archetypal world of Jung. We have to be effective; we also have to be in harmony with nature. To do both of these things at the same time is as difficult as any demand we can make upon ourselves. Our natural tendency, therefore, will be to take sides with one of them against the other, but if we do we shall neither enjoy their drama properly nor make the best use of it. This will be still more evident when we continue their dialogue briefly into the subject of religion.

Offhand it would seem that Freud had no use at all for religion. He traced its origin to the small child's helplessness before the outer world and to its dependence on its parents. He rejected religion specifically as an immaturity and an illusion, an inability to stand on one's own feet. He said, "Science is not an illusion. But it would be an illusion to suppose that we can get anywhere else what it cannot give us." To an American friend he wrote: "To me the moral has always appeared as self-evident." In other words, he took morality for granted and reasoned that if he could get along without religion, why couldn't other men? In this, I believe it can be demonstrated, he drew upon the *unconscious religion* concealed in his scientific credo, upon the unanalyzed faith that he got from his laboratory training.

"Unconscious religion" is a phrase used more and more today. Anti-communists use it to explain communists—along with such words as "fanaticism," "auto-da-fé," and "'grand inquisitors." Few intellectuals apply it, however, to themselves; they prefer to think that they have rationally transcended all religious motivations, which at least will never trouble *them*. In other words, the repressions of the nineteenth century have been reversed in the twentieth. They are no longer sexual, they are religious. To deny the many-sided urge toward erotic gratification would now correctly be considered absurd. No absurdity, however, is found in a denial of the urge toward purpose, toward symbolism, toward the necessary ingredients of the will to go on. This blind spot is one of the less fortunate of Freud's legacies.

Actually, however, without knowing it, he himself made important contributions to religious thought. Three of his most familiar concepts will illustrate what I mean. The first he borrowed from Havelock Ellis and extended. *Narcissism* is a deeply imaginative attempt to deal with the problem of evil. The inescapability of self could hardly be better symbolized than by this amazingly astute reference to the self-love that must follow us wherever we go. It is a splendid instance of the biological honesty that is indispensable to true spirituality.

His *superego* likewise provides a valuable distinction between morbid self-criticism and the healthy self-criticism needed for making truly responsible moral decisions. History is full of weaklings terrorized and crippled by power-seeking priesthoods through perverted appeals to conscience. Every ecclesiastical reformation has been in part a purge of a corrupt misuse of the sense of guilt. And this is no longer solely a religious problem but now an acute political one.

Finally, Freud's *death instinct*, when juxtaposed to its opposite, the life instinct, or Eros in its fullest sense, is seen as exactly the kind of symbolic tool that Freud's realism was brilliantly equipped to add to our thought. No one can fail to learn much about his own psychological rhythms by observing the alternations of these two opposing instincts within himself. And this kind of systole-diastole insight can lead to a philosophic balance that is not far from the idea expressed by Dante in *The Divine Comedy.* "In His will is our peace." There was much unconscious religion indeed in Freud.

There is in everyone. We are all full of it, according to our temperaments, and we shall be happier—or better able to choose a tragedy worthy of us—if we become aware of it. This was the discovery of Jung, which he announced at a time when such a point of view had become scientifically scandalous. He said he had found proof of the therapeutic effect of genuine religious experience—of the role played by faith, not in immaturity but in maturity. He made an issue of it. He announced cures. He spoke of highly educated patients who had been freed of their anxiety when they discovered the limits of reason, when they rediscovered symbolism and mystery. He wrote:

"I take carefully into account the symbols produced by the unconscious mind. They are the only things able to convince the critical mind of modern people. . . . The thing that cures a neurosis must be as convincing as the neurosis; and since the latter is only too real, the helpful experience must be of equal reality."

Jung, however, was by no means a naïve, uncritical enthusiast of the religious life. He did not point the way to easy faith. Like William James, he saw religion as a force, subject to the laws of the mind, which could lead either to good or to evil. He explored the different responses to it in different types of men. In the face of Freud's attempt to dismiss it as an illusion, he drove home his empirical discovery that it was a fact, a fact that could not be conveniently traced to the nursery and forgotten. In this matter it seems to me that he was right, and that Freud's own life and work prove his point.

On the other hand, how many people can afford to live in the epicurean detachment that Jung's prescription implies? This is a question raised by Jung's opponents. Economically, the whole trend of modern life is against his attitude, which is bound to become rarer and rarer. And would not such detachment lead to a washing of the hands, in the elegant manner of Pontius Pilate, of the urgent political and social problems that must be faced if the common-wealth is to advance in decency and justice? A civic stance acquired in lucky, war-free isolation is apt to be irrelevant. Jung's program-matic introversion is an anachronistic luxury that could only be afforded in times free of unrest, times not at all like our own. To cling to it now is mere nostalgia. Such criticism seems to be the core of the opposition to Jung.

The core of the opposition to Freud seems to be that people are not as simple as he saw them, but many rootless moderns have embraced his oversimplifications with a monomaniacal devotion that is now in the process of dehumanizing them. Our urbanized culture is producing overpragmatic monsters whose cynical first question is "What's in it for me?" Freud's reality principle, there-fore, except for some overimpressionable and overprivileged intel-lectuals, is only so many words. In practice, together with the ethical lobotomy that usually accompanies it, it has led to a deplorable opportunism that will soon lay waste, and often in the name of de-cency and justice, whatever remains of the moral foundations of society.

There is plainly an element of truth in both these oppositions. Both of them are emotional, both of them are exaggerated, but in each there is enough basis in fact to have made it possible to ration-alize them into full-scale hatreds. That is why most people's attitude toward psychology's most heated debate remains bitterly one-sided. It is so much easier to emotionalize our inner conflicts. Is so hard to live with them, to see their pros and cons, to weave them patiently together.

How to weave them together? That, together with the inter-weaving of still other theories by still other men, is *the* problem of comparative psychology. It calls for a union of tension and relaxa-tion. The thought of Freud is essentially tense. It is a product of struggle, of a life that was not permitted much calm. There is a sense of urgency about it, and its goal is less happiness than effec-tiveness. It is far more revolutionary than its opposite, at least in social impact. It is more startling, more dramatic, more in the idiom of our century. It prepares men for survival in a time of general shipwreck. It is above all practical: one is called upon to eliminate one's irrational impulses, by becoming aware of their childhood origins, and to strengthen the conscious mind. It is only in this way that one can accomplish anything worth while, right any wrongs, eradicate any ignorance, make an impression on an indifferent universe.

The thought of Jung is essentially relaxed. It is addressed to those who wish to fulfill their inner potentialities even in an era of drastic change. It refuses to get alarmed over financial and political crises. It is a product of relative tranquillity. It puts a minimum of emphasis on social adaptation, which it regards as a necessary first hurdle rather than as a life work, and a maximum of emphasis on internal development. It is especially addressed to people over thirty-five, and it finds scientific sanction for love of fate and attunement to nature.

To weave together such entirely different attitudes may be necessary for the creation of a truly successful human being, but it will obviously be an infrequent accomplishment. No wonder most people would rather quarrel ignorantly about it.

But there is another reason why Freud and Jung continue to provide a convenient battleground for quickly stirred emotions. They not only embody some of our most central dramas; in their combination of elderliness and wisdom they are both father figures par excellence. At heart we are childish, we want to confer magic on imaginary papas.

An unrecorded part of history is the expropriation of magic. The priest took it away from the medicine man, and the medical man took it away from the priest. For most of us the mind-doctor does not have as much of it as the body-doctor, because he does not scare us as much. But for those who get caught up in psychological problems this is not true. The mind-doctor turns into the most awesome figure of all, especially when he is a theorist, a name. We shall be happier, I think—or at least more ourselves—when we stop conferring magic on anyone. We are born partisan. We do not have to remain so.

Only a very small minority is capable of this kind of self-conquest. Science depends on a victory over one's emotions, but few scientists are capable of it. And nonscientists have to master a new and difficult language before they can even ask themselves the questions that automobiles and steroids have brought along with them, as part of the cost of progress. It is not surprising that in countries where this kind of debate is not permitted there is no noticeable protest against its exclusion, and in countries where it is permitted almost no one cares to admit the intimacy of its issues, that is, almost no one takes it seriously. The stake may ultimately be survival, and not only moral but physical survival; nevertheless the work is too hard. One deduction alone is possible: Only a few of us really want to live.

II

The Psychopomps

7

Reinitiation

The new science of the mind suffers from semantic confusions which do not cause its representatives to lower their voices. Gifted men have made brilliant new discoveries that may not be recognized as theirs unless they are given brilliant new names. All describe the same reality, but all find different words for it. Our psychopomps, our guides through the chaos of the underworld, require interpretation.

Another confusion comes from the fact that our fast-moving century has already wrought vast changes in the psychological climate. In some circles (in parts of New York, for instance) the sexual revolution is old stuff that long ago generated new problems in ethics and education; in other circles (in parts of the Deep South) it has barely begun. In still others (in parts of France) it was not needed. Some people have never heard of the unconscious; others use the word so often that it no longer has any meaning.

Fortunately, the exceptional reader is not troubled by these difficulties. He can find the perspective that transforms them into the dramatic enhancements of an exciting group-search. He can also appreciate the strange fate that has overtaken the unconscious.

To visit the temples of the unconscious is like visiting a temple to Jupiter Ammon, much venerated some twenty centuries ago, whose solemn images are now being rubbed away by the abrasives of the Libyan desert, while the silence is only broken by a distant prayer from a mosque. The ancient temple is in ruins; its god no longer exists; no one believes in him any more. It is almost the same with the unconscious.

No one could go about his job, for a while at least, if he really believed in the unconscious. It might flatten him out. He might make all sorts of mistakes, fail to show up at the office, forget about his bills, fight with his wife, and, perhaps, wake up in a mental home. He might call his behavior ecstatic, but the official word would be something else. For reasons of social order, therefore, the unconscious is distributed in small, routine portions, like a newer Eucharist. Its orgiastic potencies are offset by grim adjustment to drab "reality." In war time it is used to get fliers back on their bomber runs with a minimum loss of time out for crack-ups. In peace it is used to put typists back at their typewriters, husbands back with wives, priests back in pulpits, partisans back in parties. Its headier elements have been discreetly drained off. Fortunately, only a small minority is aware of its Dionysian excitations. The Organization Man never misses them, and it is at him, of course, that psychiatry is aimed. What would happen to us all if *he* cracked up? Even the jokes we make about him are merely a tribute to the steadiness of nerve, orderliness of family life, payment of debt, and general reliability that he symbolizes and that we all—even our poets when they are honest—demand. We cannot afford to have the Organization Man go haywire. Too much blessed irregularity *depends* on his admirable lack of imagination. His monotonous bass makes possible our off-beat adventures. It is a chastening thought that has ballasted the Remnant in every civilization that has endured.

No one who feels scorn for the Organization Man will take on the tasks of the Remnant. Snobbishness has no meaning for the discerning few, who recognize as much dignity in routine tasks as in tasks which win more acclaim. They also feel no guilt toward the working class, because they have never despised it or taken advantage of it. The task of the Remnant is to carry a high degree of consciousness with as much steadiness as the worker finds for his simpler proletarian work and the Organization Man for his simpler bourgeois work. But this task requires imagination and tension as well as steadiness. In terms of psychological open-mindedness it means that the Remnant cannot tolerate the discreet damping-down of the unconscious that is necessary for simpler souls, in the interests of a stable society. On the contrary, the Remnant must stand a full exposure to the unconscious, in time, when it is ready for it, because only thus can it attain its full stature. The road to its kind of maturity is through maximum risk.

It is difficult to speculate on the exact nature of the Remnant.

I see the Remnant as made up chiefly of former outcasts who now form the innermost core of their society, Ishmaels no longer in flight. Unless a man is born at variance with his society, he will never understand it. Unless he later consents to serve it, in his own best way, he will never take root. To survive, therefore, he must become *bilingual*; that is, master the language of his people, and also master the new international language of the mind, which can at last make him feel at home with his people—and himself.

But now the introduction is over. The reinitiation begins. We approach Acheron.

8

The Novels of Sigmund Freud

It is immediately clear what one can learn from Sigmund Freud: the need for personal fitness in a time of incessant war. Freud's is a militant message, a call to action. It is of particular value to those who must live in a highly competitive society, who are not as simple as most businessmen, but must make their mark in a place that is dominated by businessmen. Also, its unrelenting insistence on early family influences has been on the whole a healthful coming-down-to-earth for a prosperous and abstraction-loving society which liked to imagine that the economic ability to leave home early meant a final rupture with disagreeable conflicts with one's parents, a wiping clean of bloodstains. Freud reminds idealists of their animal origins. But above all, he provides a clear *ideological* explanation of man for a new class of uprooted intellectuals who must apprehend ideologically or not at all.

This is the best way to understand, I think, his enormous appeal in the United States, where he has incomparably more appeal than anywhere else in the world. The first task of the individual is to survive, and Freud has given the embryonic individual in the United States a strong, lucidly defined technique which takes him back to his earliest memories and enables him to adapt himself realistically to a society which confuses most people with its curious combination of sentiment and practicality. Freud invites the young American to see himself tough-mindedly, as the unreleasable victim of a biological tragedy, so that he may, if he is strong-willed enough, gain a sure footing on a slippery terrain.

In addition to harsh, uncompromising self-appraisal, however, Freud also offers a promise that enhances his popularity among his

many readers. (His *Basic Works* is a perennial best seller in nearly
every college book store.) This promise outweighs in importance,
at least for a far-sighted few, his frank discussions of sex. It is the
promise of success. What he is saying to the attentive young American might be summed up like this: "Get clear about your relations
to your mother and father, your brothers and sisters, and all the
rest of your family. Get clear about your Oedipus complex. Don't
be afraid of the word 'incest.' Face the fact that your id has much
more to say about what you do than your ego. Clarify your superego,
so that it doesn't waste itself on trifles, on mere amenities. Understand the power of the death instinct. See the sexual truth about
yourself, and don't be stupidly ashamed of it. Face up to the ghastly
sordidness, the disgusting vulgarity of being a human being—and
your reward will be that you will have the answers while your soft-
headed contemporaries are merely fooling around with words. Traps
are being laid for you every day. A great swindle called either by the
name of a church or of a political system or some other institution
is seeking every second to take you in with its calming mythology,
but if you will just see things clearly, the way psychoanalysis has
shown you, you need not be a fool any longer. You can adjust to
this great swindle. You can even make money, and in no petty sums.
You can acquire prestige. You can beat the game—and enjoy the
infinite satisfaction of watching the great majority crawl on its belly
toward you. All you need is to be clear and strong."

So realistic a program, carrying scientific weight and the intangible
authority of centuries of tested rabbinical wisdom, will not go un-
heeded by a member of our rather spindly-educated class, provided
he is not loaded down, if only through lip service, by too many
social demands. A politician or a businessman, for instance, can
hardly take such hardheaded theories to heart, however hardheaded
he may be in actual practice. The implications would destroy the
illusions he needs as a member of society. In a land where public
approval is usually essential to success, the practical man has a low
tolerance of doctrinal antinomy. He must believe to a remarkable
degree in what he says. If, however, he is an uprooted intellectual
of the type that now plays such a role in our arts and sciences,
though not in our more public professions, he can quite easily
tolerate such "Machiavellism," as it would once have been called;
indeed, his subsistence may depend on it. He is restricted to an
audience of his own kind, but at least he cuts a figure there and

believes that his "cynical" ideas will trickle down in time to the slower-witted masses. That is why there is so much confusion in all public discussions of psychoanalysis. The highbrow is saying that the middlebrow is corrupt in practice, connives at all sorts of cheap peddlers' tricks in education, literature, science, and is worse than sloppy in his separation of genuine quality from false. The middle-brow retorts that the highbrow is corrupt in theory, stands convicted by his own words, and has no authentic relation to the community, which loathes him. It is a familiar debate which originates not only in talent and character but in social status, for one's position in it is closely related to whether one is an outsider, an insider or (perhaps the most powerful class now) an outsider on his way in. Naturally, in the circumstances, little is said about psychoanalysis.

How is a hypothetical young American, eager for a radical en-counter with himself, to respond to the challenge of Freud? Nature supplies the answer, nature metamorphosed as social fate. Unless the young person is at odds with his society, and in an important way, there is little chance that he will even imagine a radical en-counter with himself. However, if he is thrown athwart his culture and forced to use intensive self-exploration as a way to survive, he will certainly find himself sympathetic to Freud. The displaced American cannot afford to go without what Freud offers him. Even if he is too complex to remain content with it, he must at least be willing to undergo a genuine exposure to it. Whether he gets it through psychoanalysis or self-analysis will rest with him. Those who doubt the efficacy of self-analysis are right in many cases, but when they *insist* they reveal the fanatic's secret doubt of his own beliefs. Freud himself, in his later days, did not oppose self-analysis.

A line from John Dewey comes to mind: "We think because we have to think." It is the present, perhaps unprecedented athwart-ness of talented Americans that is forcing them to think. They have been born into conditions which seem at first considerably more benevolent than experience proves them to be. They learn to distrust what they formerly took on faith. Their plight might be described by an image taken from another day. They thought they were living in a terrestrial paradise, but it turned out to be more like an inferno. If purgatory may be seen as a medieval, otherworldly, metaphorical anticipation of modern psychology, then a present-day American can only hope to reach Paradise (consciousness, the kingdom of heaven that is within you) by patiently climbing Mount Purgatorio with a succession of guides at his side, one of the first of whom will be Freud. We are obliged to think psychologically in a way that no one could have been expected to foresee.

It is true, however, that Freud's importance would diminish if the economic and cultural struggle were to grow less acute in the United States. We should agree then with those abroad who think our interest in him is exaggerated. A delightful *détente* would have arrived. Business would become less competitive, heads of unfriendly foreign powers would not bang shoes on desks, the Monroe Doctrine would be painlessly reinstalled, puritans would relax comfortably after the manner of Mexicans and Italians, have-nots would expect nothing of haves, Broadway would reject plays that had trivial or banal themes, television would give more time to biochemistry than to Tombstone Gulch, commercials would be eliminated, we could all lean back in our sulkies and let the reins fall down on the horse's back. There would be no need for the tough-mindedness that Freud inculcates more effectively than any other thinker of our time. However, his publishers go on ordering new editions as if there were little likelihood of the millennium. In time his public may decline, but certainly not for quite a while.

He is better understood if regarded not as a lawgiver but as a poet. It is not inaccurate to speak of his "novels" in the sense that he combatted an old mythology with one of his own creation, and drew more upon his own inner depths than upon his observations, a bench mark of superior fiction. He wrote Horatio Alger stories for intellectuals: stories with a message, "You too can win success in a cruel and stupid world, in spite of the handicap of brains."

He did not believe he was contributing a new mythology to replace an old one. He believed he was putting an end to mythology of every kind. He believed he was contributing facts, irrefutable facts, codified as scientific laws which could be extended and refined but never essentially changed. He identified himself so closely with his role of outsider working his way into a position of authority through clarity of positivistic insight (never once did he question his own unconscious philosophic suppositions, which, scientifically, was like the behavior of a chemist who experiments without sterilizing his test tubes) that he was quite incapable of regarding his dearest conclusions with the relativity that would be forced, by sheer complexity of the human material, upon a similarly gifted novelist. He wanted clear answers, an unquestionable method. He believed he could *explain* man once and for all. Or at least begin such an explanation, lay the groundwork for it.

Such optimism belongs more to the nineteenth century, with its credo of inevitable progress toward the light through mass education, than to our own day, when there is not only more skepticism about the intellectual powers of the masses but also a much more realistic appreciation of the myth-making needs involved in all communication, however austere, abstract or "scientific." Freud, ironically, contributed to our better understanding of the nature of communication, and himself complained of the metaphorical language forced upon him when he had a discovery to announce, but he could not go further in his glimpses into the irrational nature of life; he was still, in his personal creed, a rationalist. The nature of his limitations will become clearer when we examine the successful resistance of Franz Kafka, who was drenched, through his friends, in Freudian thought, but held his own against it, thanks to his familiarity with Kierkegaard, and was able to make a literary contribution that would have been most certainly snuffed out by surrender to Freud's more popular mode of thought.

Not only was Freud obliged to use metaphors, he also was obliged to use myths, even while he was shaking the pillars of the pantheon by "setting Acheron in an uproar." In his determined quest of converts he became an artist, obliged by his craft to use the best words at his command, and to seek the greatest possible influence for them through subtle emotional devices. In his keener moments of self-analysis, as when he said that he always needed an enemy to bring out his best work, he appreciated the mythopoeic and all-too-human nature of his talent; but was less convincing when he insisted on the scientific universality of his discoveries, or otherwise acted the part of a simple empiricist who had come down from a new Sinai with sterilized tablets that would never be set aside because pure observation and mathematical deduction alone had produced them. On the whole, his intensity of presentation is at least as powerful as his insight, which as we shall see has shrunk a little in the wash. As a scientist he is assured of a high place in history, but as a thinker he may be in danger of the oblivion that more than one man of letters has predicted for him—Van Wyck Brooks, for instance, in *From a Writer's Notebook*, where it is implied that Freud's emphasis on cause rather than significance will inevitably work against his fame, because exploration does not have the final value of meaning. As a morality poet of the inner world, however, a creator of new scourges against self-delusion, Freud will certainly live.

So far there has been so much myth-making *about* him that it is not always easy to see what sort of myth-maker he was. Even in so worshipful a biography as that by Ernest Jones, however, it is possible at times to glimpse the man behind the public front. There is the much-discussed scene in the Park Hotel in Munich on 24 November 1912 when "he began reproaching the two Swiss, Jung and Riklin, for writing articles expounding psychoanalysis without mentioning his name. Jung replied that they had thought it unnecessary to do so, it being so well known, but Freud had sensed already the first signs of the dissension that was to follow a year later. He persisted, and I remember thinking he was taking the matter rather personally. Suddenly, to our consternation, he fell on the floor in a dead faint. The sturdy Jung carried him to a couch in the lounge, where he soon revived. His first words as he was coming to were strange: 'How sweet it must be to die.'"

Later he reviewed the scene in the light of the latent homosexuality in himself that he thought it had revealed. In other words, his alert mind was doing with it what any alert mind tries to do at such moments; it was trying to understand, to assimilate, to use. To me he is more attractive in humiliation than when he is treated as an immortal. At such a moment we see an artist at work, a hard-pressed, lonely, sometimes hysterical artist who hammered out his message of fortitude and clarity from keen personal distress. He is not the mythical all-wise father figure in a frock coat to whom patients could spontaneously transfer their affections; he is caught in a temporary breakdown of the very kind that he loved to detect in others. And he recovers from it quickly with an idea about the joy of dying.

Indispensable to his continuing influence is the style that he found for his ideas. This style, which was goldsmithed in bitter conflict with the imperial caste system, the clerically-dominated sloth-and-peasant torpor of a moribund Austria-Hungary, early acquired the ideological edge already needed in the new intellectual lingua franca that was forming. Like Marx, Freud was not content to make scientific observations. With true genius he turned them into images that would be retained by any mind capable of comprehending them. He also burned with prophetic zeal to destroy the falsities he had suffered in a hostile society. To accomplish this purpose, he reduced his subject—in his case, man—to a negotiable currency in the thought exchanges of his time. Meanwhile, indirectly, he offered a weapon to scientifically trained outsiders who wanted to get in.

In this work his heritage was not only Jewish but German. He built on German thought and he used German words. It is significant that despite his travels and his anglophilia he quite provincially —and unlike many other scientists at the same time—*believed* in his country's cause in World War I and enthusiastically sent forth his sons to fight for it. And when Austria's might faltered, he transferred his admiration to the Germans. There is no evidence that he appreciated the tragic severance of German culture from the human standards that a psychophysician would be expected to regard as normal. He seems to have been too deeply engrossed in the development of his ideas to be aware of his own effect on the social values that he desired but that his ideas were none the less attacking. It is a prerogative of genius of which too much can be made by hostile critics. With his psychology he had created a tool that permitted him to open up an enormous portion of nature and history, but he himself saw only that portion which he was predisposed to consider, not that which might have interfered with his effectiveness. Thus an evaluation of his style must consider the programmatic egocentricity that German culture gave it.

Today the world is not as deeply impressed with German culture as it was before 1914 and 1933. Its curious juxtaposition of learning and madness has been driven home to the whole world. Though not incapable of the same evils, we have noted that culture of truly prodigious proportions can coexist with stupidity, cowardice, violence and unperturbed indifference to others. Freud himself was later to suffer personally from this kind of culture and to be publicly disabused of his earlier faith in it. It was too late however for him to draw logical conclusions; he died soon after; and there is no evidence that he could have drawn them without a change of heart. He himself was by no means entirely free of the one-sidedness, the anti-feminism, the failure to integrate thought and feeling, the inhumanity, the fanaticism that so often disfigured this great culture. The scornful polemical tone of much of his writing suggests its effect on him, not to mention his inability to tolerate legitimate differences of opinion, his callous (by American standards) treatment of his wife, or his behavior when he seemed to be getting the worst of an argument. Quite aside from cultural influences upon him, Freud was a man who had to be one-up on everybody else. He could not stand to lose. He wanted—and got—both the extraordinary respect due a German professor and the almost messianic reverence due a possibly lineal descendant of Jeremiah.

He was aware of some of his own greediness, and made brilliant use of it from time to time in his writings—and later regretted his indiscretion. With wonderful inconsistency he wanted to be applauded for the depth of his insight, yet never to give the impression that it involved a personal confession. He therefore couched his confessional insights in the form of an *attack*, an irrefutable *scientific* attack upon the self-deceptions of his reader. Strategically, and with consummate cunning, he also limited all human endeavor to his specialty and to his own particular way of looking at his specialty.

Many ambitious minds have attempted this, but few have had his success. He succeeded for a long time, both because of the nature of his extraordinary talents and because certain tides in the *Zeitgeist* were running with him. It was a time when the breakdown of an established order, once dominated by Christian theology, was creating a vacuum in men's minds, when men were required to throw out so many familiar thoughts that they had either to rethink everything or to fill up their minds with new secular ideologies that eagerly sprang up. In psychology the thought of Freud, shaped in a struggle with a hostile and reactionary environment, weighted with the pontifical solemnity of German science, and intensified with the protest of a recently reborn Jewish prophetism, proved a more effective ideology than any other. It was skillfully suited to fill more than one mental void. A striking American example is provided by the playwright Eugene O'Neill, who, having broken with Catholicism, restocked his theatrical imagination with literal recitations of Freud's ideas.

As a recent centennial book, *Freud and the 20th Century*, suggests, the chief response that he still evokes among his admirers is hero worship. Whether that response is helpful to the Remnant will be one of the questions we shall explore in the ensuing chapters, as we put his brilliant fictions next to other fictions produced by his dissident disciples. Dramatic encounter with its opponents, I hope, is still the best way to expound an idea.

One of the strongest statements of hero worship in the centennial volume is that by Stanley Edgar Hyman: "It is my belief that the writings of Sigmund Freud once again make a tragic view possible for the modern mind." Hyman attacks the dissident disciples for having watered down the original vigor and darkness of Freud's vision; Horney, Fromm and Sullivan have sweetened their therapy with the sickening optimism that seems to overtake all robust thought in the United States. Freud's therapy, he says, wisely did not offer "true happiness" but merely "modest relief from neurotic difficulties." He praises Lionel Trilling "who has been uniquely distinguished among modern literary critics by his defense of Freudian orthodoxy against bowdlerization and revision," and ends with an eloquent challenge:

"If Freud showed us that life was nasty, brutish, and short, and had always been, he was only holding the mirror up to our own faces, saying what the great philosophers and the great tragic writers have always said. If we are serious, our reaction to this bitter truth is neither to avoid it with one or another anodyne, nor to kill ourselves, but to set out humbly through the great tragic rhythm of pride and fall, so curiously alike in psychoanalysis and literature."

Since this seems to epitomize the considered opinion of a group of able present-day Freudians, it will deserve the closest scrutiny in the ensuing chapters, when we seek to understand why the revisionists disagreed with Freud. A many-sided debate begins. An attempt will be made, however, to restrict it to essentials.

9

Adler and Women

If the twentieth century had not been a disappointment to those who had great expectations for it, Alfred Adler's ideas might today be more influential than Sigmund Freud's. Adler's reputation has suffered the fate of all "liberal" thought in a time of repeated catastrophe. Despite the keenness of many of his insights, which suggested that he was indeed capable of "understanding human nature"—the title of one of his books—his view of the world was not sufficiently somber, and he never mastered the art of tough-minded ideology. He took the "will to power" from Nietzsche and used it with remarkable skill, but for the laudable and unrealizable purpose of freeing society from it. Unlike the cooler-hearted Freud, who disabused himself of earlier illusions about education, normality, and the value of his own therapy (though he did not confess, publicly at least, that he was at the same time identifying himself with an elite), Adler stuck to his beliefs in education, democracy, sturdy commonsense, and the attainment of happiness through reason.

That is why he provokes so much scorn in certain intellectual circles today, which have reacted to reactionary times with a savage contempt for hope of any kind, and especially for hope they once shared. It is also why he remains a seminal force among the revisionists. After his death in Scotland in 1937, when he seemed a remote victim of the conflicting totalitarian forces which exiled him from Vienna (the Nazis) and killed his daughter (the Bolsheviks), his school was scattered and his influence appeared at an end; yet it continues and, as we shall see, it looks as if it will continue to continue.

Adler raises issues that are fundamental to psychology and will

most likely never be settled once and for all. They are everyday
social issues. To understand them it is best to begin with their
spokesman. Adler might be described as a man who healed himself
through psychological analysis and could not understand emotionally
why others—and indeed the whole world—did not do likewise. (Intellectually, he understood all too well.) From a withdrawn, quarrel-
some, overambitious young physician who always had a book or a
pen in his hand the minute his medical duties permitted, he developed into a benign world figure, at home with all kinds of people,
entrusted with a post of leadership in the Vienna school system, and
much more given to talking than to writing. The testimony of
hostile medical colleagues and of a friendly domestic is in accord
on this point. He himself writes that as his mental health improved
he stopped dreaming. He was the first disciple to break with Freud,
and after the break it became clear that he had never accepted some
of Freud's most important ideas. Freud retaliated by describing
him publicly as a diagnostician with but one idea: "whether a person
is a homosexual, or a necrophilist, or an anxiety-ridden hysteric, or
a shut-in obsessional, or a raving madman—in every case the Individual Psychologist of the Adlerian persuasion will assign the motive
force of his condition to the fact that he wants to assert himself, to
overcompensate for his inferiority, to be on top, and to move over
from the feminine to the masculine."

Adler had earned the wrath of his former master by saying that
Freud's Oedipus complex, the focal point of psychoanalytic theory,
revealed that Freud had been a pampered child. Our times have
grown soft, Adler said; we produce a great many spoiled children
today, and Freud is one of them. His young mother was nearer his
own age than that of his elderly father (who had married a second
time) and therefore it was only natural that when young Sigmund
was cosseted by her he developed the desires to possess her and to do
away with his father. He grew up in familially unusual and socially
decadent circumstances, and then presumed to extract an ironclad
scientific law from them.

This interpretation is typical of Adler, who might be described
as a hearty, romantic moralist, actively disgusted by the shut-in,
sickly atmosphere that he perceived in Freud's repetitious insistence
on infantile sexuality as a crucial factor in the determination of
character. He believed that the self-indulgence he found in an
apparently austere Freud was a sign of bad education. The favorable

response that greeted the Oedipus complex meant merely that a great many other people had been similarly spoiled into sexual precocity of one kind or another. It reinforced them in their private weaknesses. "For by endorsing the theory they were thereby confirmed in their own way of life."

The tragic tough-mindedness that Freud advocated was, therefore, in Adler's eyes not nearly as tough as it seemed; it was soggy at the core; it came from making impossible childish demands on life and then at the first disappointment it pulled a long face and complained that the cards were stacked against everyone. Characteristically it avoided political commitment, found fault brilliantly with those who did attempt to improve the social condition of man, and retreated into an empty, gloomy preoccupation with unconquerable evil which prevented any action at all—in a word, permitted the spoiled child to go on in a private fantasy of his own superiority to a world which had not humored his every wish.

If, however, Adler was sensitive to the progress of his career, as compared to the progress of Freud's, a fear must have hidden behind this analysis, a fear that "the spoiled child" had after all been shrewder than he had been, that in a time of social disintegration a public-spirited citizen would surely lose out, in the competitive struggle for fame, to a gloomy pessimist who found a weak spot in everyone's armor and made the most of it. (Marcel Proust was to cause similar misgivings among social-minded literary critics who had called him a mere "dressmaker.") Adler had bet on the individual's use of reason to extricate himself from a sea of troubles; Freud had bet on the individual's inability to cope with it. Freud moved toward a "metapsychology" for those who had written off their "social feeling" as meritorious but unworkable; Adler was left holding a bag full of noble sentiments. Freud despised the romantic ardor of the revolutionist; Adler had nothing else. Meanwhile men who had never heard of either of them, and cared less, moved in.

The Freud-Adler duel is by no means ended, despite the wish of ex-communists to declare it a complete victory for Freud. Former revolutionaries have washed their hands of their former opinions so thoroughly that Adler, who often appealed to them more in the nineteen thirties than Freud did, has had to pay dearly for their change of heart. In Adlerian terms it would be easy to analyze them. They never were real revolutionaries but opportunists, who sought to use the revolution, which they then thought inevitable, for their own purposes. They possessed no "social feeling;" by comparison Freud, who worked for his patients and developed his ideas in important books, was full of it. So they were not then genuine Adlerians and they are not now genuine Freudians; they were always selfish human beings who are now exploiting a trend toward aestheticism in the same way that they once exploited a trend toward politics. They make a touchstone of the word "tragic" and judge a psychologist by how skillfully he shows that life is Hobbesianly repugnant and has always been so.

Adler has lost this duel, and not only because he forfeited the support of those spoilt children who have switched their allegiance, as the dirtiness of politics became evident, from men of state to men of letters. Adler has also lost this duel because he failed to sustain the individual in the way that his psychology specifically promised, at a time of profound disillusionment, when individuals learned to put no trust in princes of any kind. Too often it was found that his analysis did not go deep enough and had to fall back on that expedient which seems still to be the chief resource of similarly superficial Pavlovian psychiatry in the Soviet Union: the expedient of exhortation. Also, as his own mental health improved and he turned away from writing and toward talking, his writing suffered, and he produced books which were flimsy in thought and sleazy in style. By no literary standard could they be put next to those of Freud. The demon of simplism possessed him at a period when men's problems were becoming more complex then ever before, when merely to state them required the greatest subtlety of expression, not to mention the patience and capacity to master the many new learned disciplines they had brought into being.

Nor was it adequate to say, when he replied to charges of oversimplification, that his simplicity was deliberate and artful. "I have taken forty years to make my psychology simple," he replied on such occasions, according to his biographer Phyllis Bottome. "I might make it still more simple. I might say, 'All neurosis is vanity' —but this also might not be understood." That was excellent as one more expression of his stout-hearted faith in the healing effect of the moral challenge; but it was couched in language that many patients mistrusted; it contributed more to his own jovial sense of well-being than to an understanding of his patients' anxiety. It implied the curability of evil. For all the wisdom that Adler displays at moments, here and there in his books, there is in them a residual base of naïve Rousseauism, a belief in man's essential goodness which has been corrupted by bad institutions but will return when the institutions are rebuilt. A belief also in the Enlightenment—without the qualifications that might give it meaning today. This was an important part of his socialist faith, of his own "style of life," and no doubt of his own "guiding fiction."

At the present moment the pessimism of Freud and his grave doubts as to the perfectibility of man seem to have won this debate beyond question. In fact, those in the camp of the new Freudian orthodoxy write as if the issue had been settled once and for all. "We made a mistake. We thought man could be improved and the world changed, but now we see the error of our ways. Freud was right all along. We now see that life *is* as sick and foul as he said it was, and we are trying to go on from there." That is the way their reasoning goes.

It is highly unlikely that this issue has been settled once and for all—if for no other reason than that at least half of the population, the female half of the population, will never agree to Freud's misanthropy. The function of women is entirely different from the function of an isolated thinker. No matter how profound his thoughts, he finally speaks for himself and a few others like him, rather than for the large-bosomed sorority who are charged with the responsibility of bringing babies into the world and training them to live in it. Such a thinker can no more pretend to inform us authoritatively about the nature of things than the simplest hausfrau. And certainly he will be a poor thinker—an atavistic throwback to patriarchal days—if he forgets that women can only perform their necessary functions in an atmosphere of hope, and that the atmosphere of hope that they do actually create out of their biologically induced will to believe is as continuous a reality as any of his gloomy insights or dismal laws. Even if the world were blown up on schedule at the exact hour he predicted, we would count on their naïveté to help rebuild it. And we would count on it with the same empirical assurance that permits us to be confident of the movement of the stars, the boiling point of water, the arrival of puberty, the Second Law of Thermodynamics.

Woman's need of hope, then, is a scientific fact like a plant's need of water; a fact that calls for constant action, social and individual, to avoid its debasement. To expect that it is ever going to be diminished, or should be diminished, is a sick form of masculine pretentiousness, not unrelated to the madness that drove the German people into two disastrous world wars. The anti-feminine temper of the Freudian movement, which insisted upon a strict exclusion of *feeling*, is now confronted, as our story will make clear, with a few of the things it left out. One of them is its vulgarizing effect upon women. Another is its sterilizing effect upon man. The kind of man whose rather doubtful masculinity was reassured by patriarchal exclusiveness will perhaps realize, if he can be made aware of anyone but himself, that he is being confronted with a major reason for his unreasoning despair.

Unfortunately, Adler did not appreciate the full implications of his thought, and let it lapse into socialist optimism that was quickly refuted by political events. He was a brilliant, but sloppy thinker. Actually, a warm-hearted inclusion of woman's need for hope and a scientific inclusion of feeling in psychology do not preclude a tragic sense of life. On the contrary, they are needed, as we shall see, to make a true tragic sense of life possible.

10

Jung and Comedy

Jung's manner is strikingly unlike Freud's gloom. Jung is hearty; for him the forces of the unconscious are not always dark and primitive; they can also, if understood, liberate and dignify. Dreams are not always infantile wish-fulfillments; they can also be adultly teleological, i.e., work toward a cure and a release of creative power. And he does not consider religion an "illusion" if it succeeds, as he reports it has succeeded with many of his patients, in healing their neuroses. To continue an earlier quotation, "The thing that cures a neurosis must be as convincing as the neurosis; and since the latter is only too real, the helpful experience must be of equal reality. But what is the difference between a real illusion and a healing religious experience? It is merely a difference in words. You can say, for instance, that life is a disease with a very bad prognosis, it lingers on for years to end in death; or that normality is a generally prevailing constitutional defect; or that man is an animal with a fatally overgrown brain. This kind of thinking is the prerogative of habitual grumblers with bad digestions. Nobody can know what the ultimate things are. We must, therefore, take them as we experience them. And if such experience helps to make our life healthier, more beautiful, more complete and more satisfactory to yourself and to those you love, you may safely say: 'This was the grace of God.' "

This will hearten the tender-minded and dismay the tough-minded, to whom it will seem to endorse, too unguardedly, just those obscurantist and regressive forces which are only too ready to kite such an appeal into a blank check for any kind of religiosity and, by extension, any kind of political exploitation of religiosity.

Progressives find that it descends to polite demagogy and attempts to ingratiate its author with the more conservative members of the Yale University audience which first heard it. Headlined it might read: Scientist Okays God. Even by private standards, with no reference to possible abuses or distortions, such a statement suggests that one's inner voice is more reliable than anyone but a well-disciplined mystic, who would hardly need such encouragement, has any right to expect. It reiterates the confidence of the "inner-directed." Are not the insane asylums full of those who imagine they have a direct pipeline to the Holy Ghost? Do not the milder cases of religious certitude join our army of sensitive ineffectuals, who have shrunk away from the healthy give-and-take of the marketplace into one elegant retreat or another? Is it not reckless to encourage them in their soul-searching, their art-major mandalas? All this seems like a decadent form of upper-class Protestantism when put next to the stern counsels of Freud, who warns specifically against such immature self-deceptions. Such, at least, has been some of the response to it.

Adler's criterion of "social interest" would also make short work of such a self-appointed search for "private meaning." More gently than Freud, but with equal firmness, he would point out that each of us must meet the test of what we do "when confronted by the unavoidable problems of humanity." If we retreat into purely decorative dilettantism we cannot lay claim to the possession of great souls. If much has been given us, then we have failed all the more lamentably. We may indeed be the worst failures of whom he writes: "no one else is benefited by the achievement of their aims, and their interest stops short at their own persons."

It soon becomes apparent that three kinds of ethics are ensnarled here, and ensnarled so humanly that the capacity to think clearly about them is far more difficult than professionals will admit. The first is the insistence on grim truth-seeking of Freud, the second the insistence on friendly teamwork of Adler, the third the insistence on personal development of Jung. Each of them is so heavily loaded, in the context of our own lives, with our own preoccupations— usually unconscious ancestral bequests and therefore all the more explosive—that when we attempt to discuss them we are really painting our family tree. Moreover, each of these men was exceptionally gifted, and shaped his thoughts with exceptional skill—with the special cunning that comes to a strong one-sided mind when it is out to prove that it alone is right. (I overlook their more modest disclaimers as mere tricks of the trade, to beguile the unwary.) Each of these men spoke from his own portion of the unconscious more persuasively than when he spoke from his intelligence. Which is one more reason why they are best understood when seen as myth-makers, not scientists.

To return to Jung, his reply to Freud and Adler has been clear. He has said that he encounters many patients who respond best to a Freudian analysis, many patients who respond best to an Adlerian analysis, and still others, usually in middle age, who "are suffering from no clinically definable neurosis, but from the senselessness and emptiness of their lives." This, he thinks, "can well be described as the general neurosis of our time," and has led to his distinction between the "personal unconscious," that Malebolge of primitive aggressions and timorous repressions, and the "collective uncon-scious," the potential Paradiso which contains within it the seeds of rebirth that can conquer emptiness and replace it with purpose. He finds the theories of Freud, even in their later, revised form, too simple. Man is not only a social creature, he says in effect, and not only a hard-pressed mediator between Eros and Thanatos. He also has a life of his own, and it can be a happy one.

In a sense Jung has been a more practical psychologist than the other two. He has used his science to achieve personal serenity. Adler's triumph was brief. Freud certainly enjoyed the excitement of his great discoveries and the professional satisfaction of being put on Darwin's level, but the whole tenor of his work suggests a grave personal disappointment, even among the lineaments of gratified ambition. His heroic sublimation did not bring the joy that his name may have promised him in boyhood. But Jung has been *happy*. No one can read his works without feeling his active enjoy-ment of life. He has achieved a harmony with nature that seems almost classical. It has not commended him to our crisis-ridden intellectuals. He has been called *bourgeois*. His style has been de-scribed as Brahmsian. Existentialists protest that he excludes the reek of pre-1914 euphoria. It is plain that he is not in the modern temper, which though nominally anti-Christian seems to demand of its spiritual heroes an Agony in the Garden and a Crucifixion—or at least a very painful compulsion neurosis such as was suffered by those Christ-obsessed flagellants, Kierkegaard, Nietzsche, Dostoevsky, Van Gogh. The bucolic contentment of Jung hardly commends him for martyrdom, and it is martyrs that we—or at least a respected group of moralists among us—demand these days. The obscure sexual difficulties of Freud, as well as his cancer and his rescue in extreme old age from a brutal soldiery, are more to the taste of a generation that under the guidance of Albert Camus has made a hero of Sisyphus. (Adler does not count for much with that generation, which appears to regard him as a Foolish Virgin.)

The real reason why this generation is anti-Jung is that he does not help them in their drive for a success that might, they hope, compensate them for their unhappiness. Jung actually encourages the pleasure principle by his endorsement of a leisurely Goethean search for metaphysical values, by his hospitality to Vedanta, Taoism and Zen, by his scholarly research in Gnosticism and alchemy, by his speculations on the "archetypes," on synchronicity, on the psychoid, in short by learned investigations that would require years of contemplation and perhaps a private income. He writes as if there were no hurry at all—for a generation continually rediscovering that it has "so little time." Olympian methods of this nature are not suited to those who refuse to be students all their lives, who feel they must make their mark, and certainly their livelihood, now or never. For such down-to-earth souls the Freudian ban on the pleasure principle and its early puritan replacement by the reality principle are distinctly preferable. We only live once, and even if we *have* made our mark, we have to go on making it again and again. It is all very well to play down success—*if* you have it. Otherwise you are ignored, and after a while the public's attitude toward you becomes your own. Jung offers a nice consolation prize for the losers, something like hothouse gardening in the wintertime. He has nothing to say to those who want to win. Such charges have been made repeatedly against him.

Our realistic belief in success, success repeatedly reestablished in the press and daily proclaimed by possessions, provides the id-core of much opposition to Jung. Another source is the desire to communicate idiomatically with one's contemporaries. Jung appears to be advocating a new brand of otherworldliness. Such is not the case. Actually Jung advocates success here and now, but of an unpopular kind; private, unrecognized, estranging success; success that means, unless one is well cushioned against the disapproval of the populace, failure and poverty. His ideas are not easily apprehended by a mind conditioned by ambition or journalism. They invite, in fact, the repudiation they so frequently encounter, and sometimes not merely because of their nature, but because of the almost perverse and provocative way their author has phrased them. The quotation from his Yale lectures will have indicated how he enjoys, safe in his privileged coign of vantage, violating the intellectual tabus of more exposed scholars. His works abound in such prankish ambiguities, one of which, about Hitler, was notoriously infelicitous. But it is the unpopular substance of his ideas that creates most of his enemies. Numerically there is a smaller but more important resistance among those who are greatly stimulated by his thought but, since they want to communicate with a contemporary audience which demands that ideas be given a flesh-and-blood reality, such as his do not have, are forced to realize that these, like his archetypes, must be translated into the language of our day. It is a tribute to his enormous fertility of concept, a fertility that was most certainly helped by his nation's aloofness from struggle.

Jung does not conceal his mistrust of the unaided ego, that cornerstone of Freud's fortress against darkness and regression. Even before Freud came along, an ego-psychology was helping to strengthen the West by increasing its technical skills and redoubling its Faustian will to control the forces of nature; but now, Jung suggests, this exploitative mentality, though the East is at present feverishly trying to imitate it, has reached the point of diminishing personal returns. He therefore finds reasons to respect—though not to copy—the psychological procedures of an earlier East which is on the defensive today even in Asia. Such procedures, which seek to reinforce the ego with unused powers in the mind, increase our perspective on individual fulfillment here and now. They may not advance our technical effectiveness in a market place that requires sedulous adjustment to its frenzied competition; but they may help to make life worth living.

Indirectly Joseph Campbell described Freud's position when he wrote in *The Hero with a Thousand Faces*: "Modern literature is devoted, in great measure, to a courageous, open-eyed observation of the sickeningly broken figurations that abound before us, around us, and within. . . . And there is no make-believe about heaven, future bliss, and compensation. . . . In comparison with all this, our little stories of achievement seem pitiful. . . . Hence we are not disposed to assign to comedy the high rank of tragedy." Indirectly Campbell described Jung's position when he wrote: "The happy ending of the fairy tale, the myth, and the divine comedy of the soul, is to be read, not as a contradiction, but as a transcendence of the universal tragedy of man. The objective world remains what it was, but, because of a shift in emphasis within the subject, is beheld as though transformed. Where formerly life and death contended, now enduring being is made manifest. . . . The dreadful mutilations are then seen as shadows, only, of an immanent, imperishable eternity; time yields to glory; and the world sings with the prodigious, angelic, but perhaps finally monotonous, siren music of the spheres."

The distinguishing feature of Jung's psychology, as we have noted, is the "collective unconscious," which he says takes us out of our ego-preoccupations, reaches back to remotest antiquity, and contains the potentials of health and integration. To clarify the "personal unconscious," as Freud does, is not enough, Jung says, but must be continued into the spontaneous, archetypal symbolism that unites all men and offers transcendence of the more banal and frustrative portions of existence. Understood and used intelligently, this symbolism can fill the spiritual vacuum that is modern man's birthright. A tasteful preference for tragedy can be a safe academic formula, rather than a confrontation of both disaster *and* glory. Tragedy will come inevitably wherever there is life, but as a concept it means nothing unless it follows a conscious struggle against it in its frequently neurotic forms. Archetypal symbolism contains the seeds of faith, but does not lead to easy serenity—rather to a lifelong, controversial value-search that tragically estranges the individual from society and resembles existentialism in its trials. Later we shall see that a new school of "Existential Analysis" has come into being, and that it has much in common with Jung's mistrust of a lucrative, egodominated "mind-body split."

Such reasoning will not mean much to most people who only want to think of psychology when they suffer from some serious and elusive disorder. It also offends the practical nature of most Americans because it does not seem to apply to their everyday problems, which, when psychiatric in origin, can be dealt with by a licensed psychiatrist. Groundlings of this sort are apt to think of Jung, when they think of him at all, as addicted to la-di-da introspection, which, at first glance, is all his psychology seems to be. The devotion of his prodigious scholarship and insight to such remote matters as faith, not to mention the Gnostics and the alchemists, at a time when our psychiatry is unable to cope with such immediate matters as divorce, alcoholism, sexual deviations, delinquency, immaturity and escapism, appears to be nothing but another escapism.

Only an uninformed reading will find it so. Actually as a psychiatrist with enormous clinical experience, Jung knows very well what our everyday problems are; his books deal with them continually. His later works, for example, throw much new light on our latest social problems, the origin of wars, and what caused the atomic physicists to create the instrument that makes us all uneasy. Readers are still put off, however, by his seemingly oblivious manner, which grandly overlooks prevailing economic and biological orientations and coins a private language. Examination also discovers that he has not a few blind spots, can antagonize both the religious and the antireligious, attracts a cult of irresponsible devotees, can be rather insensitive on matters of literature and art, and has taken a position that must be termed esoteric. Upon closer examination, his esotericism seems deliberate—and farsighted.

Politically, he is neither the obscurantist nor the reactionary that he has been called, but he does *not* have faith in the masses. (Neither did Freud.) He believes that Western man is possessed by unconscious forces that have "robbed him of all free will." (Will, incidentally, he defines as the "sum of psychic energy disposable to consciousness," which seems an excellent example of the manner in which an ancient philosophic issue can be clarified by a psychologist. If you are not free, it is because your mind is still relatively "primitive." If you wish to be free, the way to it is through a new kind of "culture and moral education.") "And this state of unconscious possession will go on until we . . . become scared of our godalmightiness. Such a change can only begin with individuals, for the masses are blind brutes, as we know to our cost. It seems to me of some importance, therefore, that a few individuals, or people individually, should begin to understand that there are contents which do not belong to the ego-personality but must be ascribed to a psychic non-ego."

Modern man, he says, has lost faith in all ready-made symbols, but he cannot be healed by the reduction of his ailments to any single cause, however helpful it may seem at first. To become healthy and free, man must draw upon mental resources which come from "a psychic non-ego" that unites him to other men and to nature. This seems dubious to those bound by medical charts and newspaper statistics and the shopkeepers' trust in immediate tangible success, but is none the less real. To be of lasting use, psychiatry should aid in building a bridge to the new, untried faith that we must find for ourselves if we are not to be destroyed by our ignorance of the true dynamics of the psyche, which are far subtler—both more destructive and more regenerative—than Freud presents them in a tidy meccano-like system.

Since the correction of our ignorance would require a long period of humble study and personal dislocation, it is not difficult to see why few undertake it. To be truly effective, Jung's therapy means many more years of tough self-discipline than Freud's, because it calls for both a Freudian adjustment and a Jungian break with accepted social goals. Thus nothing is so understandable as the opposition of practical folk, who are more subject to the objective psyche's demons than their daily tasks will allow them to admit. When they enlist psychiatry they want a patchwork job. Meanwhile we go on producing "hollow men" who will never be able to give us the leadership we need. Nearly all Jungian patients are timid introverts seeking unnoticed secession.

Actually, there can be no "comic" transcendence of tragedy except in exceptional moments preceded and followed by suffering. There is not so much difference between Freud and Jung on this point as there seems to be, though Jung counsels a greater trust in the helpful processes in nature. Time exaggerated the difference of the two men on this issue. Freud reacted against the old arrogance of religion—which he had keenly felt in Austria—when he dismissed it as an illusion. Jung reacted against the new arrogance of science—which he had keenly felt, somewhat later, in Switzerland—when he said that under certain circumstances religion could be healthy.

He was also less identified with a strictly medical point of view than Freud. He had begun his career as a classical scholar, before studying medicine, and his continuing closeness to the soil increased his detachment about his profession. "Whoever is rooted in the soil endures." Compared with Freud's equally bannerlike "Men are strong so long as they represent a strong idea," this suggests an attitude that we shall be getting soon from one of our novelists. "Remoteness from the unconscious, and therefore from the determining influence of history, means an uprooted state. This is the danger . . . confronting every individual who through one-sidedness in any kind of ism loses his relation to the dark, maternal, earthly origin of his being." It is one of Jung's leading ideas, and it is also one of

D. H. Lawrence's. It goes with the genial, relaxed therapy that Jung seems to have practiced. One of his favorite maxims is the Latin form of "Nature heals, the physician only treats." It also suggests a more historical attitude toward the unconscious than was possible to the more harassed, more dramatic Freud—a difference that can be traced, as we shall see, to their religious backgrounds. In addition, it may explain why Jung was not able to accept Freud's original emphasis on sex.

Freud genuinely believed that Jung was guilty of expediency or puritanism when he wished, as Freud put it, to "soft-pedal" sex. What Freud could not realize was that his own emphasis on sex as a factor in psychopathology was in part a consequence of his struggle with puritanism; or that to Jung, who was much less of a puritan than he, sexual disorders could at times be merely symptomatic of still larger disturbances—disturbances which originated in an up-rooting, both physical and spiritual, of which the patient was still less aware than of his erotic misfortunes. Freud believed, because his own career had been mostly limited to city laboratories and city clinics and city neuroses, that Jung wished to play safe. Actually, it would have been more expedient at that time—1912—for Jung to soft-pedal his differences with Freud, and not to insist upon his own interpretations. But Jung had to express his own relationship to nature, and Freud had to express his, and so their rupture occurred. It was a great shock to both of them. That much is made clear by the amount each has written about it. But it was also a stimulant, it put them on their mettle, and each continued to influence the other —at a distance. So much the better for us: in their imperfect retinas is our vision.

Nevertheless it is a *practical* disadvantage to be nonpartisan in this debate. It makes one seem remote. Today only fanatics get an eager hearing—from exactly the same kind of fanatic. Nothing else will *send* anybody. We listen to ideas as we listen to jazz; we want them to transport us. This is the way things are. People do not even try to be "fair" any more. It seems too professorial. This, not World War I, produced the Lost Generation. This, not World War II, produced the Mislaid Generation. This, not the stuffiness of squares, produces beatniks. To be "beat" is a specialization too, a quest for a personal style so far underwater that any reminder of a community of fellow beings is regarded as an amphibious insult. We secede from society, but we begin by seceding from ourselves.

The effect of this double alienation upon our arts and sciences has received as much critical comment as any other phenomenon of our times. Generally our intellectuals—for example, our obscure poets and our obscure physicists—are attacked as arid and abstract. Actually, however, when they are examined closely they prove to be intensely emotional beings who have crammed lifetimes of feeling into an algebraic poem or a technical book review intelligible to only a few other professionals. Since no steady flow of expression is permitted them by the tight rules of the game they play, they usually have to cede the right to be heard above the crowd to loudmouthed popularizers who merely translate their ideas into platitudes or megatons. Their ideas are nuggets of feeling that need to be alloyed with baser metals for mass consumption. So our true poets are driven into conversation with one another—in symbols almost as rarely understood as those of the physicists—and run the risk of coterie dry rot, unless they can find a way to break their double alienation, from self and society.

Whether Jung's ideas can help them or the scientists remains to be seen. His archetypes are addressed directly to this problem, as a step toward freeing the mind from its immediate surroundings and enabling it to reroot itself in universal history. His typology, with its intricate crisscross of the functions of thought, feeling, intuition, sensation with extroversion and introversion, is also a guide for finding everyman's place in nature. His picture of the feminine portion of man, the *anima*, and the masculine portion of woman, the *animus*, together with his *persona*, or the mask presented to society, and his detailed account of the process of individuation—all of these are so plainly the product of one man's struggle for meaning, with his patients providing the details, that a similarly troubled reader cannot help but follow him with warm sympathy and admiration. "Do not think carnally," he is saying, "or you will be flesh, but think symbolically, and then you will be spirit." If you look clearly at the many determinisms that surround you, you need no longer be at their mercy. You also need not be blindly partisan.

Women will find in Jung an attention to their problems that Adler merely suggests—not their social problems, however, but their personal ones. Much of Jung is addressed to intellectual women who must absorb as harmoniously as possible a disagreeably mannish *animus* if they are to attain their full, complex stature as human beings. Such "priestesses" are subject to much satire from those who would in effect restrict them to the Hitlerian three K's, but this kind of envious vulgarity means nothing to Jung. He is also not greatly interested in the problems of children, or in the conventional "homemaker"; but unusual women and the fine points of marriage get more attention from him than from any other psychologist. As might be expected from such a curious man, he is also interested in random phenomena that cannot be explained satisfactorily by scientific causality, by possible toxic factors in schizophrenia, by the symbolism of the mass, by the possible relationship of horoscopes to failure in marriage, by the psychic effect of departed redskins on the behavior of present-day American whites. But that is a very small list of his investigations, the broad sweep of which may not have been equalled since the Renaissance.

From the standpoint of the Remnant, I think, the most challenging contribution of Jung is his adaptation of the Polynesian word *mana* (extra-physical power or extraordinary effectiveness) in what he calls "the mana-personality." A few human beings become mana-personalities, he says, through their capacity to control internal forces that formerly may have made their behavior unpredictable but now qualify them to serve as leaders. Such people have descended successfully into their own lower depths, made the "night sea journey" required of the hero, and now they are our best guides. They *know*, they have been there. Nothing human is alien to them. Their humanity is now working *for* them.

Mana is closely related to the "autonomy" that Riesman expects the lonely crowd to develop: "The very conditions that produce other-direction on the part of the majority today, who are heteronomous—that is, guided by voices other than their own—may also produce a 'saving remnant' who are increasingly autonomous, and who find their strength in the face of their minority position in the modern world of power." But it is not merely as easy or as vague as that, Jung says. We must acquire an intimate understanding of internal forces that are remarkably similar in everyone. As similar, in fact, as the bodily processes of seeing or digesting or breathing. We must wrest power from these internal forces and confer it, not upon a self-inflated ego, but upon our portion of the impersonal. Does it seem simple? It is the most difficult achievement of all. A Remnant will not be produced by "conditions" but by precise self-study and ancient religious methods of self-reliance brought up to date.

11

Otto Rank:
the Laocoön of Ideology

Otto Rank was the third famous psychologist to break with Freud. It took him longer to effect his separation from his master, to whom he was almost a son for some twenty years. When he broke, his direction was more like that of Jung than that of Adler—towards philosophy and the humanities rather than towards statecraft and pedagogy. Rank sought a solidly based belief, "beyond psychology," which he came to regard as something to be surpassed; a belief that would sustain him in the dark hours that he recorded with agony when he was intellectually "fatherless" and on his own; when the stern guidance formerly obtained from Freud had to be replaced by the guidance of his own mind.

The personal slant which we seek habitually in our study of artists, and have found equally in evidence in Freud, Adler and Jung, is still more noticeable in the case of Rank, who seems at times quite neurotic, by his own definition, in his inability to cope with the invisible forces that attacked him when he achieved his independence. During that tortured but productive culmination, in bitter revulsion against the Bunsen-burner calm of Freud, whom he considered impenetrably self-deceived about the true problems of man, the former disciple wrote with palpable anguish: ". . . our seeking the truth in human motives for acting and thinking is destructive. With the truth, one cannot live. To be able to live one needs illusions. . . . The neurotic, as distinguished from the creative man of will . . . , is not the voluntary seeker of truth, but the forced, unhappy finder of it." More than once we receive the impression that Rank himself was an unhappy finder of truths which cut short his life at fifty-five, poisoned his fifteen years of freedom, and posthumously became his major contribution. He suggests the writhing figure of Laocoön, destroyed by the serpents of an "ideology" that he had learned to detest but could not escape.

Near the end he was on his way to a personal vocabulary that seems to have been forced upon him by his problems. That word "ideology" recurs frequently and with more than one tortured meaning in his later work. At the age of twenty-one, however, he was open to ideological training, and succeeding precociously at it, when he met Freud. Freud has described the meeting in his *History of the Psychoanalytic Movement*. Rank had read three books of his, which were reflected in a manuscript of his own called *The Artist*. Freud liked the manuscript and took the youthful engineering student under his wing during the early years of psychoanalysis. He opened an agreeable career to him, threw important editorships his way, and treated him like his own seventh child. The brilliance of Rank was generally conceded, even in a group of men who, to judge by their own accounts, must have formed one of the most censorious apostolates in history. (Freud called them *"la crapule."*) He proved of increasing value to Freud, especially after the defections in 1911 and 1912 of Adler and Jung, when Rank's talents as a cultural critic were needed to offset the scholarship of Jung. Nevertheless a familiar drama was restaged in 1924 when Rank published *The Trauma of Birth*, which brought on such a sneering attack in the Freudian press, though not from Freud himself to whom the book was dedicated, that the thin-skinned Rank fled to Paris on a temporary journey that proved to be permanent exile from Vienna. Later he moved to New York, where he published a series of books that broke violently with some of Freud's best-known ideas. He died in America in 1939, during the same disastrous year which saw Freud die in England and Hitler open his attack on the world.

Most critics emphasize the contradictions and confusions in Rank's thought. He began by accepting Freud's concept of the unconscious, later called for the exercise of rational will within "a psychology of consciousness," and finally put his faith in the irrational "mythical stuff" that he said the individual in today's cultural crisis must find within himself or perish. It is only too easy to discover these confusions, if we consider Rank as a systematic thinker, but we do so at the risk of overlooking the stiffly-worded but pene-

trating insights that he succeeded in leaving behind him, in unpopular books and manuscripts published only after his death, as a
delayed bequest of a minor but genuine hero. Rank did not possess
the stature to create a system; and besides, he was fed up with
systems. He had given most of his mature years to a system, and
decided it did not work. In type he was a son, and when he became
a rebellious son he left his mark. Lately a few admirers are attempting to build him up as a prophet who has already led the world
"beyond psychology," as if its new and largely untried disciplines
had so soon become obsolete, and as if more gifted men of letters had
not indicated the way beyond it earlier and with better language and
surer knowledge.

Such an attempt provides one more instance of the relative in-
sularity of psychology when it is confronted with problems that
artists face every day. The polytechnician with an avocation for art,
the divided "son" who waited until he was forty to break with "papa,"
became vulnerable, after his break, in a way that every honest man
of letters expects as a matter of course. No longer protected from a
harsh world (though as a famous man he was instantly able to get
a lucrative practice as a lay analyst), he let out a new kind of scream,
the scream of the unsmocked scientist, the confessor who finds
himself, after years of authority, on the wrong side of the confessional. He was ridiculous but admirable, certainly more admirable
than those who clung to orthodoxy to avoid a similar comedown.
(A comedown that now seems inevitable for many other scientists
and technicians.)

The chief direction of his new thinking was away from neat biological reductions and towards the unchartable paths of *Weltanschauung*, which Freud had specifically rejected. Years of skepticism
erupted in the conclusion that "the individual therapy for the
neurosis is philosophical, which Freud will not admit because he
thinks in the medical ideology in which he has grown up. But he
himself has found that the neurosis presents not a medical but a
moral problem. . . . The patient needs a world view and will always
need it, because man always needs belief, and this so much the more,
the more increasing self-consciousness brings him to doubt." It is not
difficult to hear echoes of Adler and Jung here, as well as of patients
who had also come to such conclusions. And soon they will erupt
still more vigorously in the concentration camps, where faith was
needed if the prisoner was to survive.

But to return to Rank: "The irreconcilable conflict in which psycholoanalysis itself is caught arises because it wants to be theory and therapy at the same time and this is just as irreconcilable as truth with reality." In other words, "truth," when stripped of feeling and faith and other scientifically inconvenient "illusions," becomes destructive if aimed at anyone not armed with Freud's obsessional faith in science, his own unconscious religion, his own "illusions." Freud does not realize how much nihilism he is helping to disseminate. Therefore there must be a fuller concept of truth that will enable it to hold its own with reality. Wearing the heavy mail of his doctoral dissertation style, Rank sets forth on a quest of a new kind of truth that will not crumple on contact with reality, or be impossible to live with; and some years later, in the last months of his life in fact, finds it in the hidden "mythical stuff" that gives the artist his irrational confidence and his unshakable sense of vocation.

This last appears to have been even more mysterious and convincing to him than Freud's strategic monomania had been in the good old days of filial piety. It did not lead Rank to give his blessing to any living practitioners of the arts, or to cease from trying to discourage them from following "an outworn ideology." Nor did it lead him to attempt to practice an art himself, or to criticize the works of art of his own day, except to imply by silence that they did not deserve criticism; but at least it did give him a glimpse of the inner conviction that he himself had not been able to find in a lifetime of hard search.

By comparison with the speculations of such artists as Yeats and Lawrence, his reports are academic. But they do have the merit, appreciated by those who lack a key to the symbolic language of the poets—that is, those who are so estranged from themselves that poetry does not speak to them—of putting what would be self-evident to poets into the ideological language that is now required by most "educated" people before they will even consider a newly-expressed idea. Science-based ideology is our new Latin, and as necessary to international communication as Latin was in another day. Its chief linguistic source today, however, is High German, and its native heath the No Man's Land between knowledge and being, between culture and instinct, between mind and body, that is so often found in the better universities. It would prefer to be a dead language, but that is impossible so long as it can be quickly translated—most notably by Germans or Russians—into political action.

Like other tongues, it is rarely mastered by lazy or otherwise occupied Anglo-Saxons. In science it lends itself more readily to the water-tight system of a Freud than to the diaristic notes of a Rank, who forfeited some of his earlier fluency in it as soon as he sought to bridge the gap between knowledge and being—as soon, in short, as he was exposed to an artist's trials.

In a late book entitled *Psychology and the Soul* he calls psychology "a predominantly negative and disintegrative ideology . . . an ideology of resentment in Nietzsche's sense. It becomes increasingly unable to maintain even itself, and finally, as the last natural science, ideology, it destroys itself." Man, however, can overcome death "ideologically" through his will to immortality. And in his last work, *Beyond Psychology*, he writes of "ideologies" that "more than anything else seem to carry the whole rationalization that man needs in order to live irrationally."

It is a curious use of language which is also found in many other pages, equally perplexing. The reader will want to know what it means. I think it means that Rank was stuck with words and attitudes that would take him no further, words and attitudes that had worked well enough so long as he did not take off the heavy underwear that Freud had sewn him into, so long as he did not bare himself to the prevailing wind that certain others had been feeling all their lives. Rank sends chills down the orthodox spine; he is the fool who tried to go it alone. Most admirably he lacked the saving mediocrity that was to spare another revisionist, as our chronicle unfolds, a similar punishment. He waded, not beyond psychology, but beyond his own psychological depth. The pathos of his last letters reads at times like that of a patient, not a doctor.

His sufferings were the evidence of his courage and the genesis of his insight. His insight, as we shall see, was in many instances truly prophetic.

12

A French Intruder

The appearance of a French name upon this distinctly Germanic roster might call for apology, if the trend of recent history did not require it. To vault so lightly from one bank of the Rhine to the other would be inexcusable, at least among those harassed system lovers who want order at all costs, were it not for the already marked demand among ex-Freudians for a psychologically-grounded metaphysics that is not unpalatable to scientific discipline. A brief half century after Freud first announced his radically biological psychology in *The Interpretation of Dreams* there appeared a radically metaphysical psychology which went still further in the direction indicated by Jung and Rank. It was restricted neither by Jung's empiricism nor by Rank's irrationalism. Along with the related and simultaneous movement of Existential Analysis, it raised issues that must be considered by the Remnant. Its author was French, and he arrived at his psychology through the most desperate personal need. His name was Hubert Benoit.

Actually, the introduction of a French name throws our whole chronicle into a different perspective. This is so not only because it recalls the original debt of the young Freud to Charcot and Janet, during his student days in France, when he borrowed so much from them that Janet accused him of theft; but also because it helps to rescue the unconscious from heavy-handed doctors who suggest learnedly that it is theirs alone to interpret. A French name recalls such uninstructed amateurs as Montaigne, Molière, La Bruyère, La Rochefoucauld, Fénelon, Stendhal, Proust, and their "chaotic"—the word is Lionel Trilling's for the "mass of psychological insights which literature has accumulated through the centuries"—efforts to assist our understanding of man. As opposed to the "egotism" that Santayana found almost everywhere in German philosophy, and that may also be discerned in Germanic psychology, a French name recalls the humility and sanity of Montaigne, who wrote: "He who sets before him, as in a picture, this vast image of our mother Nature in her entire majesty; who reads in her aspect such universal and continued variety; who discerns himself therein, and not himself only but a whole kingdom, to be but a most delicate dot—he alone esteems things according to the just measure of their greatness."

Whatever his own merits, the introduction of Hubert Benoit means that we have left temporarily those northerly and easterly regions where the individual can see himself quite easily as more than a dot; where he may even need to simulate egotism if he does not feel it, in order to be heard; where culture and instinct are so habitually divorced that ideas have a value of their own, quite distinct from the life and art that express them. We enter a southerly and westerly region where there are distinctly fewer puritan sexual repressions (though by no means a complete absence of them) that call for de-Victorianization. There is, therefore, a less urgent need for Freud's kind of therapy. It is also a region with a strong intellectual tradition, a fruitful tension between the Church and the Revolution, and a habit of keen satirical analysis that prevents ideas from staying too long out of bounds. To say this is not to imply that France or any other relatively unpuritan country can handle its steadily increasing problems of mental hygiene without availing itself of the discoveries of modern psychology. On the contrary, it is quite obvious to the student of contemporary trends that these discoveries will be needed in time not only by the French, the Italians, the Spaniards, and other Latins, but by the Arabs, the Congolese, the Russians, and even by the Hindus, who originally contributed the idea of the unconscious to the West. (As historians have frequently shown, this was done through the translation of the Upanishads that influenced Schopenhauer, and through him Nietzsche, and through him Freud.) The mental dislocations that follow technology, whether in Europe or in once colonial lands, will naturally call for the best knowledge of the mind available. This means that our psychiatric methods must be broadened to fit other traditions. Vedanta may come back some day to a Calcutta as smoky and effi-

cient as Pittsburgh once was—if that is possible in a hot country—in
the form of a psychiatrist from Punxsutawney, Pa., wearing the caste
marks of a new kind of Brahmin.

Benoit is a Frenchman who needed psychological help that he
did not find in the French tradition. Personal distress sent his mind
in quest of a clarity that he did not find among the psychologists
discussed here. As a surgeon he had been operating in a hospital at
Saint-Lô, during the Allied landings in 1944, when a bomb scored a
direct hit on the hospital and on him. It took two years and a series
of operations to put him back on his feet, and only by good fortune
were his two legs finally saved. He still has difficulty standing, and
his right hand is partially paralyzed. It was impossible for him to
continue as a surgeon, and so he returned to a previous secondary
interest in psychology as a substitute occupation. Slowly he began
to practice psychiatry and to develop the ideas that he had won
during his crippling and his convalescence: ideas which might be
summarized roughly as the thesis that man is fundamentally "a
metaphysical animal" whose psychic disorders can, in every case, be
traced to errors in philosophy. Such ideas were in the air: the Existential Analysts were making similar discoveries. His work with his
patients further convinced him that he was on the right track, that
others also needed the clarity he had found. When he discovered
Zen Buddhism in a book by D. T. Suzuki he had a complete metaphysical system, based on the primacy of the mind, without any
references to God, to use as a stalking horse for his own eager
thoughts. In 1951 he published *The Supreme Doctrine: Psychological Studies in Zen Thought*, which was written with traditional Zen
irreverence toward the Zen masters who had midwifed his program.
It is not brilliantly written; it attempts to spell out the unspellable,
to say what the Zen masters left unsaid; it is badly translated into
English; it leaves one in doubt as to whether he has personally experienced the satori, or enlightenment, on which Zen rests; it also
seems addressed more to himself, like a notebook, than to anyone
else; and yet it is an important document, truly required reading for
anyone who wants to swing freely among the many branches of the
forbidden tree.

The alert Jung, incomparably the best scholar among the psychologists, had already discovered Zen as a therapeutic tool and, though
praising its discipline and toughness, had warned against it. In 1934
he published his foreword to Suzuki's first European book, *Introduc-*

tion to Zen Buddhism. Earlier, in 1929, he had commented at length on Richard Wilhelm's German translation of an ancient Chinese text, *The Secret of the Golden Flower,* with a specific caution against "Western imitation of the East" of the very kind attempted by Benoit. In the Suzuki foreword he wrote: "Great as is the value of Zen Buddhism for the understanding of the religious transformation process, its use among Western people is very improbable. I have no doubt that the satori experience does occur in the West, for we too have men who scent ultimate ends and will spare themselves no pains to draw near to them. But they will keep silence, not only out of shyness but because they know that any attempt to convey their experience to others would be hopeless. . . . A direct transmission of Zen to Western conditions is neither commendable nor even possible." Benoit concedes that communication of "enlightenment" is also considered impossible by the Zen masters, and then proceeds to attempt it. (When I questioned him in Paris, as part of a program of seeing in the flesh as many of the psychologists discussed here as possible, Benoit explained this as a personal necessity. He also said that he preferred Freud to Jung, whom he found unreadable.)

The personal desperation that entered into Benoit's decision is reflected in this passage from *The Supreme Doctrine:* "If I observe myself I see that I struggle incessantly and instinctively in order to succeed . . . I conduct myself as if my hopes were legitimate, as if the real good which I need (Realization, satori) were to be found in the satisfaction of these hopes. Nevertheless just the contrary is true; my hopes lie to me, they are part of a vicious circle in which I wear myself out in useless efforts. . . . My perfect joy awaits me in the annihilation of my hopes.

"One must understand thoroughly that the total disaster in the midst of which satori awaits us does not necessarily coincide with a practical exterior disaster. . . . The realizing disaster does not consist in the practical ruin of hopes which would continue to exist in us (this would lead to suicide, not satori), but in the annihilation of the hopes themselves. . . . The man who has become really desperate, who no longer expects anything of the world of phenomena, is flooded by the perfect joy which he at last ceases to oppose."

One wonders parenthetically how far this state is from the acceptance of the reality principle that Freud advocates as a step to sublimation and creation and how far from the surrender to the impersonal Self that Jung advocates for similar purposes? Inescapably comparative psychology finds a greater agreement on essentials than any textbook would dare to suggest, however great the differences in approach and terminology, and however preferable it is to retain these differences, rather than sacrifice them to some forced and precipitate unanimity.

Imagination, says Benoit, is the greatest barrier to enlightenment. "It is in the failure to master the imagination," he writes in a passage from his *Psychanalyse et Metaphysique* which has been translated excellently by Aldous Huxley, "that human servitude resides. . . . Man is born with the potentiality of self-awareness, but without the immediate possibility of enjoying it. (He is ice and not yet water.) . . . But man would refuse to go on living, would do away with himself, if this inability to enjoy self-awareness were not compensated by something else—by some *ersatz* enjoyment which imposes on him and so makes him bear his lot with patience. . . . Imagination is a kind of inner cinema film which creates an appearance of wholeness. . . . Imagination does not bring realization, but only the fallacious hope of realization. . . . The work of liberation must consist of an unremitting struggle against these automatisms on the image plane.

"This work must be carried out as a practical exercise undertaken at times when the subject can withdraw from the immediate excitations of the outer world.

"The exercise. Alone, in a quiet place, muscularly relaxed (lying down or comfortably seated), I watch the emergence within myself of mental images, permitting my imagination to produce *whatever it likes*. It is as though I were to say to my image-making mind, 'Do what you please, but I am going to watch you doing it.' "

This is a process which Jung would call "withdrawing one's projections." It is also, as we shall see when we come to the literary response to the psychologists, closely related to the act of poetry as described by Yeats. It is a process which leads to true self-knowledge, Benoit says, and finally as much liberation as is possible on earth. He warns against "discipline" or "humility" or "asceticism," which will only get in the way. It is enough to give one's mind free play consciously and to develop an attitude of "active neutrality." "Man rules by dividing: refusing to take sides with any of his mental forces, he permits them to neutralize one another. . . . It is not for divine reason to overthrow nature, but to place itself above nature; and when it succeeds in taking this exalted position, nature will joyously submit."

He goes on in *The Supreme Doctrine*: "I see that at bottom all my negative states are humiliations, and that I have taken steps up to the present to give them other names." He counsels us to face our humiliations; they have within them the seeds of health and liberation. Face them, especially in their homeliest forms, and we are free. "The individual dies for the birth of the universal. . . . Let us recall that the 'nature of things' is for us the best, the most affectionate, the most humiliating of masters; it surrounds us with its vigilant assistance. The only task incumbent upon us is to understand reality and to let ourselves be transformed by it."

Thus our anxieties are not overlooked but put to work. What seemed like high-falutin' oriental mysticism turns out to be a plain, everyday dose of "reality" that has nothing to commend it to any escapist. (It is not difficult to understand why Benoit is not popular among "Dharma bums," those spoilt-child skimmers of the Zen cream of whom Jack Kerouac writes.) In his urgent personal need Benoit ranged "beyond psychology" to an extent not advised by Jung and not imagined by Rank—and found himself back once again among personal fantasies as painful to subdue as any described by Freud. *His* "mythical stuff" was humiliation—and the ability to live with it. What stimulated him was what crushed Rank: reality. In his *atterrissage* he seemed more French than ever, one more hardy flowering of *le sol gaulois*.

He is valuable to the Remnant for his description (a bit closer to our idiom than Suzuki's) of the steps that may lead to *satori*. Whether or not he has himself had this experience, he has provided an amazingly clear manual on what the mind must do if it is to employ its own restless energy to achieve ripeness. "For Zen the normal spontaneous evolution of man results in satori. . . . But my imaginative activity counteracts this profound genesis . . . which would otherwise accumulate until the explosion of satori. . . . It is enough that we think correctly, or more exactly that we cease to think wrongly." With schoolman's exactitude he tells us what it means to think wrongly and how our errors can be corrected. He makes a precise technique available.

We Americans need this, I believe, as much as he did. We too have suffered a great shock. We may be incapable of *satori*, in the Japanese sense, but we are capable of enlightenment. Moreover, we

have been denied, more than Europeans, precise techniques of consciousness. Our initiation rites are cruder. In this respect we are *not*
rich. A few decades ago we were too emotional, one way or another,
about Freud's analysis, because our radical secularization—from 1776
onwards—had deprived us of earlier religious pictures of the mind
and we needed a workable, up-to-date psychology. (That of William
James was beautiful but not sufficiently skeptical.)

Now, however, that Freud's narrowness becomes increasingly evident to all except a rather limited type of human being (often with
an axe to grind) we need a broader psychology, such as the present
book is trying to assemble from many different schools. This need is
felt especially by the Remnant. Most of us cannot even think about
satori, but the Remnant can. The books being bought today indicate
that it has already begun to do so. That is why it can learn so much
from Benoit's precise technique for making the most of one's
natural powers.

13

The Americanization
of Erich Fromm

Like some old witch's tale, the legend of George Grosz is often retold
by painters as an example of the peculiar hazards of the New World.
Grosz was the artist whose savage caricatures of Germany in the
nineteen twenties brought him the world-wide admiration of connoisseurs. He was compared to Daumier. Then Hitler rose to power
and Grosz left Germany for America, where his painting underwent
a transformation. It was no longer animated by hate but by love; it
turned from the frailty of man to the beauty of nature; it became not
savage but gentle—and no one with critical taste admired it any
more. It appealed to a peace-loving bourgeoisie. The artist himself
said he felt better while doing it, but his fellow artists said it was
not new or intense, as his earlier work had been, and its only value
was a warning: "Don't be nice. Don't be Americanized. When you
feel 'healthy' you can be sure of one thing—you're slipping!"

Erich Fromm came to America from Germany at about the same
time. A great reputation did not precede him; he was younger than
Grosz; but his first book to appear in English—*Escape from Freedom* (1941), which dealt largely with Nazi Germany—made him
famous. And ever since certain highbrow critics have been suggesting
either that he has slipped or *never was* any good anyway. The better
quarterlies attack his "easy rationalistic optimism" and his "cheerier
illusions." Yet he continues to reach a large and growing public
with books that appear with some regularity, and his lectures are
oversubscribed far in advance. Does his American popularity have
anything in common with that of Grosz? Does it merely mean a

deceptive kind of "health"? The answer, I think, is not as simple as it might appear to either highbrows (his critics) or middlebrows (his supporters). There are, first of all, the questions: Does he attempt to popularize things that cannot be popularized? Does he suffer from a preacherish determination to say the morally correct thing? Does he sacrifice disagreeable truth to a desire to reach a big audience? I am afraid the answer must be "yes" to each of these questions. On the other hand, it would be unjust to lose sight of the educational task he has set himself, because it is a task that we must all face.

As a writer Fromm is a man with a distinct gift: the gift of simplifying complex subjects so that they may be understood by considerable numbers of men. (In the field of political journalism Walter Lippmann has a similar gift.) There is a constant need in our society for such a gift, which can be exercised honorably. No one could fairly accuse Fromm of dishonorably exercising his gift. For example, when he discusses religion he is often guilty of superficiality and lack of imagination, but, on the other hand, he never descends to the "peace of mind" or "peace of soul" level of Rabbi Liebman and Bishop Sheen. On the contrary, he brings into play his extensive experience as a psychoanalyst, and he is, by report, a very gifted one, to combat just such best-seller nostrums. During the fight he develops a useful distinction between authoritarian religion and humanistic religion that because of its homely psychiatric precision will illumniate the subject for all honest readers, whether they are convinced churchgoers or agnostic intellectuals. His analysis of "authoritarian" rigidity of mind may well have provoked certain overemphatic highbrow attacks on him, since the well-worn path of a number of highbrows has gone from one authority to another.

Fromm gets his gift, as every writer does, from his own deepest self and his own deepest imagination. Fromm's imagination is semi-popular. It stops short of Rabbi Liebman and Bishop Sheen, and it also stops short of Freud and Jung. When it attempts mistakenly to match the latter two in theory, it cuts them down to its own size, a size that has not been unaffected by the hopes of reaching a large audience in America. Fromm's mind is above all practical; he has no use for Jung's sophisticated moral "relativities," or for the lonely perspective which caused an ageing Freud to withdraw his earlier claims for the effectiveness of his own therapy. On the contrary, Fromm sees psychoanalysis as a still potent weapon in the fight against the authoritarian mind, and he also sees the fight as one that can be won. "While Freud assumes that the conflict arising from the child's incestuous strivings is rooted in his nature and thus unavoidable, we believe that in a cultural situation in which respect for the integrity of every individual—hence of every child—is realized, the Oedipus complex will belong to the past."

In short, he is interested in changing the "cultural situation" and thereby assuring the maturity and "integrity of every individual." He believes, moreover, that this can be done, though naturally not right away. Despite the qualifications, we are no longer in the gloom that encircled Freud and drove Jung to his Gnostic Alps. We are back with Alfred Adler. Hope has returned from her hidingplace and brought with her plans for a realizable future.

The highbrows who snicker at this merely reveal their own social ignorance. A man whose natural sympathies are with practical people has expressed the not too blatantly encouraging message they want to hear. Another disguised panacea may be on the way, and another disguised disillusionment may be sure to follow it, but meanwhile there has been another injection of hope vitamins from a recognized scientific authority, and the Organization Man shows up for work on Monday morning. What is more, he whistles while he works and does not feel all alone. When has the art of public healing ever done more? Instead of being jeered by our intellectuals, Fromm's services to our society should be recognized. His occasional pretentiousness should not be allowed to antagonize the critical mind, and he should be valued as one of those workaday artisans of public opinion who actually help to make democracy work.

His psychology is geared to readers who would like to hope, after reading *The Lonely Crowd*, that the "other-directed" people described there with so much telling detail will be able to develop, as Riesman also hopes, "autonomy out of other-direction." In other words, that the multitudinous new conformists who now seek to cure their anxiety by gregariousness will "discover that their own thoughts and their own lives are quite as interesting as other people's, that, indeed, they can no more assuage their loneliness in a crowd of peers than one can assuage one's thirst by drinking sea water," and that when they have made this discovery "then we might expect them to become more attentive to their own feelings and aspirations." Fromm attacks this central problem of democracy on a psychological level that goes deeper than Riesman's sociological approach, which indeed appears to owe a debt to him. He is the man who told us in *Escape From Freedom* that Germany was taken over by the Nazis because it feared the responsibility of freedom, and later in *The Sane Society* (1955) that life in our American "twentieth-century Democracy constitutes another escape from freedom" with a predominant note of "robotism." Thus our much-publicized conformity is his main target. He does not wash his hands of it, as so many of our once "socially conscious" intellectuals now do. On the contrary he attacks it with all the tools of a psychotherapy weighted with his own special studies in anthropology. He relates it also to his latest readings in sociology, philosophy, symbolism, and theology.

He has a faith in his tools that more complex psychiatrists have sometimes come to lack. For example, Rank would have considered naïve his statement, "Indeed to help man to discern truth from falsehood in himself is the basic aim of psychoanalysis, a therapeutic method which is an empirical application of the statement, 'The truth shall make you free.'" Rank, as we have seen, had made the shattering discovery, "With the truth, one cannot live," because he believed reality was such a tough antagonist that the naked psychoanalytic truth about oneself, unaided by "illusion" or the artist's "mythical stuff," destroyed one's capacity to survive. Was it sheer perversity, or mere weakness, that led Rank to such unmanly admissions? Or was it a superior insight into the true nature of existence, forever denied to more thick-skinned idealists like Fromm? The answer, I think, lies in difference in temperament, difference in evolutionary development, difference in social function.

Fromm certainly does not share Rank's doubt. "Psychoanalysis has given the concept of truth a new dimension. In preanalytic thinking a person could be considered to speak the truth if he believed in what he was saying. Psychoanalysis has shown that subjective conviction is by no means a sufficient criterion of sincerity. A person can believe that he acts out of a sense of justice and yet be motivated by cruelty. He can believe that he is motivated by love and yet be driven by a craving for masochistic dependence. . . . In fact most rationalizations are held to be true by the person who uses them. . . . Furthermore in the psychoanalytic process a person learns to recognize which of his ideas have an emotional matrix and which are only conventional clichés without root in his character structure and therefore without substance and weight. The psycho-analytic process . . . is based on the principle that mental health and happiness cannot be achieved unless we scrutinize our thinking and feeling to detect whether we rationalize and whether our beliefs are rooted in our feeling."

This kind of faith, which holds out so much hope to a growing number of people who feel confused about the world and them-selves, would not have satisfied Rank. Rank would have found it elementary and misleading. He had tried the same method for many years, and believed it had let him down. Freud also, as we have seen, was finally only slightly more sanguine about his own invention.

Even Freud's later skepticism does not trouble Fromm. He finds Freud to be, when subjected to the psychoanalysis that he escaped during his lifetime, very neurotic indeed, so much so that his great contributions were compromised by his unloving egocentricity. In his book about the Founder (1959) Fromm shows little patience with Freud's self-deceptions, which he thinks left a bad legacy to us all. *Sigmund Freud's Mission* employs the enormous skill of an expert working analyst to present Freud's character as Fromm sees it and to draw some moral conclusions. It is a book which reveals much about both men.

When it first appeared it met with a chorus of resistance not un-related to that which originally shouted down Richard Aldington's book on T. E. Lawrence. Now Lawrence is seen somewhat less heroically by everyone, even in England. Perhaps Fromm's work will finally have the same effect on Freud's reputation and serve to di-minish his almost hypnotic appeal. Even if it should prove ulti-mately to be motivated by a misguided desire to replace Freud's image with Fromm's, it will have to be regarded as a closely docu-mented account of serious personal limitations. Though they were concealed behind the impressive robes of scientific theory by a man of extraordinary talent, a talent not lacking in histrionic embellish-ments, these limitations have affected us all. Fromm has told us what happens to the patients when the physician fails to heal himself.

His portrait of Freud goes further than Adler's in its depiction of the career of a "spoiled child" who saw the world too unquestion-ingly in terms of his own limitations. Freud's great courage and passion for truth were compromised, he implies, and at the same time made strangely palatable to other spoiled children who now venerate him for neurotic reasons of their own, by his blind spots towards women, towards feeling, towards his own destructive and frequently dishonest competitiveness. Taking a cue from Karen Horney, Fromm says that Freud's theories about women were "Naïve rationalization of male prejudice, especially of the male who needs to dominate in order to hide his fear of women." Taking a cue from Helen Walker Puner, Fromm says that Freud treated his wife almost as coldly as if she were a child-bearing servant—with boredom and condescension. In disagreement with Bruno Bettelheim, who insists that Freud committed adultery with his wife's more intellectual sister, Minna, during their frequent holidays alone, Fromm believes with Ernest Jones that Freud's sex life dried up soon after his marriage, and that he was only too glad to be beyond the reach of unruly passions that might have conflicted with his icy, world-conquering concentration on the unconscious life of others. Any betrayal of feeling meant an embarrassing upthrust of the unconscious in the physician as well as a retardation of his progress toward supreme intellectual dominance; and it was Freud's ambition to stretch the whole world out on a horsehair couch and to have it at the mercy of his penetrating but self-vindicatory diagnosis. Even his benefactors must be put in their place. The fatherly Breuer, who "gave Freud the most important suggestion he ever received in his life, a suggestion which formed the basis of the central idea of psychoanalysis," and also lent him money, finally was repudiated with such savagery that the official biographer (Jones) has suppressed some of the letters. The friendly Fliess, who gave him years of attentive comradeship, as well as an important idea about the bisexual constitution of the race, which Freud first rejected and then appropriated without thanks, met with similarly rough treatment as soon as he "criticized Freud's method by saying that Freud read his own thoughts into his patients."

Fromm finds in Freud a confused "dependence on men" which was not homosexual, as Freud himself thought it, but an unresolved inner conflict; "he desired to be independent; he hated to be a protégé—and at the same time he wanted to be protected, admired, cared for" to such an extent that he became for a while dependent, in a sense, even upon his disciple Jung, which was why he fainted when Jung disagreed with him in Munich. The break with Jung was inevitable, however, because Freud "was a rationalist and his concern with the understanding of the unconscious was based on his wish to control and subdue it. Jung, on the other hand, belonged to the romantic, antirationalistic tradition. He is suspicious of reason and intellect, and the unconscious, representing the nonrational, to him is the deepest source of wisdom; for him, analytic therapy has the function of helping the patient to get in touch with this source of nonrational wisdom, and to benefit from this contact. Jung's interest in the unconscious was the admiring one of the romantic; Freud's, the critical one of the rationalist."

When Jung left the psychoanalytic movement, "Freud remarked: 'Does one know today with whom Columbus sailed when he discovered America?'" When Adler died, and Arnold Zweig "expressed how moved he was by Adler's death, Freud wrote: 'I don't understand your sympathy for Adler. For a Jew-boy out of a Viennese suburb a death in Aberdeen is an unheard-of career in itself, and a proof of how far he had got on. The world really rewarded him richly for his service in having contradicted psychoanalysis.'"

Fromm calls Freud a rebel, not a revolutionary, because he had not freed himself "from attachment to authority and from the wish to dominate others. . . . While he defied authorities and enjoyed this defiance, he was at the same time deeply impressed by the existing social order and its authorities. To receive the title of professor, and to find recognition from the existing authorities, were of utmost concern to him, although in a strange unawareness of his own desires he denied it."

The effect of his personality upon his movement was to burden it with a dogmatic attitude which would not even listen with patience to Ferenczi's timid—and subsequently validated—discovery that the patient needed love as a condition for a cure. Freud's "authoritarian" imprint also left unfortunate ritualisms and idolizations of himself that have turned his movement into an "entrenched bureaucracy which inherited Freud's mantle, without possessing his creativity, nor the radicalism of his original conception." His discovery of the unconscious "was applied to a small sector of reality, man's libidinal strivings and their repression, but little or not at all to the wider reality of human existence and to social and political phenomena."

Soon after this charge we come to Fromm's own point of view: "The understanding of the unconscious of the individual presupposes and necessitates the critical analysis of his society." He is finally dissatisfied with Freud, not only because of his defects of character but because these defects led his movement to "stagnate" in a "liberal middle-class attitude toward society. . . . Freudians saw the individual unconscious, and were blind to the social unconscious; orthodox Marxists, on the contrary, were keenly aware of the unconscious factors in social behavior, but remarkably blind in their appreciation of individual motivation. This led to a deterioration of Marxist theory and practice, just as the reverse process has led to the deterioration of psychoanalytic theory and therapy."

A final implication of the book is that Fromm could straighten out both the Freudians and the Marxists, if they would only let him, and then these two great progressive forces, reactivated, could lead mankind to a better life for everyone, far beyond the infantilism of the Oedipus complex and all neurotic doubts about the curative powers of reason. Of all the men discussed here he alone seems to have been unshaken in his self-confidence by the events of our day. In recent years his imperturbability has been increased by relative isolation in Mexico. It would be interesting to know how much of his confidence belongs to *him*, to some unreachable part of his own self-love, and how much can be attributed to his residence among the hope-demanding inhabitants of the Western Hemisphere.

14

Karen Horney: A Lost Cause

The attack of Fromm upon Freud's attitude toward women owes its existence to the late Karen Horney. It was Karen Horney who first called attention to Freud's astonishing blind spots about women and gave feminine psychology a chance to be appreciated in its own language, written by a woman for other women. Now that she is dead, however, her pioneer work can all too easily be dismissed by woman-fearing men, and few women have the ingenuity needed to defend her. Indeed most intellectual women are estranged from those very feminine inner depths that would help them appreciate what she has done for them. So Karen Horney has rather quickly become a lost cause in a land that is supposed to be dominated by its women. The exploration of this paradox is not likely to make anyone rejoice.

Karen Horney is still another example of how the United States profited by the madness of Hitler's Germany. She came to America in the nineteen thirties, after practicing as a Freudian analyst in Berlin from the early nineteen twenties. After some years in Chicago she went to New York, where in 1939 she wrote: "My desire to make a critical evaluation of psychoanalytical theories had its origin in a dissatisfaction with therapeutic results. . . . I had my first active doubts . . . when I read Freud's concept of feminine psychology." She then begins a restatement of this celebrated concept: "According to Freud the most upsetting occurrence in the development of the little girl is the discovery that other human beings have a penis, while she has none. 'The discovery of her castration is the turning-point in the life of the girl.' She reacts to this discovery with a definite wish to have a penis too, with the hope that it will still grow, and with an envy of those more fortunate beings who possess one. In the normal development penis-envy does not continue as such: after recognizing her 'deficiency as an unalterable fact, the girl transfers the wish for a penis to a wish for a child.'

". . . Happiness during pregnancy . . . is referred to as symbolic gratification in the possession of a penis (the penis being a child). When the delivery is delayed for functional reasons, it is suspected that the woman does not want to separate herself from the penis-child. On the other hand, motherhood may be rejected because it is a reminder of femininity."

After describing still more fanciful extensions of the penis-envy theory, Horney proceeds to an equally detailed refutation of it, first as having been drawn entirely from the observation of neurotic women whose bossiness, henpecking and ambition might be attributed incorrectly to such an "ultimate" cause, second, as a superficial diagnosis which many a woman will prefer to a deeper one, "because it is so much easier for a patient to think that nature has given her an unfair deal than to realize that she actually makes excessive demands on the environment and is furious whenever they are not complied with." Finally, some years later, Horney's refutation, which began on purely therapeutic grounds, was expressed in the cogent phrase: "There are just as many men who suffer from womb-envy as women who suffer from penis-envy."

Here, at last, the slowly emancipated woman analyst, freed not only from her original reverence for her master but from her early Germanic subservience to his sex, speaks out in New World tones the real core of her resistance to his theory: She tells him that it is really primitive and rather insane of him to imagine that his sex is the original one or the more enviable one; and that his own preoccupation with his books (his self-delivered children) is the best proof of it. It is a good moment in the history of modern psychology when the modest female clinician, who wisely disavows theoretical gifts, in effect tells the old seer that his one-sided idea came from his identification with a patriarchal faith which was dinned into him as a youth in the daily prayer: "Lord, I thank Thee for not having made me a woman!"

Obviously the discussion has now reached a level where argument, if it is to have any value at all, must begin by acknowledging its subjective base. By implication Horney is now challenging all that Freud says because it comes from a man and a particular kind of man. Though she continues to feel the greatest gratitude and respect, she no longer is bowled over by his genius. She also calls into question the capacity of a genius to have truly durable insight, except within its very special competence.

Adler had made a similar point, and Horney acknowledges the Adlerian slant of her therapy. For Jung she has little use, although Jung went much further than she to introduce a better understanding of woman into a subject that could be no more than half-alive without it. This was because Jung seemed too remote from the daily fight in which her patients were involved; and she was above all a practical and maternal therapist who got her bearings from the unfortunate people who had come to her for help. (In New York at least most Jungian patients are introverts and most Horney patients considerably more extraverted, though perhaps not so much so as the typical Freudian patient.) There is no evidence that she had read Benoit, who was being translated shortly before the time of her death, or that she would have been able to use his austerely metaphysical approach if she had, but his emphasis upon the curative powers of a faced humiliation comes very close, in many ways, to the warm, friendly but unsparing bath of everyday reality that she seems to draw for her readers. Reality did not terrify her, as it did Rank, or call for mythology to cope with it.

On the contrary, as a woman—and it is significant that she came into her own after her menopause—it seemed to her the most salutary thing of all, the kind of healing that family life can give. She was a kind of Cybele, M.D. She carried the dynamics of the psyche into much more homely detail than Freud ever did, and with a concrete fullness that makes her delightful to read. Perhaps she puts less stress on sex than he did because as a woman she was naturally more down to earth about it than any man could be, especially a man so highly puritanized, so neurotically obsessed with it as he. Therefore she refused it the theoretical place of honor, which she awarded instead to *self-love*. Again in this respect she was like the French, unpuritanized Benoit, who also finds the refinements of self-love more crippling than the refinements of repressed eroticism. So, having been given by Fromm a cultural focus to replace Freud's sexual focus, she was ready to add the calming voice of woman—a natural peace-lover, because it is her children who get killed in war—to a furious debate. Other women psychologists had ably entered the debate, among them M. Esther Harding, Clara Thompson, and

Helene Deutsch, but Karen Horney made perhaps a more original contribution than any other member of her sex. By comparison with the women artists who have spoken more spontaneously in unimpeded use of the imagination, she may seem relatively constricted; there may also have been some foolhardiness in her trespass of traditionally masculine thought-preserves; but for all that she brought an important point to view that only a very limited kind of man will reject.

"Woman lived for centuries under conditions in which she was kept away from great economic and political responsibilities and restricted to a private emotional sphere of life . . . her work was done within the confines of the family circle and was therefore based only on emotionalism, in contradistinction to more impersonal matter-of-fact relations . . . love and devotion came to be regarded as specifically feminine ideals and virtues . . . to woman—since her relations to men and children were her only gateway to happiness, security and prestige—love represented a realistic value, which in man's sphere can be compared to his activities relating to earning capacities. . . .

"Hence there were, and to some extent still are, realistic reasons in our culture why woman is bound to overrate love and to expect more from it than it can possibly give, and why she is more afraid of losing love than man is. . . .

"We should consider it neurotic if men became frightened or depressed when they approached the fifth decade. In a woman this is regarded as natural, and in a way it is natural so long as attractiveness represents a unique value. . . . It prevents woman from evaluating qualities which are outside the erotic sphere, qualities best characterized by the terms maturity, poise, independence, autonomy in judgment, wisdom. Woman can scarcely take the task of the development of her personality as seriously as she does her love life if she constantly entertains a devaluating attitude toward her mature years, and considers them as her declining years."

Horney goes on to develop a much more intricate picture than Freud's of feminine psychology, as seen in actual therapeutic problems. A mere "engineer" by comparison with his amazing skill at "pure science," she was more interested in therapy than he, who frankly confessed it did not attract him. Her books are therefore best read as masterly clinical notes, as perhaps the most consummate descriptions of neurotic conflicts that her branch of medical science has as yet produced. One searches them in vain for a systematic picture of woman's mind; on the whole she prudently shies away from such an unfeminine task. One gets instead intimate portraits of particular women, observed with a skill that we have come to expect of good novelists—portraits in which cultural factors play a more important part than biological factors. Perhaps, for subjective reasons, the latter were simply not as exciting to her imagination as the former; and perhaps, again for subjective reasons, the biological factors meant so much to Freud because he had been denied the earthy, wordless understanding of sex that can come so naturally to a woman. Aside from such debatable speculations, she certainly decided, for medical reasons, that her women patients needed much more than "penis-envy" to explain their mental illnesses, and that they frequently became neurotic because they developed flattering pictures of themselves through their anxiety about their status as sweethearts, wives, and mothers. She also decided that the best way, on the whole, to treat them was to help them to enjoy the happiness that came so spontaneously to a woman attuned to her destiny both as an egg-bearer and as a human being with a mind of her own.

I must confess I was surprised and disappointed when I discovered that she disagreed with Freud about the "death instinct." As I have already indicated, I consider this insight of great value. When I tried to put myself in her place, however, I could understand the *motherly* motivations and perhaps the earthy wisdom that made her attack the "destruction instinct," that "derivate of the death instinct." "Freud left no doubt about its meaning: man has an innate drive toward evil, aggressiveness, destructiveness, cruelty. 'The bit of truth behind all this—one so eagerly denied—is that men are not gentle, friendly creatures wishing for love, who simply defend themselves if they are attacked, but that a powerful measure of desire for aggression has to be reckoned with as part of their instinctual endowment. The result is that their neighbor is to them not only a possible helper or sexual object, but also a temptation to them to gratify their aggressiveness on him, to exploit his capacity for work without recompense, to use him sexually without his consent, to seize his possessions, to humiliate him, to cause him pain, to torture and to kill him! . . . Hatred is at the bottom of all the relations of affection and love between human beings.' . . .

"Freud . . . fails to see that disputing the contention that man is destructive by nature does not mean asserting the contrary, that he is good by nature. Freud also fails to see that the assumption of a destruction instinct may appeal to people emotionally because it can relieve them of feelings of responsibility and guilt, and because it can free them from the necessity of facing the real reasons for their destructive impulses." She then argues that "the extent and frequency of destructiveness are *not* proof that it is instinctual. . . . The more anxiety is released by psychoanalysis, the more the patient becomes capable of affection and genuine tolerance for himself and others. He is no longer destructive. But if the destructiveness were instinctual, how could it vanish?" She then returns to her faith in therapy—and man: "If we want to injure or kill, we do so because we are or feel endangered, humiliated, abused; because we are or feel rejected and treated unjustly; because we are or feel interfered with in wishes which are of vital importance to us. That is, if we wish to destroy, it is in order to defend our safety or our happiness or what appears to us as such. Generally speaking, it is for the sake of life and not for the sake of destruction.

"The theory of a destruction instinct is not only unsubstantiated, not only contradictory to facts, but is positively harmful in its implications . . . it implies that making a patient free to express his hostility is an aim in itself. . . . Such an assumption paralyzes any effort to search in the specific cultural conditions for reasons which make for destructiveness. It must also paralyze efforts to change anything in these conditions. If man is inherently destructive and consequently unhappy, why strive for a better future?"

Here she states what has become a standard objection to Freud: that he impedes intelligent political and social action, that he gained a greater shock value for his ideas by presenting them with unqualified pessimism, and perhaps satisfied some obscure punitive impulse in his own overdisciplined mind, but really wrote more capriciously than his chilly style and all his familiar maneuvers of conscientious medical circumspection would suggest. In short, by implication, that he *faked* when it suited him to do so, and after he had succeeded in drawing an amazing amount of adulation to himself with mesmeric skill—he indeed became the pampered scene-stealer that Adler saw in him.

How much sound reasoning can be found in her motherly hope will be decided in time. The events of recent years have not been kind to any hope at all, though perhaps our minds have misused our disasters as sickly as she suggests. A familiar criticism of Horney is that she shares Rousseau's faith that man is born good but is the victim of bad institutions. Actually, she specifies that she does not imply that "man is good by nature," and she never comes forward with a social program. Her emphasis is on what the patient can do about himself, rather than on what he might do about society. The hope she holds out to him seems to me more like a professional carrot to a layman donkey than anything else; in that sense, all good physicians are romantics. It is therefore hard to believe that she is really being charged with Rousseauism; what is being objected to, I think, is her introduction of feminine unpredictables into a tidily male preserve. When she reminds us of the occasional capacity of human beings for love and heroism, she makes it hard for our neo-orthodox tragedians.

But love and heroism have existed, do exist, and may exist in the future. To assume the contrary is merely to wish one's own crabbedness on the unborn. When a woman healer, with a woman's natural desire to believe that such victories can be won here and now, puts her accent more on the chances of victory than on the chances of defeat, she merely is offering a little animal warmth to unthawed lives that, to judge by the reports pouring in from social workers and novelists, have been numbed by continual defeat. Surely a responsible educator's first obligation is to remind such people of the possibility of less tundra-like conditions, however seldom they are achieved.

It is true that we Americans, eager to escape our Antenora, usually misuse any kind of hope and convert it into a drug for avoiding the recognition of our deeper frustrations. Our compulsive optimism may be doing us more harm than the poppy ever did to China. Even the best psychotherapy can be—and doubtless often is—put to bad use. That is hardly a reason to discontinue offering it. It must be made available, and in the natural style of the therapist. A just appraisal of Horney would find, I think, that the main direction of her analysis was not toward romantic escapism but toward a sober attempt to combat a cultural blizzard. Men and women were becoming physically so frozen that to suggest the possibility of the lonely crowd's ever achieving "autonomy" was much more "romantic"—and much more dangerous.

Women should be the first to appreciate Horney's heroic attempt to translate the dry discoveries of her science into the language of feeling. Alas, her brief acceptance among them is on the wane.

American women, whose pathetic "matriarchal" substitutes for genuine fulfillment have been journalistically misrepresented, have not rallied strongly to her or to any other woman psychologist. Our matriarchs seem easily satisfied with instalment plan purchases, television flattery and an optimism she does not carry. As yet our women read little of a serious nature. Perhaps a national disaster will some day change this, and the public-library status of Karen Horney as well, but at present she is not in great demand.

15

Harry Stack Sullivan
and the Human Pyramid

In *The Art of Loving* Fromm compares Sullivan favorably to Freud
in his concept of love, and asks: "What is the meaning of love and
intimacy in Sullivan's concept?" He then quotes Sullivan: "Intimacy
is that type of situation involving two people which permits validation of all components of personal worth. Validation of personal
worth requires a type of relationship which I call collaboration, by
which I mean clearly formulated adjustments of one's behavior to
the expressed needs of the other person in pursuit of increasingly
identical—that is, more and more nearly mutual satisfaction, and in
the maintenance of increasingly similar security operations."

This kind of language, which carries jargon beyond the bureau-
crat's dream, cries out for quotation, in an introduction to Sullivan,
for what it reveals of the amazingly intricate attempt of a man,
described by many colleagues as one of the most gifted of his day,
to shape his style so that it would say exactly what *he* wanted it to
say, without concern for the reader. It also reveals something of the
circumstances in which he worked. Sullivan reached his conclusions
and put them repellently on paper at a time and in a place where
other-directedness was the new tyrant and a mass-influenced psychology would have no more of the bold, myth-making metaphors
that had once been welcomed so eagerly from Europe. Vertical
Teutonic symbols have been replaced by flat American abstractions.
Each word looks sweaty and uncomfortable. Imagery has been
sacrificed to machine-tooled precision. Linguistically, Sullivan is a
true American, a product of the tongue-twisting mechanic's paradise that in earlier days gave birth to the Book of Mormon and

Mary Baker Eddy. His land, however, has developed some new ailments, and he, as its newest mind doctor, is trying to find the right jawbreakers to describe them.

A literary analogy may be helpful: Henry Miller on the subject of the American character. He is sitting in a park in Jacksonville, Florida. "The benches were littered . . . with the dregs of humanity—not the seedy sort as in London or New York, not the picturesque sort that dot the quais of Paris, but the pulpy, blemished American variety which issues from the respectable middle class: *Clean clots of phlegm*, so to speak. The kind that tries to elevate the mind even when there is no mind left. . . . The American type par excellence. . . . Not a speck of human dignity left."

Here is Sullivan on the same subject: "We, the people of the United States, in particular, would quite certainly exterminate ourselves before we could devise and disseminate adequate substitutes for our now ubiquitous security processes." Translated into the language of our ancestors, he is saying that without our many instantaneous ways of kidding ourselves, we Americans would find it impossible to go on living, and indeed death itself would be preferable to the truth that Rank, on coming to these shores, also found impossible to live with. And this because ours is "an increasingly incoherent social organization."

Miller fled to a lonely promontory on the Pacific. Sullivan belonged to a profession that had been formed to combat the situation he found, and so he stayed in his clinic, saw hundreds of patients, had a recognized social function, as well as a steady sufficiency of cash in his pockets (unlike Miller) and developed a speech that could only be "prehended" by the members of his own Latiniform tribe. Much more work has gone into it than into Miller's, which, though better than most of *his* tribe's, is signposted with so many stereotypes of thought and expression that it "flows" naturally into what Sullivan would call the "syntaxic mode," that is, the recognizable method by which we put the loose ends of darkly perceived experience into some sort of "consensually validated" order. To employ Freud's criterion of good writing, Miller's style creates less anxiety than Sullivan's and is therefore more acceptable. But Sullivan has more that is new to say than Miller, on this occasion, and would most surely have starved if he had had to compete in the literary market under the handicap of so cruelly inhuman a style. The reviewers would have expressed their anxiety in a horse laugh, and the public would not have touched him. Fortunately' for him, science occupies a place of honor in our culture that literature does not, and so he was free to torture the language with impervious medical humor—and with no loss of fortune or face. The result takes about the same time to learn as Serbo-Croatian, but is worth the trouble, if any member of the Remnant should want to avail himself of Sullivan's remarkable understanding of the lower teammates of the human pyramid which makes it possible for a few to stand on their shoulders and perform the higher acrobatics.

Sullivan concentrated on our common underpinning, both in the lower orders of society and in the forgotten development of every individual. To read him attentively is to encounter, in agonizingly new proximity, those unfortunate people who are so profoundly immersed in tragedy that they could not possibly speak of it, people who reveal "that from very early in life something has apparently been going terribly wrong in the part of their life which is partitioned to sleep—that is, they have night terrors. . . . The term, night terror, applies to the situation in which one awakes from some utterly unknown events in practically primordial terror; in this state, one is on the border of complete disintegration of personality—in other words, there are almost no evidences of any particular competence and one is almost disorganized, since one is actually in a state of panic." On the whole it is a world of the most modest catastrophe that Sullivan describes, nothing that would lend itself to literature, or at least literature as it has been traditionally conceived. One begins to understand why Aristotle insisted on the noble birth of the protagonist in tragedy; he was making a biological point, even more than a social one. The characters in Sullivan's theatre are so low in the scale of human evolution, at least from an external standpoint, that the bums in Samuel Beckett's theater seem by comparison magnificent mutations, aristocrats of body structure and freedom of will. Sullivan studies his dramatis personae in an ultimate extremity of alienation and despair.

But Sullivan shows us not only our humblest teammates of the human pyramid; he also shows us ourselves when we too were so helpless, for example, that the anxiety we took in by empathy from our disturbed mother's nipple might be sufficiently disabling to debar us permanently from the loftier gymnastics on the top of the heap. The inescapable hazards in the development of every individual are described with such authenticity of detail, from infancy through

adolescence, that it is difficult to understand how Sullivan, because
he uttered a word of modest therapeutic encouragement now and
then, was ever accused of putting psychoanalysis into the Emersonian
"optative mode." On the contrary, the whole drift of Sullivan's
thought, as his sentence about the modern American character in-
dicates, is that we are so prone to self-deception that the dangers
implicit in faulty evolution and poor education have been enor-
mously increased, and indeed our future prospects are not good at all.

"Anxiety relates to the whole field of interpersonal interaction;
that is, anxiety about *anything* in the mother induces anxiety in the
infant. . . . For example . . . a telegram announcing something of
very serious moment to the prestige or peace of mind of the mother
may induce a state of anxiety in her which induces anxiety in the
infant. . . . Now looking at it from the infant's standpoint . . .
the outcome of ordinarily appropriate and adequate behavior when
hungry—namely, crying-when-hungry—has produced the wrong nipple, a very evil situation with very unpleasant and unsatisfactory
consequences." And the attention given these everyday nursery
hazards is extended to thousands of other overlooked events that
continue through childhood and into late adolescence, always with
an emphasis upon disasters which pass up no one and may have the
most far-reaching harmful effects. If anything, Sullivan is *over*-
preoccupied with the defenselessness of man and does not give
nearly enough time to the consciousness that a few people construct
as a step toward self-arming.

The reason for this is that he is primarily a social psychiatrist,
more interested in mass problems than in those which hamper a
privileged few from the fullest possible self-fulfillment. In that sense
he has little to say to a Remnant, except that his picture of the
primordial terror from which we all try to emerge may help more
concretely than the program of Marx, for example, to reunite the
individual and society. Our alienated individuals leapt on the Marxist bandwagon in the nineteen thirties because they thought it might
heal their psychic wounds by giving them a specific political goal
and a proved technique for achieving it. They hoped to be cured
of Chekhovian drift in the way they thought Maxim Gorky had.
Now they realize that this kind of cure encounters many more complications in a highly advanced technology, with long-standing traditions of political freedom, secular thought and bourgeois customs,
than it did in Russia, where one kind of theocracy was quickly ex-

changed for another with secular labels. And even in Russia the day came when the individual got no kind of cure except the permanent one of the firing squad. (Gorky, we now hear, received the distinction of poison.) So the individual in America—and elsewhere if he is not totally blind—has his work cut out for him, and can understand its complexity better by reviewing his own life in the painstaking way that Sullivan suggests. "Interpersonal" clarity is needed even by the best minds. To imagine that you know all that matters about your childhood once you have mastered the intricacies of the Oedipus complex: that is the new post-Freudian daydream. As we shall see, there are *many* necessary ways back to one's earliest days. Sullivan's is not mapped by one's desire for personal effectiveness against competitors, but by one's need to see even one's competitors as part of one's kin. A distinctive note in Sullivan's work—he is said to have been latently homosexual—is feminine, almost maternal.

Riesman has acutely observed that Sullivan singles out, in the contemporary American superego, not the potent parental images which so impressed Freud, but the much more tyrannous figures of the "peer group." In other words, a young American is more likely to be dominated by what his "chums" value than by what his father and mother value. It is an interesting observation, suggestive more of Fromm's anthropologism than Freud's biologism, and it helps along Riesman's study of the new other-directed conformists. But Sullivan also emphasizes biological factors, and ones that Freud did not see, with the result that his psychiatric "system," if it can be called that, is by common consent an exceptionally flexible one, more in the American pragmatic manner than in the European ideological manner. As such it is considerably harder to describe. A few comparisons may help to fix some of its protean methods in the mind.

As his style suggests, he tried to make himself into a photographic plate that would record *everything*. Too much is eluding us, he seems to be saying; we must not miss anything! Therefore his pages appear quite formless by comparison with those of Freud, who always knows exactly what he is doing and how, by classic masculine devices of concision, to get the best possible effect out of it. It is only later that, considerably extending our frame of reference, we can see form in Sullivan, a somewhat Proustian form, but even then it gives a bare minimum of reading pleasure. As an author he is limited to his own peer group, the psychiatrists. He was not trying to set Acheron in an uproar, or as that Virgilian phrase might be translated today, to let all hell loose. He merely wanted to help a few sick people.

He is still further away from Adler's tonic simplism, which aimed at a final liberation from medicine and psychology, as far as that was possible. Sullivan seems to have been the kind of physician who could not live without patients, and to have given no attention at all to reducing complex psychological problems to more easily stated moral ones. He inherited an unpredictable world at about the same time that Adler's collapsed.

He is most remote of all from Jung's bridge between psychology and metaphysics. An up-to-date member of the Remnant, no longer content with positivism, will know at once what Jung is talking about, whether or not he agrees with it, but Sullivan will seem to him gibberish, unless he recognizes the value of a humbling bath in the same tub as a preponderantly sick and terrified humanity. Sullivan's stress is on anxiety, the million anxieties that we all feel at one time or another. Most Jungians could do worse than to consider his lowly untouchables.

The chaos that Rank discovered in the New World, and that may have contributed to his undoing, was exactly what Sullivan, the only child of an old, distinguished, and vanishing American family, needed for his personal survival. It gave him an act of leadership to perform. Fromm, less sensitive but more resilient than Rank, could join in the same task with Sullivan. Fromm, however, was a European who continued to see problems ideologically, while Sullivan saw them as so new and so fundamental that the old approaches would no longer do. Sullivan may serve as an example of the Remnant in action. In many ways he resembles Horney most closely of all, not only in his almost maternal sympathy but in his mental-hospital note of hope. He too seems to say that people *can* change, if they try hard enough, but actually there are so many catches to his encouragement (and hers) that only a very anxious person, pretty far gone, would take it literally, through an act of oversimplification. With the psychological methods of Zen, as imagined by Benoit, he has nothing at all in common—though he may be useful to those Americans who believe that they can fly first-class to *satori* without stopping off at the homelier problems that we all inherit, even in God's country. Kerouac's Dharma bums could get a lot from going back to Sullivan's sour nipples.

16

William Sheldon
and the Human Physique

If David Riesman had wanted a psychologist model for his picture of the "inner-directed" resistant to the "other-directed" rebellion of the masses, he could have found an eloquent example on his own doorstep, either at Harvard or the University of Chicago, in William Sheldon. As the only other native American beside Sullivan to be presented in this gallery, Sheldon draws a portrait painter's attention away from the lowly members of our national circus troupe who attracted Sullivan and focuses it instead on a much more traditional aspect of the United States—the settling, the flowering, and the Indian summer of New England.

Born in Rhode Island to a scientist father and held at his christening by William James, Sheldon represents a conscious effort—in a region of our country which once provided most of our intellectual leadership—to reassert the moral values on which its authority formerly rested, but in a new style, significantly that of science rather than that of literature. Sheldon conducts a rear-guard attack, documented with photographs and statistics, upon the advancing big city hordes of overstimulation, overproduction, overconsumption, overpopulation and overexpression. Like that other distinguished Yankee, the poet E. E. Cummings, he came to New York and formed a private enclave there, to study at first hand the largest and most confident group of immigrants who had disturbed his sylvan repose and who had, in effect, stolen his ancestral land away from him. Again like Cummings, he studied them with patrician disgust and rather boyish affection. He came to some independent, disturbing conclusions that recommend themselves to those who wish to be as free from the new democratic tabus as from more traditional ones.

Unsupported by any significant popular movement, and therefore rendered both desperate and free by his loneliness, Sheldon raises touchy issues that anyone who has been intimidated by the Left would much rather ignore. Unfortunately for him, few American intellectuals have not been intimidated by the Left, because our Right is so reactionary and so illiterate that it has never been able to reach them. It has also failed to reach them because our Left speaks both a language of the heart that comes from our predominantly romantic literary traditions and a language of social progress that would align every thinker with the workers rather than with the bosses. Sheldon might get some support from the New Conservatives who, taking stock of the failure of Marxist landing parties to stay long on our shores, have tried to formulate a neo-Burkean program that would save the best in liberalism with some hardheaded rethinking; but the New Conservatives have not been able to maintain their beachheads either, because they try to fit a program that came from an agrarian gentry to an economy that is dominated by a more fluid, a more prosperous, and a more demoralizing finance capitalism. Sheldon might also appeal to Jungian fugitives from the market place, and in fact he started out, in his first book, as pretty much of a Jungian himself; but he was not content with mere complaints against the vulgarians who had taken over his homeland; he soon passed to the attack—and to the use of ultra-objective methods quite unlike the transformation mysteries of the Greeks, which have received so much study in Switzerland.

His methods and his discoveries were respected up to a point— but since they did not fit in with the desires of any determined minority (a clear prerequisite for impingement on our cultural chaos) he soon found himself almost as alone as when he started. His discoveries, however, remain, despite their failure to mobilize a party. He has not known how to give them the literary cachet that Eliot, for example, found for a more reactionary statement of a New Englander's emotions. Thus he never won the continuing support of the teachers of English, who were flattered profoundly by Eliot's purism and became the mainstays of his movement. Sheldon also failed to establish a school of psychiatry, and so lost that mainstay, too. But his discoveries will interest those isolated independents who want to know what his well-documented research has discovered about the conditions of individual development amid a hostile mass.

He differed from Sullivan in still another way. Despite the Yankee ingenuity of his methods, he was not content to follow the usual American path; he was not content to make only *technical* contributions. He did not, like Sullivan, eschew theory in the grand old-fashioned European manner and bury himself in the minutiae of "interpersonal" observations. He soon lost interest in psychiatry, turned instead to "constitutional psychology," called himself a biologist, and sought bolder ways to make his theories stick. He had even less interest in healing than Freud, and he also came to the conclusion that Freud's influence on America, through its effect on socially necessary inhibitions, was doing more harm than good. He could be personally affectionate toward individual voices in big-city dissonance, but the moral import of their communal cacophony dismayed him. It did not harmonize at all with the gentler music he had heard in the forest primeval as a junior state ornithologist; it meant degeneracy. Psychologically it had been encouraged by "the new Freudian religion of self-expressiveness." Next to such a grandiose challenge, the task of helping a few neurotics to realize that they suffered more from the "animectomy complex"— his neologism for the fear that one has lost one's soul—than from the Oedipus complex seemed of secondary importance. So in his first book, Sheldon launched a full-scale offensive against the most successful psychology of all, the Freudian.

His book comes out of an Anglo-Saxon tradition that does not as a rule think ideologically, that is casual and even deliberately amateurish, but for all that, and in spite of a possibly excessive exuberance, *Psychology and the Promethean Will* is a gifted performance. If our study of the mind were not still in a barbarous state, it would have been welcomed long ago, by its antagonists, as an interesting if crude rejoinder, in a lively American style, to the more systematic thought of Europe. It is the kind of book that makes dialogue possible. For example, its imaginative variations, better than Jung's, on the Spitteler theme of Prometheus v. Epimetheus would have illuminated the highbrow-middle brow debate and perhaps generated a little mutual tolerance among the debaters. Novelists and playwrights might have lifted more than one scene from his dramatic struggle between the "character-phile" and the "waster," those anticipations of Riesman's types which however stress character rather than conditions.

His first book was written in a youthfully confident mood which can now, at a time of religious "revival," all too easily be confused with current moralistic oversimplifications. The "waster" enemies, drawn from the Roaring Twenties, were depicted as formidable because they followed the line of least resistance and came at a curve in history which favored the triumph of their loud self-indulgence. Nevertheless the book's final emphasis lay rather on the conscious person's ability to transcend an unfavorable time than on the possibility of his defeat. In its search for a fruitful union between medicine and an enlightened theology it reiterated a familiar hope of advanced Protestantism. In the two companion volumes that followed it, after a decade of research, *The Varieties of Human Physique* and *The Varieties of Temperament*, there were darker implications, though still enough grounds for sober religious hope to cause Aldous Huxley to praise them in *The Perennial Philosophy* as constituting a system of human classification that surpassed the previous typologies of Jung and Ernst Kretschmer, that indeed was "more comprehensive, more flexibly adequate to the complex facts than all those which preceded it." Huxley also leaned on Sheldon's discoveries in the theoretical parts of this quasi-anthology of mystical thought, which may be his own most ambitious book.

With his study of temperament Sheldon made a major contribution to psychology and emerged as a world figure. It is crammed with closely observed detail, and so immediately useable that some readers regard it as a mere parlor trick. To take it literally *would* reduce it to a conversation piece, but if handled with intelligence it can put a brilliant new interpretation on familiar events. An example of Huxley's use of it will demonstrate this.

In Sheldon's description of the aggressive, noisy, ruthless, energetic, power-loving muscleman who is his second psychophysical type (the somatotonic) it is difficult not to recognize certain traits that had formerly been found in "the waster." "Somatotonia is the craving for vigorous action and (when fully admitted to consciousness) the resolution to subdue the environment to one's own will. Successful somatotonics are conquerors. . . . Somatotonic people tend to lack introspective insight. They are like loaded guns and they want to be pointed somewhere and set off." He says that the somatotonic often fears self-knowledge more than death itself, and therefore prefers to "go quickly" rather than find out what manner of man he is. "People who show this trait are cut off from insight into their own internal organic life. . . . Such people . . . not infrequently break down suddenly. . . . In mental pathology, somatotonics tend to become manic or hysterical. . . . Somatotonic people experience sudden 'conversions' of all sorts." He finds this type so dominant today that he writes, "Up to the time of the 'somatotonic revolution' which became so readily apparent at about the period of the first World War, we were attempting, so far as the conscious rationalization was concerned, to live out a religious ideal based essentially on cerebretonia [his word for a thinnish, repressed, intellectual type], although complicated by an undercurrent of sublimated viscerotonia [love of man]." (This is his word for a fattish, emotional, alimentary type.) "But for some time now, as is especially obvious in Germany, a vigorous religious movement has been afoot which is based squarely on unsublimated somatotonia."

Huxley put capitals on one of his phrases, and wrote: "The 'Somatotonic Revolution' has been greatly accelerated by technological advances. These have served to turn men's attention outward, and have encouraged the belief in a material apocalypse, a progress toward a mechanized New Jerusalem. . . . In a world peopled by cerebretonics, living an inward-turning life in a state of holy, or even unholy, indifference to their material surroundings, mass production would be doomed. That is why advertisers consistently support the Somatotonic Revolution. . . . Nazi education, which was education specifically for war, aimed at encouraging the manifestations of somatotonia in those most richly endowed with it, and making the rest of the population feel ashamed. . . . During the war the enemies of Nazism have had to borrow from the Nazi educational philosophy. . . . Never has somatotonia been so widely or so systematically encouraged as at the present time. Indeed, most societies in the past discouraged somatotonia, because they did not wish to be destroyed by the unrestrained aggressiveness of their most active minority."

Huxley's imaginative use of Sheldon's work suggests some of its possible values. Temperament is only one factor in social thought, but it is an important one that would do much to humanize and make more predictable those large historical forces that too often remain in the realm of abstraction. Also, unlike Riesman's more popular reassurances, it alerts the Remnant to its strengths, and its

weaknesses. The study of temperament and its complex relationship to the body is even now being integrated by skillful psychiatrists with Freud's discoveries about oral, anal, and genital types,
with Jung's extroverts and introverts, with Horney's division of people into those who move toward, against, and away from others.
Classification may be only a preliminary, long-distance technique,
but we need cameras with telelenses as well as microlenses.

Other uses of Sheldon's methods were illustrated in his next book,
which studied one of our most serious social problems—and produced some distinctly new discoveries. On its surface *Varieties of
Delinquent Youth* is only an exceptionally well-documented, well-
illustrated study of two hundred bad boys in Boston. It gives the
significant data about them with remarkable thoroughness and in a
new kind of scientific shorthand. Minor examples of this are "*t*" for
skin texture, which is related to sensibility, and "AMI" for a quality frequently exploited by delinquents (and the boy Fausts), Appeal to the Maternal Instinct. The book applies the "constitutional
psychology" methods that were developed by Kretschmer and others
and later refined by Sheldon. These methods stress subtle and often
unnoticed relationships between body structure and temperament
and psychiatry. Thus *all* of the criminal types under study turned out
to have a similar body structure. Sheldon says of his procedure that
it "reverses that of psychoanalysis, in which the analyst starts with
conscious reactions and proceeds toward the 'unconscious.' By the
unconscious I *think* psychoanalysts mean the body, however shocking the thought may be to psychoanalysts. The body is really an ob-
jectification, a tangible record, of the most longstanding and deeply
established habits that have been laid down during a succession of
generations."

This thesis, which in actual case histories he balances with exceptional gifts of common sense, humor, compassion, and insight,
leads to subtle measurements and revealing statistics. Discontented
with the facile "slums-breed-crime-and-a-better-economy-will-eliminate-
slums" theory that has been enough for so many of us, Sheldon
pushes into the disturbing biological factors that help to create not
only slums but the slum mentality. Almost all of the two hundred
delinquents, he finds, for example, came from delinquent parents; a
high percentage of them had grossly fat mothers; and another high
percentage suffered from a "medical insufficiency," or inherently
weak constitution, that had been accumulating for generations.

But he is not content with the data collected on the specific subject of delinquency. In the belief that an exhaustive study of it may throw light on even weightier human problems, he employs his findings as a basis for speculation on such matters as cancer, psychoanalysis, Christian theology, and war. "Delinquency," he says, "may reside in the cellular morphogenotype," and develops some highly suggestive ideas on the relationship between cellular misbehavior in the bad boy and in the cancer patient. These thoughts carry professional weight, since as director of the Constitution Clinic at Columbia University he has been one of the chief continuators of the work of George Draper in predicting the kinds of disease each type of flesh is heir to. On the environmental approach of the Freudians he writes: "So long as the psychoanalytic priesthood holds its power and dominates the mentality of the social work profession . . . it will be almost impossible to get at the problem of delinquency. For whatever else may be true of the delinquency I saw in Boston, it is mainly in the germ plasm." He criticizes Freudianism for encouraging a socially destructive "Dionysian" attitude and Christian theology for encouraging hebephrenia, or avoidance of the psychological tensions that make for maturity. Of war he writes: "We have explosively quadrupled the load of human gut and soma on a planet that was already groaning with that commodity. Human life has thus been so cheapened and so inflated that in many quarters of the earth it already has a negative value. That is to say, it is as ready for war as steam is ready to escape from an overheated boiler."

In brief he attacks the greatest tabu of our democracy by opening the forbidden subject of heredity. At a time (1950) when the Soviet Union officially sponsored illiterate obscurantism on this very subject (Lysenko's theories, since repudiated, even officially, though Lysenko is once more in favor) an American scientist addressed his own best energies to it—and met with violent opposition. Instead of being congratulated for using our relative freedom wisely, to investigate some of the measurable facts that obstruct our efforts to build a strong society, he received open abuse. The scientific community did not like to be forced to realize that the growth of medical skill had meant the sudden population of the earth with vast quantities of inferior flesh that helped to create delinquency and war. Also, he brought up the question of responsibility, thus antagonizing the boy Fausts, who naturally prefer the painless futurism of *The Lonely Crowd*.

His book was denounced as a reactionary plea for genocidal wars —and other unlovely things. The resistance to it was inevitable. No one likes to hear that more and more people are born into bad bodies, bad characters, bad destinies. Now, however, despite the needlessly provocative way in which he sometimes stated his findings, there is more inclination to consider and use them. Some day perhaps we shall be willing to think about another statistical implication of his: that the great majority of the human race is biologically unfit to make the decisions that life in a present-day democracy demands of them. That single telelens shot makes most close-ups of the subject seem rather unimportant. It also provides an objective charter for the Remnant.

17

The Existentialists

In 1958 Rollo May introduced to the United States a volume called *Existence*: A New Dimension in Psychiatry and Psychology. May has been intimately associated with the work of Fromm and Sullivan, and at the beginning of his career was a student of theology under Paul Tillich. His first psychiatric study *The Meaning of Anxiety* (1950) prompted his former teacher to reply with *The Courage To Be* (1952) which also treats anxiety as primarily existential—that is, implicit in man's condition—rather than primarily neurotic. The friendly dialogue between May and Tillich coincided with a new psychiatric movement in Europe which was debating the same issues; and it is some of the documents of the new movement, written chiefly by Ludwig Binswanger, Eugene Minkowski, and Erwin Straus, and grouped under Existential Analysis, that May has assembled and introduced in *Existence*. It is an important movement which continues the impressive trend among psychiatrists and patients, already noted here, towards a closer connection between psychology and philosophy. It came spontaneously into being, out of the needs of patients, when a number of European psychiatrists discovered that many patients did not get well until they encountered insights that came from the philosophers Kierkegaard, Nietzsche, and Heidegger. The specific warning of Freud, that philosophy had no place in psychoanalysis, was "transcended," and the patients got better. In place of Jung's discreetly restrained preparation for ontology, the new healers substituted a direct plunge into it, and the effect was noticeable. Or at least such a claim was made.

The relevance of Existential Analysis to the United States will be understood by any American resistant to conformity. May sketches the rise of existentialism in Europe in the nineteenth and twentieth centuries as a protest against the way human beings were compartmentalized by rationalism, which had gained philosophic ascendancy during the rise of science and technology, because it efficiently tightened man's grip on nature. This kind of rationalism, he suggests, causes ultimately the most serious psychiatric problems in a science-loving, highly-industrialized America. Our greatest danger lies in our overreadiness to be estranged from ourselves through abuse of our powers of reason.

Marx protested against the misuse of human beings economically; Kierkegaard protested against the misuse of the human being psychologically. Since he spoke for the masses, Marx has already had an enormous effect on laws and customs, even in capitalist countries. Since he spoke for the individual, Kierkegaard is still not understood generally, and may never be. He called attention to something much subtler, and today much more important—the willingness of the individual to be treated as an object, if only he can be spared loneliness and dark thoughts. Against a popular current that permitted him to die in almost total obscurity, Kierkegaard demanded supreme athleticism of man.

"Existentialism," says May, "is the endeavor to understand man by cutting below the cleavage between subject and object which has bedeviled Western thought and science since shortly after the Renaissance. This cleavage Binswanger calls 'the cancer of all psychology up to now . . . the cancer of the doctrine of subject-object cleavage of the world.' The existential way of understanding human beings . . . arose specifically just over a hundred years ago in Kierkegaard's violent protest against the reigning rationalism of his day, Hegel's 'totalitarianism of reason,' to use Maritain's phrase. Kierkegaard proclaimed that Hegel's identification of abstract truth with reality was an illusion and amounted to trickery. 'Truth exists,' wrote Kierkegaard, 'only as the individual himself produces it in action.' He and the existentialists who followed him protested firmly against the rationalists and idealists who would see man only as a subject— that is, as having reality only as a thinking being. But just as strongly they fought against the tendency to treat man as an object to be calculated and controlled, exemplified in the almost overwhelming tendencies of the Western world to make human beings into anonymous units to fit like robots into the vast industrial and political collectivisms of our day."

What has been the role of psychology, until now, in this fight? "Freud held a concept of reason which came directly from the enlightenment, namely 'ecstatic reason.' . . . By the end of the nineteenth century, as Tillich demonstrates most cogently, this ecstatic character had been lost. Reason had become 'technical reason'; reason married to techniques . . . reason as an adjunct and subordinate to technical industrial progress . . . reason indeed as opposed to existence—the reason finally which Kierkegaard and Nietzsche attacked. . . . It is not unfair to say that the prevailing trend in the development of psychoanalysis in late decades, particularly after the death of Freud, has been to reject his efforts to save reason in its ecstatic form. This trend is generally unnoticed, since it fits in so well with dominant trends in our whole culture. . . . There is considerable danger that psychoanalysis and psychotherapy in general will become part of the neurosis of our day rather than part of its cure . . .

"The existential psychotherapy movement . . . is precisely the movement that protests against the tendency to identify psychotherapy with technical reason. . . . It is based on the assumption that it is possible to have a science of man which does not fragmentize man and destroy his humanity. . . . It unites science and ontology."

We can illustrate the new therapy with a case, described by Medard Boss, in which Freudian and Jungian analyses had failed. The patient was a physician who suffered from washing compulsions. After a psychotic period he responded to Existential Analysis and was eventually cured when he realized that he was not merely suffering from guilt feelings which could be explained scientifically and therefore need not concern him, but that he actually *was* guilty and of a serious existential offense—not making the most of his potentialities. In other words, he was cured when he became aware of the moral problem involved in his illness, the subtle moral problem so easily overlooked by those who want to divorce psychology from ethics. When he realized what a very hard act of "total commitment" lay ahead of him, he got well.

To understand this, May implies, it is necessary to know that existentialists regard guilt as inherent in the nature of man, and say that it must be faced as squarely as death, because it too is an inescapable part of life. Despair and the fear of meaninglessness are also great negatives that are built into us at birth; and only when we face them with courage and clarity can we hope for real joy or real solidity of achievement—unless of course we prefer well-adjusted conformity and the medals it bestows, together with the neurosis and self-deception that hide beneath its glow of sun-tanned health.

There is an emphasis on reality rather than appearance, on wholeness rather than fragmentation, that will never be popular. Sheldon's biological research, which now covers very large numbers of people, enough people to have changed the actuarial rates of insurance companies, has demonstrated that few of us have evolved psychophysically to a point where we can make the demands on ourselves that Existential Analysis requires. May expresses, however, a diplomatic hope that it will appeal to the American people, to whom its findings so strikingly apply. This is to overlook the fact that even a gifted minority of Americans would have to make imaginative extensions of its ideas, if they were to have any meaning here and now, since they were first developed in nineteenth-century Europe by two pampered, moody bachelors who were spared by early death or madness from having to live out all their own conclusions. Much interpretation is required to turn Kierkegaard and Nietzsche into useable therapists.

Some portions of Existential Analysis have been anticipated by other psychologists. To hear the existential analysts give their opinions on death, for example, is to be reminded of related opinions expressed still more forcibly by Freud in his *Thoughts for the Times on War and Death* (1916) which will be examined in the next chapter. And Jung found it "hygienic" to discover in death "a goal towards which one can strive."

"The existential analysts," writes May, "hold that the confronting of death gives the most positive reality to life itself." And he quotes Tillich: "The self-affirmation of a being is the stronger the more non-being it can take into itself." Not only are we aided thereby in making our individual existence more real, but we also have a keener experience of community. Most of us have lost this experience; we have "lost our world." This is the worst kind of alienation, which "has expressed itself for several centuries in Western man's passion to gain power *over* nature, but now shows itself in an estrangement from nature and a vague, unarticulated, and half-suppressed sense of despair of gaining any real relationship with the natural world, including one's own body."

Existential Analysis divides a man's "worlds" into three—the world of nature and biological drives, where Freud's genius has been so illuminating; the world of interrelationships between human beings, which Sullivan marked out as his special province; and the world of the individual's relationship to himself, which May says "is least adequately dealt with or understood in modern psychology." Actually this is the "world" to which Jung's "individuation" is specifically addressed, but May has little interest in Jung, perhaps because he dislikes his recommendation of harmony with nature, which can closely resemble the *euphoria* that is the special fear of the existentialist. He also fails to mention that Jung long ago used therapy of the Medard Boss kind. Or that Rank did the same.

The new therapy says that the patient must distinguish consciously between his three "worlds" and learn to interrelate them gracefully. Actually, however, any good therapy makes similar demands, and to encounter them as restated by the existentialists merely confirms an impression that all good psychiatry, of whatever school, has become fluently eclectic. The new therapy also says that the patient will be incapable of love unless his "third world" is in order, his relationship to himself. But this is another familiar demand of good psychiatrists.

The existentialists stress the patient's future. "The word of the past is an oracle uttered," said Nietzsche. "Only as builders of the future, as knowing the present, will you understand it." When translated into treatment this means, says May, "Whether or not a patient can even recall the events of the past depends upon his decision with regard to the future." His past does not come alive to him unless some meaning beckons to him from the future. The first thing in treatment, therefore, is to find "where" the patient is with regard to his future; once he is positive about that, he can be led through the past and helped over present obstacles. Our best capacities will dry up unless we can cope with our anxiety about the future, and it is essential to face our great, inescapable, existential anxieties. Later the neurotic ones may be overcome by a clarified intelligence and a reanimated will.

As persuasively introduced by May, Existential Analysis seems made to order for psychic ailments in which Americans conceivably lead the world; and it comes at a time of national disillusionment when more and more of us mistrust a pragmatic way of life which once seemed enough. We are more hospitable to ontology, in prin-

ciple, than we were; and we have had ample evidence that psychoanalysis, as now practised, often furthers self-estrangement, instead of
diminishing it. Yet the personal revolution that Existential Analysis
demands will not come any more easily for all of that; it will still
require a dislocation no less painful or "hopeless" than Kierkegaard
experienced, together with a much wider understanding of cultural
complexities than was demanded of him. Unless this is clearly appreciated, Existential Analysis cools quickly into one more academic
formula, a little more timely than its predecessors, a little more dramatic, but *safe*. Like almost everybody now, it is against conformity,
but what about economic adjustment? Ontology, that handy word
which means almost the same thing as metaphysics, without having
its disagreeable popular associations, may provide a comfortable livelihood, if one teaches it in a university or assumes it in a therapeutic
office. But what if it plays havoc with one's earning capacities, oblig-
ing one to forsake a lucrative career for a search for truth? It may as
easily wreck one's status as improve it. And what if Kierkegaard
and Nietzsche, those revived heroes, had not had enough money to
escape their social tasks and devote themselves to thought?

The charges leveled at Jung—that he encourages a highly imprac-
tical search for meaning—must also be leveled at the existentialists.
Once a man becomes passionately interested in finding an answer to
his questions, he may neglect his career. Ordinarily one doesn't find
much truth unless one does.

Blueprints from another time and place must be redrawn today if
they are to be of any use. This is especially true of blueprints for the
inner life, where Americans are least at home. Therefore the existentialists, whatever their shortcomings, are very much a step in the
right direction.

A recent book by C. P. Snow, the English novelist, *The Two Cul-
tures and the Scientific Revolution*, demonstrates this. It suffers from
the "mind-body split" with astonishing unawareness. Snow complains
that he "found Greenwich Village talking precisely the same language as Chelsea, and both having about as much communication
with M.I.T. as though the scientists spoke nothing but Tibetan."
Our literary culture and our scientific culture fail completely to
understand each other, and Western civilization is in danger of being
overthrown because our intellectual leadership has split into two
cozy but mutually exclusive jargons, while the Soviet parlays its bets
on science and disregards literature. It is a natural fear in a post-

imperial British mind of great energy, and its pro-scientific bias may have the useful effect of shocking some of our writers out of their precious Bunthorne-in-tweeds disdain for physicists and engineers. It narrows the educational problem, however, to a power struggle; it overlooks entirely the emotional *price* of technology; and it totally ignores the effect of this upon mental health. Also, it fails to observe the inner dynamics set going by large-scale industrialization; it applauds the masculinization of women by industry; it speaks condescendingly of one of our best poets (Rilke). Above all it seems quite unaware of its own willingness to exploit the most manipulative traits of the mind, at the expense of the rest of the human being. Its engaging tartness of statement makes its unawareness of the proven dangers of its attitude all the more regrettable. A mind that sees only the power problem, and never its effect upon man: this is the real anachronism.

Snow's position is typical of the new "practical" European belief that more advanced "technicization" can be accomplished in Europe without the lamentable side-effects it is having in Disneyland and Radio City. His psychological callousness reveals a warlike attitude toward nature. As usual, the unconscious attitude is what counts.

This is equally true of a French man of letters whose name is linked inseparably with that of existentialism. He is Jean-Paul Sartre, and though he is best known as a philosopher, novelist, and playwright, he has produced what he calls "existential psychoanalysis." It "rejects the hypothesis of the unconscious." One reason why it does this is to prevent people from using the unconscious as a means of escape. "People gladly have recourse to the unconscious," because they do not wish to become aware of their own "bad faith," by which he means their lies to themselves. Each human being is inescapably involved (*engagé*) in the world, and his freedom is only meaningful in so far as he commits himself (*s'engage*) to definite ends through conscious choice. We are "condemned to be free," but usually we try to escape from freedom in even worse ways than Fromm suggests in his book of that name.

"The principal result of existential psychoanalysis must be to make us repudiate the *spirit of seriousness*," which regards man as an object and subordinates him to the world. We must not only realize that "God is dead" (Nietzsche) and we are therefore on our own, to make of our lives what we will. We must also realize that we are surrounded by enemies who assume the mask of "seriousness"—that is, steal all the big ethical concepts, as well as all the power, while we are not looking—and would only too gladly assist in our complete frustration, to use us as their dupes. We must therefore become conscious of our every act, and assume full responsibility for it. Then perhaps we may become militant enough to exact some few satisfactions from our fortuitous and "absurd" existence on a bleak planet which, if it were capable of thought, would doubtless regard us as an itchy skin disease. There is no meaning to our lives except what we give to them.

This shows as little sympathy for farm workers and other simple folk as did Marx, to whom it owes much. It makes demands that few people, except those remarkably like Sartre, could satisfy. William Barrett says it "leaves man rootless. This may be because Sartre himself is the quintessence of the urban intellectual of our time. . . . He seems to breathe the air of the modern city . . . as if there were no other home for man." His psychology "misunderstands or disparages the psychology of women." Also, "alone, unjustified, and on the very margins of existence," it has "sundered itself from nature." The freedom it advocates is "rootless freedom" in the Cartesian mode.

Thus Sartre actually furthers the mind-body split that the thought of Descartes helped initiate in the seventeenth century. His militancy sounds forceful, but it offers no help in our fight against the hidden forces that misshape us. He denies the existence of such forces, of all determinisms, in fact, biological or psychological, and gives us a kind of sermon on conscious will. He is obliged to deny the existence of the unconscious. To admit its existence might lead to an unmilitant humility before nature that might expose one to one's enemies, enemies who are always on the lookout for such moments of weakness. He is too fearful of his enemies to do otherwise. He denies the possibility of genuine relatedness to others. *Others* are enemies. *All* others.

Sartre's psychology is so subjective, so nakedly confessional, so local, that it makes one appreciate the attempts of the scientists to achieve objectivity. At least they tried to mint their insights into common coinage.

Sartre performed the useful social function of rallying the youth of his country after the great defeat in 1940. He preached conscious decision to youngsters who were demoralized. He made it disgraceful to use past French glories as an evasion of present personal tasks.

It was a necessary educational work in a highly traditional land which enjoys such an ever-present sense of history, as well as so many of the good things of life, that it might have gone slack. He was a good teacher and a great gadfly. He carried the fight to the *salauds*. It is a fight that still needs to be fought, and he is going on with it. But he does not have very much to say about man. He has a great deal to say about himself, and what he has to say is fascinating when not too compulsively verbose, but his psychology is not much more than an autobiography—for those who know how to read it. It offers little of a general nature except a rather dated kind of you-can-do-it exhortation. As that, however, it is bracing.

It is a far cry from his kind of exhortation to that of Viktor Frankl, who was also roused by an encounter with the Nazis to forge a philosophy of conscious choice. Frankl's encounter was more hazardous; he survived two concentration camps and a death march. On the other hand, his mind is not nearly as subtle or original as that of Sartre. He sees things even more in black and white. The gas chambers at Auschwitz he blames on "the lecture halls of nihilistic scientists and philosophers." Freudian evasion of philosophic responsibility, he says, played into the hands of the S.S. His ideas are still more simplistic than Adler's. They might be called overstatements of Jung. Yet, as documents of moral survival under extreme pressure they deserve study, since it is not inconceivable that the Remnant may some day have to cope with similar trials.

The deliberate brutality of the concentration camps, he says, turned most of the prisoners into brutes. They suffered from "futurelessness," from rage, from apathy, from "primitiveness of the inner life" which made them think of nothing but food. On the other hand, their pathetic undernourishment purged even their dreams of sexuality. And yet "probably in every concentration camp there were individuals able to overcome their apathy and suppress their irritability. . . . Asking nothing for themselves, they went about on the grounds and in the barracks of the camp, offering a kind word here, a last crust of bread there." Such people had adopted an attitude which made it possible for them to behave unselfishly—and not to "let go." "For in every case man retains the freedom and the possibility of deciding for or against the influence of his surroundings." The others, who did "let go," who "surrendered without a struggle to the physico-psychic influences of their surroundings . . . had lost their spiritual support." In his desire to understand this spiritual support, Frankl has fashioned a "logotherapy" which works together with an existential philosophy to lead patients toward "consciousness of responsibility." His clinic at Vienna tries to help patients to find a purpose in their lives. In American terms, his writing often seems like old-fashioned uplift, with not a few echoes of the pulpit. Its justification seems to be that it was called into being by new and desperate needs that could not have been foreseen in the gentler days of the Emperor Franz Joseph. As such it is one more witness to the changing needs of our time. The positivism that flourished in the days of the Hapsburgs may now be in the process of becoming a period piece.

The contributions of existentialism to psychology are on the increase. New schools spring up every year. The further we advance into the twentieth century, the more we seem to require frank metaphysical support. Does this mean a decline in the now more popular antimetaphysical—chiefly Freudian—therapy? The answer seems to depend on how hard-pressed we are likely to become.

18

Summation for the Founder

Within less than a century modern psychology has passed from its "classical" age: a fortunate thing for the patient. The spell of its illustrious pioneers slowly loosens, and the many perceptions they bequeathed fall with increasing anonymity into our mental pharmacopeia. Freud is still good for a twenty-one gun salvo, because he plays Leopold Bloom to many a fatherless Stephen Dedalus; but he used to get forty-eight guns. Jung has his Jungfrauen, a significant change of gender; and occasionally someone tries to rescue Rank from his despair, or Adler from his hope. The martyred Wilhelm Reich has his orgone shrines in Levittown; George Groddeck is championed by an Irish poet in a Provençal *mazet*; while lonely volumes on dianetics or conditioned-reflex therapy, in adobe huts in New Mexico or stone mansions in Virginia, burn like unblessed candles to the savior that is within us all. They are being crowded out, however, by books on Zen, which is the rage at the moment, because our new unguided life is quite as hard to sustain as Harry Stack Sullivan and Henry Miller found it, and our literate public, with a sickening sense of being trapped, searches desperately for a shortcut to a sustaining "way."

Modern psychology has passed rapidly into its silver age. Its techniques get better as its glamour declines. It is losing its better-read audience, except when they fear actual madness or a serious decline of effectiveness. In most cases they turn away from it to works of art where there are not only vicarious satisfactions for those permanently estranged from themselves but a good chance to pretend that things are otherwise. Our new wealth is producing a disproportionate number of aesthetes, propelled straight from a bottle containing the right proportion of evaporated milk and "formula" to a similarly demanding attitude toward thought and the arts. Some readers understand psychology with almost no effort, and pass beyond its rigors even in adolescence to the most advanced painting, the most advanced verse, the most advanced theology. Their precocity is an improvement over that of the revolutionary youth which preceded them twenty or thirty years ago; it involves almost no risk at all, and confers an equally high sense of personal superiority. They can fit into our educational system without mental reservations while they take their loyalty oaths, and there are plenty of jobs for them. Why should they make life hard when it can be such fun?

As for politics and the social problems that disturbed their elders, everybody knows that if there is an atomic war there won't be any more problems to worry about. The best way is to "play it cool," find something you really like, read up on it, and when you have to go to work, teach it. After all, what Freud told us was not to be afraid of sex, and we certainly are not that. We are just having as much fun as we can, and without all the *complications* that look so funny in print nowadays. The people in *Lady Chatterley's Lover*—why did they make such a fuss about a simple thing?

Those who condemn such reasoning with the psychoanalytic curse "infantile" are probably right, but they also miss the point. It *is* a great self-delusion to believe that the high watermarks of a previous culture can be reached without an effort equal to that which produced them; and we may pretend to play it cool when our real desire is to cover up our inordinate anxiety in the face of a breakdown of all the cultural touchstones. We may be discovering how much sober philosophy there must be in the background, as in Plato's *Symposium* or Prince Hal's revels or Auerbach's cellar, if we are even to raise hell when we are young. Yet to preach "maturity" or to hold out the reality principle to be kissed as though it were a modern crucifix misses the point, because it merely repeats formulas that will be empty until they are put into the idiom of our day.

Except for a few scholars, the reality principle has nothing like the immediacy it once had. It suffers from metaphysical, political, and aesthetic deficiencies. The best idiom of our day is much more complex than Freud's. It has been enriched by the work of many other gifted men, both in his profession and out of it. To understand the new idiom requires a supple receptivity to many levels of experience, such as only a resourceful and self-critical Remnant can hope to find within itself. This kind of suppleness will be asked in the following brief review of what his most gifted colleagues have said in opposition to Freud, together with his own rebuttal.

First the opposition. Adler, as we have seen, accused Freud of avoiding the social and political problems that we must all live with, by the transparent expedient of dealing only with those more intimate, more boudoir aspects of life to which his neurotically constricted theories applied. His pessimism was not courageous, but an escape from large, adult-sized difficulties with which he could not cope. Hence his present success merely testifies to the failure of nerve of disciples who are so well-protected against unpleasant realities by postwar prosperity that they have a vested interest in pretending to find a complete psychology in Freud.

The Adlerian objections are continued by Horney, Fromm, and Sullivan. Horney not only rejected the archaic narrowness of Freud's analysis of women but on the whole agreed with Adler that the compensatory and cramping nature of Freud's genius had made him misunderstand a great many other things that needed common sense to be put into a more helpful perspective. As a practical therapist she found Freud's sexual interpretations and "destructive instinct" provided handy screens behind which patients could hide, instead of confronting their real problems, which usually centered in "idealized images" of themselves. She said, in effect, that Freud's antibiotics no longer worked, because germs had found new ways of outwitting them.

Fromm stressed the cultural factors that helped to make man what he was, no less than his instincts; and found that Freud had neglected these, as well as the need of the individual to find the right kind of "relatedness" to the world and to himself. Freud, he said, had not given nearly enough attention to the needs of man to find productivity and love and faith or to the institutions that frustrate these needs. Even the Oedipus complex had to be rescued from Freud's literal interpretation of "incest," if man were to use it to unlock the doors that prevented him from reaching his full stature, and if society were at last to become humane and rational. Also, Freud's neurotic personality had left a neurotic institution behind him. Sullivan, less theoretical, found some of Freud's concepts good as far as they went, but said that in practical therapy they needed extensive overhauling if they were really to help the patient.

Each in his own way, Jung, Rank, Benoit, Sheldon, and the existentialists based their chief objections to Freud on his refusal to let psychoanalysis become a philosophy of life. Rank found it destructive because it merely made patients self-conscious instead of giving them a world view and a belief that would sustain them in their daily conflicts with reality. He said it had been personally tailored to meet the needs of Freud and others content with his hand-me-downs, but actually hampered more independent beings. Benoit reversed Freud's biological emphasis, and put it instead at the other end of the spectrum, on metaphysics, thus going radically further than Rank "beyond psychology." He did not dislike Freud's atheism, since Zen has no need of God, but he found Freud's concept of the unconscious elementary and incapable of leading to true freedom.

Sheldon objected to the effect of Freudianism on America, in its encouragement of the "waster," Dionysian, expressivistic trends in our new melting-pot culture. Technically Sheldon accused Freud of neglecting the body's role in our deepest problems, of sponsoring a shallow environmentalism that, for all of his avowed pessimism, actually fitted hand in glove with the unrealistic sentimentality of social workers. The Existential Analysts said that Freudianism, especially after the death of Freud, had actually encouraged the Cartesian subject-object cleavage that is "the cancer of all psychology up to now." They also said that psychoanalysis did not go deeply enough in its study and treatment of anxiety, which, if seen as not primarily neurotic but existential, can become a source of the greatest productivity.

Except for Adler's, all of these objections came after Jung's, which are still the most comprehensive. "It was a great mistake on Freud's part to turn his back on philosophy. Not once does he criticize his premises or even the assumptions that underlie his personal outlook. . . . The sexuality which Freud describes is . . . an overemphasized sexuality piled up behind a dam; and it shrinks at once to normal proportions as soon as the way to development is opened. . . . There is nothing that can free us from this bond except that opposite urge of life, the spirit. It is not the children of the flesh, but the 'children of God' who know freedom. . . . That is what Freud would never learn, and what all those who share his outlook forbid themselves to learn. . . .

"As for Freud's idea of the 'superego,' it is a furtive attempt to smuggle in his time-honoured image of Jehovah in the dress of psychological theory. . . . It is permissible for science to divide its field of enquiry and to set up limited hypotheses; but the human psyche may not be parcelled out. . . . Scientific thought, being only one of its functions, can never exhaust all the possibilities of life."

This last was an echo of Jung's basic charge of *reductionism,* which he was the first to level at Freud. It is now leveled even by some "Freudians" at Freud: that he reduced not only dreams but all of life overmuch to his personally straitened anatomy of the mind. And thus, says Jung, since Freud denied himself the replenishments that can be found in nature and spirit, he portrayed the ego, which he called man's only instrument for achieving consciousness, as a "place of fears." "The ego is indeed the 'place of fears,' as Freud says in *The Ego and the Id,* but only so long as it has not returned to the 'father' and the 'mother.'" As his translator makes clear in a footnote, Jung here equates the "father" symbolically with spirit and the "mother" with nature. Finally he says that Freud is shipwrecked spiritually because he sourly repeats the earth-bound literalness of Nicodemus in the New Testament, instead of responding to the capacities for rebirth that Jesus found in the human spirit.

Freud's defense against his critics is an attack. After portraying Adler as a foolishly ambitious man, he says:

Adler's theory was, from the very beginning, a "system," which psychoanalysis was careful not to become. . . . Adler's theory emphasizes . . . that all libidinal feeling contains an admixture of egotism. This would have been a palpable gain if Adler had not made use of this assertion to deny, every time, the libidinal feelings in favor of the compelling ego components. His theory thus does exactly what all patients do, and what our conscious thinking always does; it rationalizes . . . in order to conceal the unconscious motives. Adler is so consistent in this, that he considers the desire to dominate the woman, to be on the top, as the mainspring of the sexual act. . . . As it is known, the principle of Adler's system states that it is the object of the self-assertion of the individual, his "will to power," in the form of the "masculine protest," to manifest itself domineeringly in the conduct of life, in character formation, and in neurosis. This "masculine protest," the Adlerian motor, is, however, nothing else but the repression detached from its psychological mechanism, which is, moreover, sexualized in addition. This is hardly in keeping with Adler's vaunted expulsion of sexuality from its place in psychic life. . . . I feel obliged to emphasize how all psychological acquisitions of psychoanalysis have been thrown to the winds by Adler. In his book, *The Nervous Character,* the unconscious still appears as a psychological peculiarity, but without any relation to his system. Later, he declared, quite logically, that it was a matter of indifference to him whether any conception be conscious or unconscious. . . . The view of life which one obtains from Adler's system is founded entirely upon the

impulse of aggression. It leaves no room at all for love. One might wonder that such a cheerless aspect of life should have received any notice
whatever; but we must not forget that humanity, oppressed by its sexual
needs, is prepared to accept anything, if only the "overcoming of sexuality" is held out as bait.

Freud then turns his attention to Jung, whom he portrays as originally full of "race prejudice" but willing to overcome it in return for
a prominent place in the psychoanalytic movement.

In 1912, Jung boasted, in a letter to me from America, that his mod-
ifications of psychoanalysis had overcome the resistances to it in many
persons, who hitherto wanted to know nothing about it. I replied that
this was nothing to boast about, that the more he sacrificed the hard
won truths of psychoanalysis, the less resistances he would encounter.
. . . The relativity of all our knowledge is a consideration which may
be used as an argument against any other science, as well as against
psychoanalysis. It originates from well-known reactionary currents of the
present day, which are inimical to science, and strives to give the appearance of superiority to which we are not entitled. . . . To emphasize
personal arbitrariness in scientific matters is bad; it evidently is an
attempt to deny psychoanalysis the value of a science. . . . Anyone
who highly regards scientific thinking will rather seek for means and
methods to restrict, if possible, the factor of personal and artificial
arbitrariness, wherever it still plays too large a part. . . . Of the two
movements under consideration here, Adler's is undoubtedly the more
important. Though radically false, it is, nevertheless, characterized by
consistency and coherence, and it is still founded on the theory of the
instincts. On the other hand, Jung's modification has slackened the connection between the phenomena and the instinctive life, besides . . . it
is so unintelligible, muddled and confused, that it is not easy to take
any attitude toward it. . . . It represents itself in a peculiarly vacillating
manner, since at one time it calls itself "a quite tame deviation, not
worthy of the row which has arisen about it" (Jung); yet, at another
time, it calls itself a new message of salvation which is to begin a new
epoch in psychoanalysis; indeed, a new philosophy of life for everything
else.

Freud did not live long enough to defend himself against the
other deviations from psychoanalysis, and never gave Rank such
rough treatment, but it must be clear that he would have been able
to reply to every opponent with equal vigor. He believed that anyone who disagreed with him suffered from a "resistance" that originated in neurotic unclarity. The other's unclarity would have to be
removed by a lengthy psychoanalysis before there could be any rational discourse. And he had significant reasons for taking an atti-

tude that in anyone else would have been dismissed as intolerably arrogant.

However neurotic Fromm found him, or perhaps *because* of his neurotic state, he really believed that he had created a science in which he had restricted every "factor of personal and artificial arbitrariness," a science which fully deserved the name because it gave the world a final criterion for determining whether a person was neurotic or not neurotic. "One says rightly that the Oedipus complex is the nuclear complex of the neurosis. . . . The task before each new human being is to master the Oedipus complex; one who cannot do this falls into a neurosis." He would have dismissed the recent statement of his admirer, Jerome S. Bruner, "Freud's mode of thought is not a theory in the conventional sense, it is a metaphor, an analogy, a way of conceiving man, a drama." He would logically have had to dismiss this as coming from as "reactionary" a relativism as Jung's. And yet the position of Jung and Bruner on this very important issue, though it has not yet dribbled down to patients, except in the form of inarticulate resistance, seems to be one that is being forced upon most able psychologists, and not, I think, because they are "reactionary" but because they have had so much humbling evidence of the inescapable relativity of their own and everyone's profoundest judgments. Ironically, Freud himself helped to point the way to this humility, but chose to disregard it when it touched upon his own discoveries.

The reason is emotional, I believe, and may bring us closer to a "nuclear" understanding of Freud. He *had* made very important discoveries in the Oedipus complex and in all the many, many, other insights that went with it; and they *were* discoveries that could be called scientific to the extent that they revealed a root cause of human failure or success, made it possible to predict behavior, lent themselves to a teachable technique, and in several other ways met our demands on scientific laws; but much more significantly, Freud felt that his discoveries had permitted him to understand human beings and their activities and their history and their possible future better than anyone else. He not only made his discoveries, he lived them. His vision was a gloomy one, but he could sustain it, and whatever misfortune came to him, he could sustain that too. And if he looked at his contemporaries, what did he see? No one who had done as much.

Any attempt therefore *on the part of anyone else* to remind him of the limitations of his work did not get through to him. He could be intensely self-critical, and he could also learn from enemies—the well-hidden influence of Jung and others on his later work would make a good study—but only in terms of what he had already done, and what he *could* do in the future. He worked within a personal and highly practical sense of his own potentialities, beside which his limitations seemed mere abstractions. He *had* the artist's "myth" that Rank despaired of. Jung's modification of his achievement, which restricted its application to those of a type similar to Freud's, therefore meant nothing to him. Its "larger view," and the moderate, reasonable, philosophical tone in which it was couched, only made Freud despise Jung, in very much the way that an effective writer often despises another who may have a broader culture or a nobler attitude but lacks the demon that makes the difference between first-rate literature and something less than that. For Freud, Jung was "muddled and confused."

This is a frequent attitude in a writer who puts a high valuation upon style and lives in a *sauve-qui-peut* time. It can be found, as we shall soon be seeing, in the life of James Joyce. After he had made his central discoveries Freud put more and more of his energy into style. The nature of his style deserves investigation. We shall find, I think, that it owes its fundamental sagacity to his youthful conflicts with Austrian stupidity. As a counter to a decaying peasant-priest-soldier society that made his career difficult, he hit upon a few intensely clever devices which occur throughout his work. These devices would mean nothing if they were not used to convey important insights, but there have been other writers who also had important insights but did not know how to express them as well.

For example, Jung writes in one of his best essays, *The Relations of the Ego and the Unconscious:*

A somewhat arrogant gentleman once came to me for treatment. He ran a business in partnership with his younger brother. Relations between the two brothers were very strained, and this was one of the essential causes of my patient's neurosis. From the information he gave me, the real reason for the tension was not altogether clear. He had all kinds of criticisms to make of his brother, whose gifts he certainly did not show in a very favorable light. The brother frequently came into his dreams, always in the role of a Bismarck, Napoleon, or Julius Caesar. His house looked like the Vatican or Yildiz Kiosk. My patient's unconscious evidently had the need to exalt the rank of the younger brother. From this I concluded that he was setting himself too high and his brother too low. The further course of analysis entirely justified this inference.

Freud never wrote so carelessly. Since the case history is one of several, the point of which matters more to him than the details, Jung treats it casually, as if speaking to learned colleagues who already are aware of a hundred such cases, and thus gives the common reader an occasional impression of a slackness which is not, however, in his style when he is on his mettle. As a writer Jung can be uneven. Freud never is. Freud is always almost paranoidally conscious of an audience whom he must not only satisfy but lead. He knows exactly where he wants to lead his readers and how to make them *want* to go there, that is, if they are intelligent enough to follow him. For example, in *Thoughts for the Times on War and Death,* he wants to lead them to the recognition that in their deepest selves, in their unconscious they are like primitives in their attitude towards death, and they will be better off if they recognize their real primitive motivations instead of deceiving themselves with falsely "civilized" ones, or rationalizations.

In addition to the devices that any expert writer would employ, Freud employs one here and elsewhere, that usually is not at the command of a writer of his erudition. Neither the fatigue of study nor the joy of discovery prevented him from knowing how to make the reader *desire* to turn away from previous convictions and accept in their stead those which Freud has carefully prepared for introduction at the proper place. In nearly every case this desire is provoked *by making the reader feel stupid* if he does not change his opinion. To lead him into a new position, favorable to psychoanalysis, Freud has played with enormous cunning on his fear of ridicule. Thus, since his greatest weapon against "resistance" is contempt, Freud sets the stage in his essay with infinite pains, so that his kind of reader—an educated person invariably, full of pride in his mental capacities—will either have to agree to the primitiveness of his own attitude toward death or have to identify himself with the many stupid people, transparently self-deceived, who "hush up" any mention of death, so that they can go on in the unconscious conviction of their own immortality. The key part of the essays begins, therefore, with a portrait of such people, and the reader soon wants to disassociate himself from them as definitively as possible. Because of this, he is finally predisposed to go along with Freud's major conclusion: "Our unconscious is just as inaccessible to the idea of our own death, as murderously minded toward the stranger, as divided or ambivalent toward the loved, as was man in earliest antiquity."

Freud was a practical psychologist in the sense that he used his own science to become a better writer. Through his knowledge of the id he learned how to make his words take up permanent residence in the minds of others. His literary skill, in fact, offers an important key to his character.

"To endure life remains, when all is said, the first duty of all living beings. Illusion can have no value if it makes this more difficult for us." The stoical Freud was not interested in happiness; he was interested in developing his ideas and putting them into the best possible form. "Men are strong so long as they represent a strong idea"—and he might have added, "express it strongly." He was resolved to write supremely well. His ideas he had produced single-handed, he believed, and his major work consisted of putting them down durably. It is not surprising that he has awakened the enthusiasm of more than one fellow writer. It *is* surprising that his style, though generally admired, though honored with the Goethe Prize, has not been analyzed, so far as I know, for what it reveals of his innermost character.

Freud took no interest in "spirit" or "rebirth" or in any grace outside his professional scope. He scorned religion as he knew it because he had already received the faith and the grace to endure life without complaint and to do a hard job with superlative skill. His unconscious religion had bestowed so many blessings on him, in the name of antireligion, that he did not feel obliged to thank it for what he had done himself. He did not need Rank's "mythical stuff"; he had it. When he sat down and wrote his books he satisfied both his own reality principle and his own pleasure principle. The grimness of his ideas satisfied the former, and the joys of creation the latter. He was sufficient unto himself.

This gave him the courage to violate scientific objectivity when he thought the situation warranted it, and when he thought he could get away with it. Emboldened by his own solution of the Oedipus complex, which to him was like the answer to the Sphinx's riddle, he felt justified in writing fiction, and whenever he needed it. His heroic quest of a coherent theory of the mind would never have been fulfilled if his methods had been as strictly empirical as he said they were. For example, in his excellent essay on war and death, as we have seen, he wanted to show that modern man was just as unrealistic about death, just as murderous, just as ambivalent as primitive man had been. He had seen more of modern men than he had seen of primitive men. In fact, he had never seen primitive men at all. He had merely read about them, and he had not read much at that. He had not lived among them, as Jung did for two years. Even his reading was limited and biased. Paul Radin, after many years of experience among primitives, disagrees specifically with Freud's armchair picture of them: that they were as compulsively subjective as modern neurotics. In *The World of Primitive Man* Radin shows a strong movement among them toward objectivity, reason, maturity. Thus only could man have become civilized.

One begins to understand what Freud was doing with material of which he had no first-hand experience. He was using imagined primitive behavior as a dreadful *metaphor* with which to awaken modern neurotics to their true condition. So his lack of solid information did not prevent him from writing with assurance that primitive man was emotionally a monster. "The death of the other man he had no objection to; it meant the annihilation of a creature hated, and primitive man had no scruples about bringing it about. He was, in truth, a very violent being, more cruel and malign than other animals. He liked to kill, and killed as a matter of course. That instinct which is said to restrain the other animals from killing or devouring their own species we need not attribute to him."

Some of this brutal picture reads like Grimm. Where did it come from? Even if all primitive men were like that, and we know that they are not, the very ardor of its presentation would help us to perceive its source. Freud *enjoyed* that portrait. Through it he expressed himself as an artist, lived out harmlessly his own murderous impulses, hypnotized his audience. There are many other such instances in his work, which would not be half as lively, or perhaps as important, without them. If he had not worked up his amazing combination of fact and fiction, he would certainly not receive so much discussion today.

He had found the fusion of fact and myth that Rank died seeking. And with it came the artist's hundred-per-cent concentration that Rank also sought. One of the biggest problems of the Remnant did not exist for Freud. That is why scholars who *wish* this problem did not exist for them hasten to encumber his memory with a disproportionate hero-worship; they hope they can hide behind his Pentateuchal robes, be carried along to Sinai. To insist upon his genius is to make a pathetic confession. He was indeed a genius, and he has much to tell us, but his genius is of a kind that seeks total conversion. Its single-minded intensity can only be absorbed with impunity by those who have elsewhere acquired a deep and wide experience of *other* intensities. His central idea is revolutionary, and cannot be smiled off; it demands an intimate trial over a period of years if it is to be understood; but it also demands correlation with many other revolutionary ideas, if it is not to produce an unfortunate kind of monomaniac. Today we are subjected to one apocalypse after another; survival requires outlasting a steady stream of fanatical prophets, each able to drown out the others. Survival may finally be chemical: the knack of mixing the right amounts of adrenalin and that earlier secretion called phlegm.

It also requires the formulation of a much more complex psychology than Freud's. The half-educated are short of breath, however, and want a *definitive* anatomy of the mind that will make it unnecessary to pick their own path through the jungle. If their every experience can be quickly identified with death wish or super-ego or penis-envy or the preconscious, they have found a ready-made path to the tragic sense of life and need not bother their heads any more. They need not bother about such complications as have been brought up by other men who did not found modern psychology, it is true, but at times were more thoughtful, more cultured, more helpful, more imaginative, more humane, more penetrating than their illustrious predecessor. There never will be a definitive anatomy of the mind; that was one of the more infantile hopes of the Founder. We had better resign ourselves to the demonstrated fact that the new "science" of psychology will always remain as bloody a battlefield as the old "science" of theology proved itself to be long ago. Utopianism is by no means restricted to political or social hopes; it is subtlest, and most harmful, when it hides behind the confidence that "some day," especially if the foundations are kind, there will be so many closely observed studies on every scientific subject that it is only a question of time before our new knowledge trickles down to the masses and the reign of reason begins.

Aside from his illusions about his own science, Freud was hard-headed, and especially in his furtherance of an undeclared literary career. If it had been openly literary, he might have stood no chance with his opposition; but under the protection of science he became a very important influence on letters. As a writer he had a big job to do: to bring every subject he encountered, every experience he had, into the orbit of his "strong idea." Overapplication to his job may have contributed to the illness that finally killed him, but it also gave him the sense of vocation that an artist of his caliber prefers to longevity or freedom from pain. Whenever he had a moment, there was always some writing to do. And the more he made his writings succeed, the more energy he discovered to round them out, to expand his idea, to alter it in some details, and to make it unpalatable to all except those who would follow him in perfect acceptance. He had what every artist wants: an audience so much at his command that they more than made up for the old wounds and the continuing enmities. He could enjoy his success and still not forget to make the most, literarily, of the wounds and the enmities. There was no secret that would not yield to his idea, and no obstacle in the path of its presentation that he could not surmount. A distinctly hysterical scholar had grown, by sheer force of character, into a great world figure.

It has been said that his fellow Jews sometimes admire Freud because he awakens more natural enthusiasm in them than they could be expected to feel for a thinker of different origins. In his own language, they can more readily identify with him. This is true of those Jews who are at the mercy of patriotic sentiments; but as we have seen, he has met with Jewish opposition from Adler, Rank, and Fromm, as firm as any other. To an outsider the trait that he seems to share with some fellow Jews is a certain toughness of mind that may be traceable to early encounters with anti-Semitism. An account of the loutish humiliation of his father by an anti-Semite appears to have made a very painful childhood impression on him. Whatever the reason, he confronted the "nuclear" problems of childhood with astonishing courage and developed a strong desire to rise above them through force of character. He wanted supremely to succeed, to vindicate himself against enemies early and late; and to succeed he found it necessary to get to the roots of his character as it had been formed in his infancy. This meant uncovering a great many nasty "instinctual drives" that he has since obliged a reluctant world to find in itself too. By persisting in an unsavory task he discovered an important clue to the root cause of immaturity in man, a clue that no one who wants to take up his full conscious burden as a human being can now afford to ignore. To that extent he has indeed made a scientific contribution; for anyone who really faces his Oedipus complex, as well as the other unpleasant "Freudian" facts that go along with it, does take a decisive step toward self-knowledge; and it is easy to distinguish those who have done this from those who have not.

Unfortunately, that is not everything that is required. The unconscious is not a single underground cave that one hunter fell into one day; it is a whole network of caves that extend throughout the earth, and its further exploration calls for many hunters, many diggers, much humility, much imagination—and at least as much time above ground as below. The school which has followed his lead—regrettably neglected in this bird's eye view—has done much to extend the work, and so have other schools.

Meanwhile they have been challenged, as we shall now see, by those who disagree profoundly with *all* the psychologists.

III

Their Natural Opponents

19

Isaiah Counting Famine

The most serious opposition to the psychologists comes from theologians and men of letters. First, however, an unrecognized source of opposition must be driven out of its hiding place, an opposition which may be attributed indirectly to our great new prosperity. In Hart Crane's poem *The Bridge* Columbus speculates on the future of the continent he is discovering—a transparent device to permit the poet to express his own fears for his country:

> —Rush down the plenitude, and you shall see
> Isaiah counting famine on his lee.

Certainly a plenitude has been rushed down on us, and certainly it has caused a famine in the reflective habits needed to give psychology meaning.

This can be illustrated by the practitioners of the new science, who have received an opportunity to become well-to-do in a short time if only they conduct themselves with proper scientific decorum, maintain their group loyalties, expand their connections, acquire a reputation for steadiness. With extraordinary speed their profession has moved from eager discoveries that suggested enormous areas for exploration to what Alfred Kazin calls "a big business, and a very smoth one" with "little original thought."

It would be wrong to expect anything else. Our period is not at all like the period which gave birth to psychoanalysis. Then there was every incentive to achieve the fullest possible consciousness; now there is every incentive to avoid it. We have seen what it can do to injure one's capacity to fit into a mutual aid society. Our minority groups now divide up our astonishing wealth among them—and pun-

142

ish any infringement of their rules with greater severity each year. Our democracy has fulfilled Emerson's description of it, "an association of mutually repellent particles." Communication between groups has become so difficult that as soon as possible, in big cities at least, Scotch Catholics see only Scotch Catholics, Socratic homosexuals see only Socratic homosexuals, Sephardic Jews see only Sephardic Jews, abstract painters see only abstract painters, representational painters see only representational painters, and even so there are well-nigh insuperable language barriers. Under such conditions holism itself becomes a specialty, and interdisciplinary movements in universities, aimed at stimulating the self-extension for which Snow ably pleads, encounter the jeer, "Dilettanti!" Anyone is a dilettante who is not anchored lucratively behind a blind spot.

Technical concentration is the only way to keep one's head above water. Any trace of hospitality to more than one subject may well mean the end of a promising talent. The sooner a man jumps on a bandwagon, the better off he will be. To jump off it is a good working definition of neurosis.

It will not do, then, to complain about the failings of the psychiatrists. They are the priests of a new church; subject to no ecclesiastical discipline except that provided by a chattel mortgage on a Cadillac. The patient who expects more of them than he gets has simply not caught on: he has to do it all himself. Whatever his original hardships, our prosperity means that he is soft, softer than he has any right to be; softer than his opposite number in other lands; and yet his softness is his salvation—if it leads finally to complete confusion before a blank wall. Then he may be ready to go "beyond psychology" in a way that the unhappy author of that phrase never knew.

20

The Oldest View

A generation ago it would have been difficult to convince anyone that psychology, because of its distrust of what people believe they know, would actually help the revival that we presently behold of the most debatable knowledge of all—theology. Now that that revival is a fact which enrolls more students at Columbia University in the once shunned theology department than in any other department, there may be more disposition to see a tie between a scientific study of the mind and a subsequent concern with original sin. The violent oscillations of a young, paper-born, paper-mistrusting culture like the American, which seems centuries away from being a true civilization able to prepare its young intelligently for their struggles, cannot account entirely for the new prestige of the science of God. Nor is it enough to suggest, as Gregory Zilboorg does, that, "Even the concept of original sin or of the original fall of man finds its empirical counterpart in the findings of psychoanalysis." This is good, but a better explanation would be that the very one-sidedness of the daring drama that Freud began, but naturally did not complete, brought about in time, and with especial rapidity in our inexperienced people, a need to live out and write in the parts of the play that he had not been able to imagine. This is a task, as we have seen, that fell heavily upon his revisionists, who were not always the murderous band of father-eating sons that he melodramatically seems to have visualized, but more often the disappointed heirs to an incomplete theory. This task has also fallen upon theologians whom his hostility helped to revitalize.

The mordant humor of our era makes it possible to enjoy the hysterical convulsions of a land that, if a cultural seismograph had been invented, would surely astonish everyone by its affection for earthquakes. Nothing can be more hazardous than to impute a personal will to a society, but one observer is convinced that beneath our portion of the earth's crust lies a vast geological pie which seems to have been fed not only by our weather but by our feelings, our thoughts, our most intimate lives. If something has been seriously lacking in our lives—as, for instance, freedom was lacking to the Negroes in the ante bellum South—there is soon an eruption, and the lava takes the form of popular expression. In the Negroes' case it was the spirituals, addressed to Jesus and heard by Lincoln. Other folk songs have come into being the same way, and this kind of upheaval has also produced ideas. Thus, unless I am mistaken, the barrenness of scientism has produced in our day an unexpected welcome, and, at times, an excessive welcome to theology. It is profoundly ironic that the kind of speculation we thought had passed out of American life with Jonathan Edwards, or certainly with Emerson, is now back in our midst and going strong. Moreover, it has something important to say about the new science which unintentionally aided its return. Since it takes the oldest view of man, it is naturally concerned with his newest discoveries about himself—and just how new and how useful they are.

But theologians are divided into as many warring camps as psychologists, and though they carry on their wars today in more polite language, they too have to be studied with some restraint if they are to help us. Two Catholic thinkers have addressed themselves impressively to the problems raised by psychoanalysis. One of them is a priest, the other a layman. The priest is Father Victor White, an English Dominican; the layman Jacques Maritain, the French writer so well-known in America.

Father White cannot let Freud's description of religion as an illusion pass unchallenged, or accept his definition of God as " 'at bottom an exalted father,' a phantasy substitute for the actual, and never wholly satisfactory, parent," but he begins his reply with an attempt to understand Freud's position: ". . . it is by no means valueless. If religion is found to be withering in Western man and society, is not this largely due to the fact that it has often become over-intellectualized, uprooted from its lowly origins in elemental, instinctive human needs and experience? Nor, perhaps, is Freud's conception of religion as a universal *neurosis* entirely without truth— once we have understood his terminology. We must remember that for him, not only religion, but dreams, unbidden phantasies, slips of the tongue and pen—everything short of an unrealizable ideal of complete consciousness is somehow abnormal and pathological. But theology will also confirm that religion, in the sense of creeds and external cults, arises from man's relative unconsciousness, from his incomprehension of—and disharmony with—the creative mind behind the universe, and from his own inner conflicts and divisions. Such religion, in theological language, is the result of man's fall from original innocence and integrity, his remoteness on this earth from Divine vision. . . . Freud was surely right in sensing that religion as we know it was somehow a sign of some radical irregularity and incompleteness in man; but unduly optimistic in supposing it could be psychoanalyzed away. Theology has perhaps been more realistic in insisting that this irregularity must be accepted together with all its consequences; more in line with the findings of depth-psychology itself in trying to keep it constantly before our consciousness if it is to be finally overcome."

Although he is grateful for Jung's hospitality to religion, Father White says: ". . . the very 'religiousness' of Jung is apt to scare off the religious-minded." Maritain and most Catholic psychotherapists believe, he says, that a distinction can be made between Freudian philosophical theory and clinical practice, and therefore prefer Freud's psychology. Father White does not; he finds that Jung's break with Freud led to a radical "revaluation of religion, and particularly of Christianity." He also believes that there is no real psychotherapy that disregards religion. He praises Jung for removing the literalness from Freud's concepts of the libido and incest. "The way is now open to us . . . no longer to conceive of God as a substitute for the physical father, but rather the physical father as the infant's first substitute for God." He reverses Freud's formula: "God is less a Big Father than the physical father a little god."

Jung "challenges us to become more conscious, more responsible, more adult in our religion—or irreligion—if we would not destroy ourselves and our fellows. Western man fools himself if he thinks he has outgrown religion and has no need of God—as he is learning in the bitter Nemesis to his pretensions of self-sufficiency. But he *has* outgrown an infantile religiosity which is no more than an escape-mechanism, an outer and theoretic compensation for inner godlessness in practice."

Father White finds, however, that the Jungian school is in danger of degenerating into a retrogressive mythology, an esoteric sect of initiates, if it fails to recognize the word made flesh, the Christian demand for the earthly realization of the symbol. He suggests certain affinities between the Jungian movement and the wealthy gnostic sects of early Christian days: "Each gnosticist sect was a chosen, superior, favored people, alone in the possession of the saving knowledge. This cut clean across the Christian conviction that Christ's life and teaching and death and rising had been for all men."

Thus Father White raises the point whether a modern Remnant would not inevitably acquire the exclusive character, the unpleasant superiority of the Gnostics. He also takes issue with Jung on two matters: he does not think that Jung has been correct in suggesting, in *Answer to Job*, that the Catholic Church has an inadequate theory of evil, and he also believes that Jung's weakness lies in his "psychologism" which leads him to regard God as an archetype, an imprint upon the mind, rather than as a reality that exists independent of the mind. On the whole, however, Father White has nothing but praise for Jung as a healer superior to Freud, an intellectual leader more imaginative than Freud, and as a discoverer of new religious land for which theologians can only be intensely grateful.

Maritain does not agree: "it seems to me that Jung and several of those who are called 'revisionists,' while they indeed are restoring essential values denied by Freud, have aggravated the confusion between the scientific realm and the philosophic and moral realms in an irremediable way, making room for a sort of scientific mythology able to produce some remarkable results in therapeutic practice, but not much healthier for the intelligence than the 'philosophy' of Freud."

Father White objects to so compartmentalized a view of man: "It does . . . seem unscientific to contend that, in the name of science, psychotherapy can and should disregard religion and moral issues. Even from the purely therapeutic standpoint it seems that a patient's religion and moral principles cannot be regarded by the practitioner as a tabu, a constant which can remain unchanged throughout the process. And we would further venture to contend that the psychotherapist who supposes otherwise is of all the most to be regarded with suspicion, for he is of all the most unconscious of his responsibilities, of the principal factors and of the inevitable outcome of any effective treatment he may give." Despite its scholarly mildness of

wording, this is a strong statement, not only to Maritain and Roland
Dalbiez, the French Catholic psychoanalyst who helped Maritain
to believe that Freudian treatment can be separated from Freud's
unstated philosophy, but to any one else, in or out of the Catholic
Church, who believes that there can be any true psychic healing that
does not penetrate the whole man, including his religious and moral
problems.

Maritain's position is different. He says that the distinction between bodily health and virtue is completely evident. "Nobody declares that palpitations of the heart are moral faults. When it is a
question of psychic health, however, it is curious to find how certain
people confuse it with virtue. Yet, already in the realm of normal
psychic life, the distinction between psychological determinism and
morality is easy to grasp. Intellectual and artistic aptitudes are in-
contestably something psychological, but they do not pertain to
morality. Nobody can be blamed morally for his lack of aptitude for
mathematics or sculpturing. The most heroic moral efforts run
aground trying to overcome the limitations of psychic capacities.
A fortiori it is the same in the realm of abnormal psychic life. Will
power counts for nothing in the presence of a feeling of depersonalization. Psychic health, far from being confused with virtue, is presupposed by it. It can be appreciated, therefore, that while ethics
sets out to realize the total and supreme good of man by means of
free will, psychotherapy sets out to realize a human good that is
partial and relative, whether psychic or physical, by means of psychological determinism. To introduce the cultivation of free will
into psychotherapy is to be guilty of confusing essences."

Thus we see that even the church which is supposed to be mono-
lithic in matters of doctrine, when confronted by the new psychology, erects two contradictory shafts of opinion, and on a site that
can be called one of great theological importance, since it looks out
on the spiritual health of men. This health can be achieved, says
Maritain, by psychoanalytic method separated sharply from psychoanalytic thought. Freud was "an admirably penetrating psychologist,
whose ideas, inspired by his astonishing instinct for discovery, are
spoiled by a radical empiricism and an erroneous metaphysics that is
unaware of itself." Father White, on the other hand, believes that
man's mind does not lend itself to such conveniently medical
methods; if a man is psychologically ill, his religion "is precisely one
of the elements or factors in the disorder," and there will be no

real psychic health until he has confronted and mastered his moral and religious problems. Maritain's might be called a short-term, practical view of the unconscious, while White mistrusts any psychotherapy which does not specifically address itself to religious integration. This may be another way of saying that Maritain is pro-Freud, while White is pro-Jung. Psychology's central debate has appeared again, and in a place where there is not supposed to be debate.

It appears also when we turn to the dogmaless Protestant theologian Paul Tillich, who is pro-Freud. Speaking for a "Protestant principle" which he regards as having antedated the creation of any church, a critical attitude toward institutions which was also manifested by Christ, Tillich approaches psychology from an existential position. Historically, he says, "the success of psychoanalysis in Protestant countries has two main reasons: (1) the rigorous moralism which developed in Protestantism after the sacramental grace was taken away and which poisons the personality through repressing vital impulses by moral law and social conventions and (2) the solitude of the deciding individual, who has to bear responsibility and guilt without the help of confession and the related forgiveness which comes from the outside."

He credits Freud with having contributed to the development of a "transmoral conscience" which he did not, however, because of his science-imposed timidity, fully understand. This transmoral conscience puts man "'beyond good and evil' in the moral sense" but makes him "good in the metaphysical (or mystical) sense that he is in unity with life universal." Tillich agrees with Heidegger that "existence as such is guilty," and that only self-deception can give a good conscience. Freud, however, was "inhibited" in his analysis of the moral conscience, too conventional to face moral problems as radically as the existentialists did.

This reverses the usual attitude toward Freud, who is not generally reproached with a lack of daring. Tillich's approach to psychotherapy is roughly comparable to that of Maritain: he recommends it to those who are not yet ready for their real problems; and he prefers it in its Freudian form, which is restricted to a technical operation. If we were philosophically clear, he suggests, we would not need it at all. Jungian therapy he seems to regard as a dubious substitute for religion which tends to draw men away from their obligation to accept their full saving burden of anxiety and guilt. It is Protestantism gone soft and exotic. In its refrain of harmony with nature it offers euphoria, which is the worst enemy of vigorous self-fulfillment; what we need is not euphoria but action. "Conscience . . . tells us only to act and to become guilty by acting, for every action is unscrupulous. . . . We *must* act, and the attitude in which we *can* act is 'resoluteness.' Resoluteness transcends the moral conscience, its arguments and prohibitions. It determines a situation instead of being determined by it. *The good, transmoral conscience consists in the acceptance of the bad, moral conscience.* . . . Is the idea of a transmoral conscience tenable? Or is it so dangerous that it cannot be maintained? But if the idea has to be dismissed, religion as well as analytic psychotherapy would have to be dismissed also; for in both of them the moral conscience is transcendent—in religion by acceptance of the divine grace which breaks through the realm of law and creates a joyful conscience; in depth psychology by the acceptance of one's own conflicts when looking at them and suffering under their ugliness without an attempt to suppress them and to hide them from one's self. Indeed, it is impossible *not* to transcend the moral conscience because it is impossible to unite a *sensitive* and a *good* conscience."

Tillich's challenge, as we have seen, has strongly influenced the American presentation of Existential Analysis by Rollo May. Tillich believes that the best way to help man to face and conquer his psychopathic anxieties is to make him aware of his existential anxieties, which he acquires by being born. If he confronts them, Tillich suggests, there will be no need for him to be neurotic. It is a way of bypassing Freud with philosophic rigor. Psychoanalysis is a mere temporary preparation for the real fight, which is first to find the "God above God," the God who appears when we have destroyed within ourselves every conventional image of God, and then to move on to "the courage to be," the courage to live "in enthusiastic unity with life in its creative and destructive power."

Reinhold Niebuhr, another Protestant theologian, born in the United States, praises Freud for correcting the illusions about man which grew up in the Enlightenment, but finds his picture of the self too narrow.

Since Freud's system is a consistently naturalistic one, it can not, despite the subtleties of its analyses of the intricacies of human selfhood, do full justice to the transcendent freedom of spirit of which the self is capable. . . . Retrospectively it is always possible to establish scientifically what pressures prompted the self to certain actions. It is only prospectively that the self is free. The moment it has acted its actions become one in a chain of cause and effect. Freud is not to be criticized for his determinism as such, though probably for the consistency of his deterministic assumptions. But the primary problem of his determinism is that he finds the causative factors in too narrow a range of subconscious motives. Meanwhile, the self acts in a large area of events and forces in which the action may be prompted by any combination of causes on many levels of economic, cultural, ethnic and other interests. The freedom of the self is in fact partly due to its ability to choose between the pressures which seek to prompt its actions. If the self is determined after it has acted, it is because it is possible to chart the particular cause which prompted its action. But the freedom of the self, as self-determining agent, is always hidden from view. . . .

Insofar as the myths of the Bible contain the stuff of history and illumine man's perennial problem arising from his position as creator and creature of history, they are bound to illumine some facets of the human situation which the most rigorous science, too closely bound to man's non-historical nature fails to illumine. In that sense the doctrine of original sin surveys a broader aspect of human nature and behavior than Freudian pessimism.

Niebuhr's view of original sin, needless to say, is not the one usually associated with that doctrine. To him, when it is relieved of the embarrassments of "outworn dogmas and myths," it can be restored to modern usefulness because it serves to defeat man's recurrent attempts to deny his humble creaturely status in history, such as can be discovered in the physiocrats of the Enlightenment, in the optimism of Herbert Spencer, in the rationalistic utopianism of Auguste Comte and in the pretensions to omniscience of contemporary Marxists. The most plausible form of the doctrine of original sin is to define this persistent and universal tendency to forget and to defy man's creaturely limitations as 'original sin.' "

Freud does not revive the errors of the Enlightenment, as Sullivan, Horney, and Fromm do, Niebuhr says, but his pessimism is inferior to Christian pessimism, when Christian pessimism is purged of its outmoded forms, because "it fails to consider man as an historical creature" and also because in many other ways it is too reductive and too narrow. Freud's great discoveries have laid the foundation for the art of healing mental disorders, but we must not expect from them either great political or great moral relevance. Niebuhr's position is finally not unlike that of Maritain and Tillich: Freud is a technician, to be employed as such but not as anything more.

The Jewish thinker Martin Buber also finds Freud's thought too narrow. In his book *Hasidism* he writes: "The psychoanalysis of our day has again taken up the Hasidic view in the form of the theory of the 'sublimation of the libido,' according to which stimuli can be diverted, and carried over into the realm of the spirit, therefore changing so to speak their form of energy. Everything here is limited to psychic events alone, while Hasidism teaches ever and again the actual contact with other essences. 'Sublimation' takes place within the man himself, the 'raising of the spark' takes place between man and the world."

The striking Hasidic phrase is another way of saying that it is not enough to become strong within ourselves, we cannot find true psychic health until we establish a religious relationship with others, and this Freud did not understand. "What can Judaism tell the world? This is its message: *You yourself must begin.* Existence will remain meaningless for you if you yourself do not penetrate into it with active love and if you do not in this way discover its meaning for yourself. . . . Meet the world with the fullness of your being, and you shall meet God. . . . If you wish to believe, love."

Though critical of Jung, Buber gives more praise to his psychology than to that of Freud. He criticizes Jung for offering "no criterion for a qualitative distinction between the two realms, the religious and the pseudo-religious," and for overstepping the boundaries of psychology in his studies of religion. He also makes two objections that Father White makes: he accuses Jung of "psychologism," that is, conceiving of God as an autonomous psychic content that does not exist independent of our minds and he finds in Jung a strain of gnosticism that he cannot approve. He calls Jung "the leading psychologist of our day," and says that he is correct in speaking "of Freud's inability to understand religious experience."

As a step to genuine religious experience Buber preaches "holy insecurity" and believes in the man "who stakes his life on his thinking." In the words of his commentator, Will Herberg, his work is a protest against "depersonalization and thingification," and he "rejects both atomistic individualism and totalitarian collectivism." "In Isaiah the Messiah is seen as the King of the remnant, from which the people will renew itself," Herberg says by way of summarizing Buber's thought on a point that touches this book. "The man who straightforwardly hates is nearer to relation than the man without hate and love."

Buber admires both Zen and Hasidism for their "positive relationship to the concrete," but finds the latter superior. Zen is better than Freudianism; it is not restricted to psychic events alone and it wisely avoids overexplicitness; but it too fails to establish the right relationship to things. Things are not given the religious significance that they obtain in Hasidism. In Hasidism "they are the abode of the holy sparks, which shall raise man up. . . . The realism of Zen is dialectic, it means annulment; the Hasidic realism is messianic, it means fulfillment. . . . Hasidism is, so far as I see, the only mysticism in which *time* is hallowed."

However far their reading or speculation ranges, all of these Catholic, Protestant, or Jewish thinkers stay within their own traditions. A theological movement has sprung up in the United States, however, led intellectually by naturalized Americans of English birth, which has broken with the Judaeo-Christian tradition in the name of what it calls Western Vedanta.

Perhaps somewhat in remote expiation of English imperialist guilt toward India, certainly with more satisfaction in Indian religious thought than in English religious thought, this movement has found in Vedanta a scientific approach to religion which satisfies both its intellectual and its mystical demands. One of its leaders, Gerald Heard, finds Western religion in ruins today because it "has made three fundamental mistakes." "Taking its cosmology from the rudimentary Hebrew world-view it tied itself to a crude Apocalypticism. . . . The Vedanta has a world-view infinitely vaster than the Hebrew and one which does not contradict the findings of science. The statement that the physical world is a construction of the human mind from a substratum, a basic unity which our animal senses break up into a manifold, is a statement which modern physics can support. The hypothesis that consciousness is *sui generis* and this particular temporal experience is an event in a series which extends beyond it in both directions, is an hypothesis that research into consciousness tends to establish. This brings us to the second great mistake of Western religion and it is even graver than the first. Western religion neglected psychology and psycho-physiology."

One reason why the West is so fascinated now by modern psychology is that we, having acquired our first glimpse of the unconscious belatedly through a translation of the Upanishads, are now desperately trying to catch up with a realistic understanding of man that India has had for centuries. Though he came after the preparatory work of Schopenhauer, Carus, von Hartmann and others, Freud

startled us, but really he told us things that we should have known
long ago, and he reported them superficially in his attempt to squeeze
the greatest possible shock value out of them. Psychologically, like
him, we are provincials. Our technical vocabulary is tiny compared
with the Indian vocabulary of psychic facts, and otherwise we behave
like boisterous newcomers to an ancient art. A few of us are beginning
to use *hathayoga* exercises to combat the stress diseases of our culture, but these must be combined with Vedantic thought to be truly
effective.

In Vedanta meditation and contemplation are basic and make a complete working psychology, while with this scientific knowledge there is,
as a modern would expect and demand, a clear realisation of the body-
mind relationship, of how man may and only may change the aperture
of consciousness by a thorough understanding of that relationship. And
all this rests, not on blind authority but upon empirical work which any
enquirer may repeat (indeed must repeat) and confirm for himself. As
Dr. Babbitt has said, it is the West which has made experiment and
religion seem an impossible combination. But once trust authority
blindly . . . and the church must first condemn all experiment and
then fall into the further graver error of persecuting and striving to
destroy all who differ from orthodoxy's ruling. This was the third and
final blunder of Western religion . . . it had to end . . . in brutal
intolerance. The Vedanta . . . not only avoids intolerance but has a
scientific case for tolerance . . . tolerance reveals that there are not
merely higher and lower types in the world, but that men of equal intelligence, integrity, and devotion inherit different methods whereby they
must make their initial approaches to the Inexpressible Ultimate.

Gerald Heard praises Sheldon's type system for helping to clarify
the differences in temperament which when understood can lead to
peace and which when not understood lead invariably to the egocentric madness of religious war. He also praises Jung for imaginatively
civilizing Freud's discoveries. In the debate between White and
the other Christian theologians he would undoubtedly agree with
White that there can be no real psychotherapy that does not consciously seek and achieve religious integration.

Another leader of Western Vedanta is Aldous Huxley, who sec-
onds Heard on his major theses. Huxley has described, in *The Perennial Philosophy*, "the metaphysic that recognizes a divine Reality
substantial to the world of things and lives and minds; the psychology that finds in the soul something similar to, or even identical
with, divine Reality; the ethic that places man's final end in the
knowledge of the immanent and transcendent Ground of all being."

Huxley's position is that Christianity has made an important contribution to "the eternal gospel" but only one contribution among many, and that its insistence upon Jesus as the sole incarnation of God, as opposed for example to Hinduism's many incarnations or to Buddhism's teaching that we are all born into a state of the highest good, if we only realize it, has led to the bloody record of the Christian tradition, to many wars of extermination, and to a dogmatic narrow-mindedness that prevents its unfortunate possessor from achieving a felicitous harmony with God.

He finds a similar narrow-mindedness in our current preoccupation with modern psychology, a narrow-mindedness that is merely a secularization of the dogmatic fanaticism that preceded it.

One of the most extraordinary, because most gratuitous, pieces of twentieth century vanity is the assumption that nobody knew anything about psychology before the days of Freud. But the real truth is that most modern psychologists understand human beings less well than did the ablest of their predecessors. Fénelon and La Rochefoucauld knew all about the surface rationalization of deep, discreditable motives in the subconscious, and were fully aware that sexuality and the will to power were, all too often, the effective forces at work under the polite mask of the *persona*. . . . Like Buddha's and St. Augustine's, Pascal's view of human virtue and rationality could not have been more realistically low. But all these men, even La Rochefoucauld, even Machiavelli, were aware of certain facts which twentieth century psychologists have chosen to ignore—the fact that human nature is tripartite, consisting of spirit as well as of mind and body; the fact that we live on the border-line between two worlds, the temporal and the eternal, the physical-vital-human and the divine; the fact that, though nothing in himself, man is "a nothing surrounded by God, indigent of God, capable of God and filled with God, if he so desires."

He has studied our psychology and written about it at length, but he turns away from it to "the mystics" who are "not only the ultimate source of our knowledge of the soul and its capacities and defects, but . . . the salt which preserves human societies from decay. . . . It is they who, dying to themselves, become capable of perpetual inspiration and so are made the instruments through which divine grace is mediated to those whose unregenerate nature is impervious to the delicate touches of the Spirit."

Unfortunately one of the most delightful contributions to religious thought of our time cannot be discussed here—for the reason that it fails to include a single reference to modern psychology. Its title is *The Descent of the Dove*: A History of the Holy Spirit in the

Church, which makes its sin of omission all the more striking. Its author, as every poet will know, was Charles Williams. His exclusion of modern scientific research into the nature of the Holy Ghost is the least felicitous and most narrowly Anglican aspect of an excellent book which is otherwise up to date. It has been reprinted, like many of the theological works discussed here, because it offers a new version of an old perspective that our once oversecularized readers now begin to demand. The chronic acuteness of our crises seems to have ushered in the age of the longest possible view. This is the most encouraging part of our current intellectual confusion, that it makes us feel a need to rethink everything, refeel everything, and begin at the beginning. In time it may somewhat offset the general trend toward a break with the past that means "early foot" and quitting badly in the stretch. In time it may become less interested in track records than in the style achieved by horse and rider.

21

Sex and Philosophy

The reply to the theologians by the psychologists is best when it speaks the new language created by our disillusionment with science. For once, Freud's position is not as well stated by himself as by another who is fluent in the new language. That other is Professor Abraham Kaplan, who defends him with a cunning that is distinctly of our own day.

Before going on to a specifically religious discussion, Kaplan attacks the ancient problem of free will. "Psychoanalysis allots man less freedom than he thought was his, but makes possible more freedom than in fact he had." Freud is by no means undermining, as his critics claim, moral responsibility; but "only the self can hold itself morally responsible," and traditional ethics was unaware of the forces at work within the self until Freud's critique of conscience forced a recognition of its destructive potentialities as well as of the conditions under which it can be rational. We know now much more about the nature of freedom, thanks to him, and it is a study that no one can afford to neglect, no one who wants to be as free as he can.

"Man's place in nature—that is the preoccupation of the religious philosophies; and it is here that Freud's naturalistic temper is most marked. There is no need to make room for faith conceived as a relation to the supernatural. Lacking an object, faith is not a relation at all, but a condition of the faithful. The psychological understanding of religious belief is to replace the logical analysis of religious truth." Unlike William James, Freud does not accept the "presumed identity of the object" of the "varieties of religious experience"; he does not believe there can be any objective cause of this kind of experience; it is simply an expression of humanity's old, old longing to be childish. Whatever a sophisticated religionist like White may say about the physical father being a substitute for God in the child's mind, the truth is that it works the other way: the child endows a fictitious God with the attributes he has found in his own father. This is the "genesis of religious belief."

"For science is a matter precisely of curiosity about the *facts*; the scientific interest can develop only with the maturity of a mind capable of sustaining the weight of the reality principle . . . religious philosophy cannot overlook the elements of infantilism so often expressed in what is conventionally identified as the religious life. . . . The peace of mind or soul recurrently promised is not the peace which passeth understanding but one which can be very well understood in psychoanalytic terms. It is the rootless security found in an external source of morality and personal integrity. . . . In Freud's perspectives, it is the outlook of a child for whom the world is still a nursery." It is neurotic, and the religious spirit will also condemn it as such, because the religious spirit does not want sick dependency but the power "to find the world worthy of our love."

"The mysticism which is the core of the religious experience is thus, to my mind, untouched by Freud's corrosive analysis of its external corruption." In other words, psychoanalysis is only challenging the Law, not the Prophets. Its insights are needed for a wholesale reconsideration of religion, and perhaps even prophecy itself can be purified by it, "as speaking, not for the god, but out of the fullness of an encompassing self." Freud may not have been anti-religious after all; just opposed to religious abuses; and naturally intent, as a psychologist, on the role of the mind as a producer of religious experience.

Kaplan thus gives a shrewd presentation of Freud's cause, a good cover-up on what some of his most sympathetic admirers have long considered his weakest point. Kaplan's presentation would be still stronger, in my opinion, if it said firmly that those religious thinkers who brush Freud aside will do well to look first very closely within themselves, within their own unconscious lives, and discover what naïve or uncouth irrationalities may hide behind their most assured utterances, before they pass on to broader issues. Academic theologians have not risked exposure to the stern self-probing required by Freud; even their best pages disclose their unconscious complacencies. Fortunately, there are other theologians who have been obliged to work out their ideas by personal need rather than by professional careers or accidents of birth. Such men have welcomed the sternest challenge of the reality principle—and also discovered its limitations.

One of the most serious of these limitations, which has a noticeably parching effect on artists and intellectuals, has escaped the attention even of the Existentialists, to whom it might most naturally have occurred. It is this: the mind-body split which ultimately has such disastrous consequences takes place more readily in a puritan than in a flesh-lover, because the puritan is more likely to adopt an attitude of suspicion or hate toward the pleasure-giving capacities of his own body, beginning with his sexual parts, and is aware that this attitude furthers his mental effectiveness, strengthens his control over nature, and gives him a practical advantage over those who are stupidly bemused by sensual delights. Receptivity to pleasure may lead finally to a poetic reverence for nature and in a few very exceptional cases to a true maturity of which the puritan will never be capable; but in the hard struggle for success it is a heavy handicap. In the same way that world political dominance has passed historically from slothful southerners to more efficient northerners who could bring off the mind-body split and reap its rewards (they also gave us the legend of Faust), personal dominance has passed to disguised puritans, who welcome the reality principle as a power device.

Disregarding its caveats as so much window dressing, they like Freud because he helps them to indulge in the sexual act (without overconcern for their partner) and not be economically weakened by it. They recognize him as a fellow puritan who encourages them in the very hypocrisy they need: the belief that they are singing "the body electric" at the very moment they are being mentally most shrewd. He enables them to take a scientific attitude toward sex and put it in its place. Thus they are released for their real passion, which is conquest, and they achieve a separation not only of body from mind but of feeling from thought, action from consequences. But a great deal more energy has been released in them by their egocentric actions than their competitors have at their command, and they employ it to proclaim the apparently moral victory they have achieved. The average sensual competitor looks at them with dazed eyes and waits stupidly for some law of retribution to take over. Meanwhile they are in command. The new puritanism, which so often calls itself antipuritanism, is in command. Power has gone to a ruling class that is sure to crumble psychically, somatically, politically, intellectually, aesthetically.

Jung has provided his own rebuttal of the theologians, who, in a sense, are trying to put him out of business. His rebuttal, however, is not couched in the discreet New Academy style that is preferred today but in a rambling manner that he has rather carelessly retained from a time when one did not have to make one's points in neat one-two-three order.

"Theology," he says, "does not help those who are looking for the key, because theology demands faith, and faith cannot be made; it is in the truest sense a gift of grace. We moderns are faced with the necessity of rediscovering the life of the spirit; we must experience it for ourselves. It is the only way in which we can break the spell of biological events." Such a rediscovery does not, however, come through an act of will; it is an experience, a fact, and the way to it is best prepared by a realistic recognition of the obstacles that stand in its path. These obstacles are within ourself, involved unconsciously with all sorts of sexual drives and power drives and other irrationalities that must be confronted before we can even hope for a preliminary understanding of our needs.

"At a time," Jung says, "when a great part of mankind is beginning to lay aside Christianity, it is worth while to realize clearly why it was ever actually accepted. It was accepted in order to escape at last from the brutality of antiquity." (A recent film by Ingmar Bergman, *The Virgin Spring,* dramatized this brutality.) "If we put Christianity aside, then that wantonness appears again of which life in our great modern cities gives us an impressive foretaste. This step is not progress but regression." We are not living in the rational period that we confidently expected. "The gigantic catastrophes that threaten us are not elemental happenings of a physical or biological kind, but are psychic events. We are threatened in a fearful way by wars and revolutions that are nothing else than psychic epidemics. At any moment a few million people may be seized by a madness, and then we have another war or a devastating revolution. Instead of being exposed to wild beasts, tumbling rocks and inundating waters, man is exposed today to the elemental forces of his own psyche."

This does not express the withdrawn outsider's attitude with which Freud confronted similar fears. Jung is not thinking how to save himself, in the midst of a general insanity, by the use of his own intelligence; he is looking for common mental reserves that may be marshaled against the danger. And he thinks that a typically Protestant action has put man in greater peril—and also in closer touch with these reserves. "The history of the development of Protestantism is one of chronic iconoclasm. One wall after another fell. And the work was not too difficult, either, when once the authority of the Church had been shattered. . . . The disintegration of Protestanism into nearly one hundred denominations is yet an infallible sign of life, and shows that the restlessness is growing." The Protestant is stripped of much of the symbolism that enriches the lives of other men, but by this very act of self-impoverishment he prepares himself for an understanding of the positive forces within the unconscious—*if* he appreciates both his arrogance and his nudity. "The Protestant has lost the sacred images expressive of important unconscious factors, together with the ritual, which, since time immemorial, has been a safe way of dealing with the unaccountable forces of the unconscious mind. A great amount of energy thus became liberated and went instantly into the old channels of curiosity and acquisitiveness, by which Europe became the mother of dragons that devoured the greater part of the earth. Since those days Protestantism has become a hotbed of schisms and at the same time, of a rapid increase in science and technics which attracted human consciousness to such an extent that it forgot the unaccountable forces of the human mind."

This is the first psychological description of that process of self-alienation which later became the chief target of Existential Analysis. When united with the philosophical description of Kierkegaard, it offers an historical understanding of our extraordinary present-day preoccupation with the unconscious. For centuries the unconscious was either ignored or exploited with such arrogant unawareness that it finally returned upon man with an archaic fury. This fury first came to the attention of medical observers in the form of hysteria that brought forth a sexual explanation from Charcot, Janet, Breuer, and Freud. The career of Freud was launched with this sexual explanation, and depth psychology began with Freud, but actually an earlier cause of this hysteria may have been religious and philosophic. Freud could not see this for three reasons: his search for a startling explanation that would have to be accepted; his ignorance of religious and philosophic history; his emotional disengagement from the mainstream of European life. As a fame-starved outsider he could develop an enormous cunning in dramatizing a limited explanation that struck home; he was also fortunate enough to arrive at a time which increasingly preferred the excitement of one-sided ideas that made easier reading than a dreary balanced view. When his ideas had made their impression he could protect them with skillful amendments and extensions perhaps often inspired by his rivals; but as one whose tradition had only recently come out of the ghetto and merged with that of Europe, he could not be expected to see the historical roots of psychopathology in a way that his fellow Jews, as they identified themselves more fully with a secularized Europe and America, began to do. He saw the biological roots, not the historical roots; and the limitations of his view made it for a while all the more powerful.

In his eightieth birthday gift to Freud, Thomas Mann said, "science had never made a discovery without being authorized and encouraged thereto by philosophy." He was speaking of Freud's great debt to Schopenhauer. Later he spoke of Jung's great debt to Freud; and in both cases he was correct. But he did not say that Freud, for all his obvious greatness, is not quite the psychological innovator he has been thought to be. The portion of the unconscious that he discovered was only part of it, the part he was equipped to see. There was another part of it which Jung, even though it is true that his works as they stand "could never have been written" without Freud's prior discoveries, was equipped to see; and this part appears to be of equal importance to everyone and possibly of greater importance to those who want to be free of positivist excesses. Also, the psychopathology that Jung discovered *brought on* much of the psychopathology that Freud discovered. Would Freud's patients have become so neurotic if their cosmos had not been troubled? The answer is no. How much does philosophic disorder have to do with sexual disorder? Very much indeed.

It may therefore be incorrect to regard Jung as a revisionist. Because of his far greater breadth, he has pioneered in a more dangerous and, to us today, a more important area than Freud's, the area of *connection* between science and philosophy. He has had the courage to go into intangibles which make the schematic mind hysterical. The disguised self-indulgence which permitted scientists of an earlier day to believe that they could live in the state of emotional unrelatedness expressed in *The Future of an Illusion*, which is one of the world's great unconscious confessions, has been re-

vealed as an inadequate way of life. In its grosser forms it has led to
the boy Fausts. The mistrust of feeling which made Freud a brilliant
observer of emotional error, and a brilliant manipulator of it in his
writings, has now doubled back on him. We once saw only the
strength it gave him; we now begin to see the weakness it concealed.
Because we have lived with his ideas as we have lived with few ideas
in our time, we have had a chance to test them. The pulpit complaints against him are still all wrong; but he has also had apprecia-
tive admirers who have learned painfully how much was left out of
his vision. When he omitted the embarrassments of faith and feeling, he left some enormous holes in his hull that sooner or later had
to let in water. Even the new puritans seem to become aware of this
now and then, as they grow prosperous enough to take stock of their
self-deceptions—and their hideous disappointments. It is no fun,
however, to have to admit that the stupid sensualists may have
been more farsighted after all.

Only the main issues in the dispute between the psychologists
and the theologians can be suggested here. The most valuable idea
that emerges for the Remnant is this: our present preference for
tough-mindedness, which can be found even among the theologians,
has become sterile. It was useful once to clear away a great deal of
superstitious nonsense, but now it urgently requires a liberal admixture of its opposite.

The need for this kind of balance, and its prehistoric origins, are
beautifully described by Joseph Campbell in *The Masks of God:
Primitive Mythology*. Our best research makes it clear, Campbell says,
that it was a civilizing dialogue between tough-minded "honest
hunters" and tender-minded shamans, or medicine men, that
brought our remote ancestors to recordable consciousness. He also
makes it clear that the tender-minded shamans provided the original
impulse. Through his "Way of Suffering" "the shaman is in a
measure released from the local system of illusions and put in touch
with mysteries of the psyche itself, which lead to wisdom concerning
both the soul and its world; and he thereby performs the necessary
function for society of moving it from stability and sterility in the
old toward new reaches and new depths of realization.

"The two types of mind, thus, are complementary: the tough-
minded, representing the inert, reactionary; and the tender, the living progressive impulse—respectively, attachment to the local and
timely and the impulse to the timeless universal." Their dialogue

has as its splendid end product "the art-work which is civilization in its flowering in time."

This leads us to where we were going anyway, to the debate between the psychologists and the artists. If the psychologists can claim a greater proximity to the unconscious than the more schematic theologians, certainly no such advantage can be claimed over the artists.

22

The Revolt of the Writers

More is written each year on the shotgun marriage between literature and psychology, but most of it appears in academic and technical publications which few people ever see. Perhaps the best anthology on the subject is *Art and Psychoanalysis*, edited by William Phillips. An outstanding feature of the book is the new dignity claimed by the writer for himself. If he once cringed before the indictments of psychoanalysis, if he once meekly concurred in the medical opinion that he was not normal, and used far too much medical jargon even in his fiction, he has now changed his tune. Both Phillips and Lionel Trilling make this clear in *Art and Psychoanalysis*. After recalling that Freud himself in later years moderated his attitude toward the artist, Trilling finds neurosis as prevalent among scientists and businessmen as among writers, and says of the poet, "what indeed suggests nothing but health, is his power of using his neuroticism. He shapes his fantasies, he gives them social form and reference." And Phillips ends with "maybe some day the neurotic artist will become a pillar of society."

This is pretty far from what Rank wrote in 1932 in *Art and Artist*: "If [the neurotic] seeks his salvation in artistic creation, instead of in the development of his personality, it is because he is still in the toils of old art-ideologies. . . . Artistic creativity does not favor the personality but impedes, since it forces upon the artist a professional ideology which more and more penetrates the human self and finally absorbs it." Our examination of Rank's personal drama has suggested how he came to this opinion.

Freud in his early work regarded the artist as an escapist, a neurotic who sought to flee from unpleasant reality by means of

165

"substitute gratifications." He was always heavily respectful of art, however, and wrote in his paper on Dostoevsky, "Unfortunately, before the problem of the creative artist, analysis must lay down its arms." Late in life he acknowledged that literary men had preceded him as discoverers of the unconscious. By this time he may have recognized how much of his scientific fame rested on his literary skill. He never went so far, however, as Phillips in readmitting the writer to normal society.

There are similar implicit reservations in the statement of his disciple Franz Alexander, who wrote in *Explorations in Psychoanalysis* (1953): "The naked unconscious, as it often appears in contemporary art, is not a suitable way of communication. It must go through the prism of the organizing portion of the personality, the conscious ego, in order to become meaningful. The artist eventually will emerge from the surrealist detour through the depths of the unconscious with a new constructive message which he cannot express in this era of doubt and confusion."

This is not quite as drastic as Rank's statement, but it amounts to much the same thing. It may not say, "Writers, stop writing! Painters, stop painting!" but it does say, "Artists, don't expect to do anything good at a time like this." Such counsel, as we shall see, has been followed by a deliberate use of "the naked unconscious" in the first American school of painting to make a world-wide impression. It has also encountered resistance among writers, who have been hearing it or something like it ever since the Golden Age. So we come upon essays by Leslie Fiedler and Stanley Edgar Hyman which indicate ways in which the writer may actually write better because of the new techniques put at his disposal by psychologists. Hyman finds "endless vistas" for better criticism. Fiedler finds hope even for the poet.

"A final way back into the world of Archetypes," he writes, "available even in our atomized culture, is an extension of the way instinctively sought by the Romantics, down through the personality of the poet, past his particular foibles and eccentricities, to his unconscious core, where he becomes one with all of us in the presence of our ancient Gods, the protagonists of fables we think we no longer believe. . . . We cannot get back into the primal Garden of unfallen Archetypes, but we can yield ourselves to the dreams and images that mean paradise regained."

This is almost a paraphrase of Jung. Since the "archetypes" of

Jung are praised so highly, not only here but in Maud Bodkin's *Archetypal Patterns in Poetry*, it should be pointed out that Jung believes the writer's chief problem is that of energy. Most writers, he says, are dismal failures as human beings because their energy has been foreclaimed by their talent. Genius imposes a discipline of its own which may mean a shocking life but a good book. Hence the *poète maudit*. The writer, knowing that he has only so much energy to spend, quickly learns to channel his into words, not deeds. Therefore we frequently witness the spectacle of a monster who has written a masterpiece because he has put his demon at the disposal of a "collective unconscious" that disregards personal fulfillment. On the other hand, he has the profound satisfaction of serving mankind by tapping common sources of myth, poetry, and spiritual reactivation.

This brings us to some of the central questions of the writer today. Does he need psychotherapy, and if he believes he does, how will he stand up under it? Will he lose his demon, as Joyce and Kafka feared he would, or reinforce it, as Trilling believes possible? Must he be content with paving the way for the "new constructive message" that Alexander hopes for, or can he come through, as Fiedler believes, even here and now? If he is about to become a "pillar of society," where will he discover the double energy required for good citizenship *and* intensity of craft? Can he achieve both "perfection of the life, and of the work?" Does he require a metaphysical initiation as well as a psychological one?

The questions are familiar, and the answers must of course be found in each writer's own mind. But a pattern is clear enough in all this discussion: the psychologists show occupational skepticism and the writers show occupational hope. If not hope for the world they live in, at least hope for their own capability to survive in it—and no more neurotically than anyone else. Their works may not please the scientist, but then, they say, for compensatory reasons that the psychologists themselves have explained, the scientific taste in literature is usually rather old-fashioned. And meanwhile writers are writing, and an increasingly complex world demands their reinterpretation.

A story about Thomas Mann is relevant, because it suggests the kind of reversal of public opinion that many writers now hope to achieve. It concerns his early autobiographical novelette *Tonio Kröger*, which deals with a writer who did not fit into his native town in northern Germany. Tonio was fond of his school chum,

Hans Hansen, but even as a boy he realized that he could never compete with Hans in robustness or acceptance by the world. As they grew up, it was only natural that the beautiful Ingeborg should prefer the strong, normal Hans to the frail, neurotic Tonio.

When he became a man Tonio went south to Munich, worked hard, and won success as a writer. Then he made a lonely return to his old home in the north, where no one knew him. He went on to Denmark for a sad holiday and there saw Hans and Ingeborg at a dance. He looked through a window and saw them, as gay as ever, in the very center of the fun. His childhood fears were realized: Hans had got everything he wanted, while Tonio merely looked on.

The story caught the world's imagination. Hans and Tonio became symbols of health and neurosis. It was translated into many languages, and its author became rich, famous, and "senatorially robust." Then he received the Nobel Prize. To celebrate the occasion he wrote a tiny volume called A Sketch of My Life (1930).

There is a passage in it which has been overlooked. I sometimes wonder if Mann himself fully appreciated its irony. He wrote of early poems "inscribed to a dear friend, the one who as Hans Hansen in Tonio Kröger, had a sort of symbolic existence, though in real life he took to drink and made a melancholy end in Africa."

Mann's sketch is significant of a craving that seems to lurk in many a writer's bosom and to have come again into the open at a time when a sinking but prosperous society has developed a vested interest in the maintenance of the arts. It is what Mann calls the craving for dignity. He speaks of it openly as his mainspring. There are colleagues of his who might make a similar confession today, if they had not been frightened by the Marxists of that awful word "bourgeois." It is not money alone that draws so many of them to the academy, nor the mere "status" they say they want. They now covet the eminence being vacated by a demoralized gentry. They want their children to be respected in a way they themselves were not. It is therefore imperative that they remove the psychologists' smear. Especially in view of what they have been observing in the psychologists themselves, the insensitiveness, the lack of imagination, the timeserving.

The best way to achieve their ends is to attack their defamers. It is hard, however, to shake off a transference, and some of our most gifted writers suffer from that, especially where Freud is concerned. Literary roughnecks have an easier time getting up from his horsehair couch; they never settled down on it. But what they say becomes more and more pointless, as the problems of consciousness press in upon them with the same ruthlessness that statesmen and businessmen and scientists must face. So our roughnecks duck the issues and fall back on easy answers. One sure trick of the best-selling author is to be anti-intellectual. It is also a sure way to dissipate whatever civilization remains to us.

Mere survival will demand in time that a few writers abstain from easy answers. They will have to learn how to pass freely between the conscious life of the world as we see it and the unconscious life of the world as we come painfully to know it. They will have to live both in the angry, confused world of will and in the serene, art-conscious world of idea. They will have to bear the full shock of scientific attack and still pour out the passionate imagery that justifies their existence. They will have to be sufficiently *bilingual* to think in the new Latin which science is slowly providing for our new Dark Ages, but still write poetically in the vulgar tongue.

Only the Remnant will realize how much re-education this means.

23

On Knowing What You Do

Twice the word "bilingual" has been used to indicate a skill required of those who hope to survive morally today. It is plainly more than an intellectual skill. It demands the "transmoral conscience" that is in turn demanded by the rejection of authority. But we have many rejectors of authority and apparently transmoral consciences who only bring grief to themselves and everyone around them. Irresponsible freedom is a typical problem of our day. It is the characteristic mistake of the half-educated, who have now turned in the other direction and are running away from freedom and towards authority.

How do responsible bilinguals differ from the half-educated? The question is best explored, I think, through the careers of two well-known American artists who died young. Abstractly it would be possible to say that bilinguality consists of "knowing what you do," in the sense of the apocryphal parable of Jesus and the man seen gathering sticks on the Sabbath: "O man, if thou knowest what thou doest, blessed art thou; but if thou knowest not, thou art cursed." Bilinguality might also be defined as a consequence of "being a lamp unto yourself," in the Buddhist phrase, or of being able, in Christian terminology, to find reliable guidance in the Holy Ghost. But such language is meaningless, for most readers today, unless it is made concrete by contemporary reference. This is especially true of those readers whose rejection of authority leads to rejection of all sacred texts.

These artists are Hart Crane and Jackson Pollock, a poet and a painter. In the case of the former it is possible to examine the biographies written by Philip Horton and Brom Weber.

Hart Crane helps us to understand "bilinguality," the capacity to speak both the language of tough-mindedness and the language of tender-mindedness, and each at the right time, because it was his lack of bilinguality that mortally wounded him as a poet and destroyed him as a man. If this *poète maudit* had been able to master both the gentle, suggestive vulgate of poetry and the hard, precise Latin of science, he might have found a way to master his steadily more crippling self-centeredness and to avoid a double suicide. A path would have been opened to that community of spirit which exists even in the most alienated times and the most atomized societies. He would have known that he was not alone, that the key had been left under the mat, if he chose to bend and pick it up. Given such a sensibility, he would still have had to live a tragedy, but it would have been a tragedy of awareness, not of ignorance, publicity, urinal eroticism, and delirium tremens. He might have ended his days a mild lecturer, or he might, like his hero Melville, have made a heroic comeback into literature, through the delayed, self-supervised initiation that seems to be required by our young civilization.

Few people know the story of the sensitive, uneducated Ohio boy who "drenched" himself in words while still in his middle teens. By the time he had reached his early twenties he had amassed a formidable verbal technique—and he had written some of the best poetry in our language. With touchingly American naïveté he determined early to "make fate" and of the "curveship" of the Brooklyn Bridge to "lend a myth to God." Reversing the usual order, he had more talent than intelligence. He possessed none of the "strategic" shrewdness of present-day litterateurs who make a hero of him and other culture victims to wheedle better allowances out of indulgent parents or guilty foundations. Hart Crane lacked slickness. Aside from his talent, he was pathetically at the mercy of circumstances: a quohaug without a shell, a Whitman-believing romantic who was tossed into our modern confusion, who wrested some acetylene images from it, could imagine no cozier tricks, despised nonliterary techniques, clung to his helplessness, dried up as a poet and killed himself.

For those other Ishmaels who do not want to be destroyed by a sometimes treacherous heritage, he may serve as a symbol of uninstructed American passion and what it can still learn, a generation or so later, from the psychologists (and their opponents) in the art

of "knowing what you do." It is true that the psychologists did not
write their books for poets. On the contrary they seem to have
written chiefly for fellow workers. But they touched inevitably on
matters of vital concern to poets—and imaginative persons of whatever occupation—because they dealt with the psychopathology they
found. In the past, poets have often deliberately overlooked their
own psychopathology, in the sometimes correct surmise that it
helped their poetry; but there is now, as we shall see, considerable
evidence that this is no longer true, that we demand more of the
poet and are only really impressed by poetry that comes from a
completed personal revolution.

To say this is not to demand complete maturity of the artist. Or
to deny him his rightful portion of the "madness" that Plato found
indispensable to his craft. But this becomes clear when we turn to
Jackson Pollock, whose uninstructed passion is still more instructive.

All psychological literature is written from the standpoint of the
psychologist. The patient appears, tells his story (all of it that fits
into the psychologist's theories), is treated and usually sent away
either "cured" or at least "helped." Not to embarrass this tradition,
which after all does have some excellent achievements to its credit,
but to speak up for the usually silent patient, the case of Jackson
Pollock is introduced as one in which psychological treatment not
only failed but had to fail. This artist availed himself of psychiatric
treatment from time to time. Nothing written here is intended to
discredit this treatment. As a matter of fact I am well acquainted
with one of his psychiatrists, whom I consider an able practitioner.
The point is that nothing could have been done to help this artist—
or many others like him. Our artists can only profit by *their own* use
of the psychologists, and this ability they usually lack. Jackson
Pollock died in 1956, at the age of forty-four. Because he was a
neighbor of mine in a Long Island village, I had a chance to become
acquainted with his life and his work over a period of years.

He died in an automobile accident that he invited. He was driving
at a speed estimated by a survivor at eighty miles an hour, over a
winding and uneven road, in a condition described as intoxication.
When a fellow passenger asked him to slow down he increased the
speed; the fellow passenger was also killed. He had driven as dan-
gerously on many other occasions, and seemed for some time to
prefer death to life. Neighbors were surprised that he was allowed
to keep a driver's license. "If there were two doors, and one was safe

and the other dangerous," another painter said afterwards, "Jackson would have gone into the dangerous one. Always." The effect of his death, when it finally came, upon his fellow artists, especially those of the same "abstract expressionist" school, was extraordinary. They grieved for him like a brother, and seemed both dazed and chastened. One of them said, "It's as if it had happened to me." Their sense of team loss seemed to suggest that he had represented, with a talent and single-mindedness that caught everyone's imagination, not only a kind of art but a way of life. As one of them put it, "He had the guts to see it through."

He also became a national symbol. Unfortunate attacks on him in the press made that clear. A symbol of what? It is difficult to say, but I believe that the answer draws nearer when his kind of avant-gardisme is put in historical perspective.

One reason why it is difficult to generalize about nations is that a national maincurrent sometimes produces minority backwaters that end by becoming more important than the popular torrent that made them necessary. A familiar example is the sensuality of the Near East—so intense and far-reaching to those who have witnessed it— which produced, by reaction, stern religions and fierce moralities that have spread all over the earth. In the United States, on the other hand, a predominant puritanism produced the antipuritan Walt Whitman, with his enormous liberating influence on poetry everywhere; and in our own times an over-all American tendency toward mechanized conformity has produced a minority of artists of uncompromising, even aggressive individuality. Jackson Pollock was one of the most spectacular—and interesting—of those artists. He dramatized no everyday problem of psychiatry but an exceptional problem which is, however, not peripheral but central, since it deals with man's struggle to be free, to be true to his deepest needs, in spite of the confusions and pressures that surround him.

A painter cannot live, even meagerly, unless he sells paintings, and today he sells more readily if he receives publicity, especially publicity in the mass media. One of the most important events in Jackson Pollock's career was an article in *Life* which suggested that he might be America's most important painter. Those who buy new painters like to be assured that they are not throwing their money away, if they do not buy solely for pleasure and if their taste is not entirely certain. After the article in *Life* Pollocks sold better. He was also praised in little magazines, by more serious critics, but most collectors today are reassured in direct proportion to the circulation of the words which tell them what to buy. The huckster is now perfectly at home in the museum. After his success, hucksterism played no small part in Jackson Pollock's life. Perhaps also in his death.

Some day our sociologists will study the strange new interest of periodicals aimed at the mass mind in the most advanced modern art, which usually takes years of study, not to mention special aptitude, to understand. The motives of the periodicals seem fairly clear; most readers are antagonized by modern art, but enjoy being antagonized ("My *kids* can do better than that!") and also like quick information and ready-made opinions, soon forgotten, on a subject that normally would not enter their ken. As for the artists, they usually detest what the periodicals write about them but recognize its business value. Sometimes they accept publicity as a substitute for a slowly recognized social function, a hard-won place in a confused cultural tradition, a chance to mature slowly under adverse circumstances; and they can hardly be condemned; but the aesthetic and moral price of such surrender is usually suicidal. "Nothing fails like success," said Scott Fitzgerald, who had had it. Jackson Pollock's attitude toward it was ambivalent; he both wanted it and hated it; and the tensions it set up within him became so painful that he longed to die and finally did. He possessed no ancestral defense against an irresponsible culture, and he was not able to cover his nakedness with a psychological or a philosophical technique.

Perhaps it was his extreme defenselessness that inspired affection and made him paint well. He could not fight back, except on canvas, and so his best energy went there. In a time of accelerated advance-guard discontent with all earlier visual symbols, his cultural impoverishment turned out to be an aesthetic advantage. He was a beatnik who won. But this did not make him a happy man—or an artist able to continue.

Perhaps all vanguardism, especially in its more flamboyant expressionist modes, is a product of despair. Let a serious artist feel cut off from most of the life around him (which is usually how he feels today) and the chances are that he will also feel a need to compensate for his deep sense of deprivation by expressing himself more violently (and more originally) than would be necessary if he could live in harmony with nature, history, and his fellow men. It may be heroic that he should do so; he makes his lifework an outcry of protest; he would rather live in hell than be prosperous and successful. (At least until these temptations appear.) If he is lucky enough to fail, he becomes part of a minority backwater that ends by being more important than the maincurrent which required it. Certainly this has been a recognizable pattern in the arts since Rimbaud's day, and perhaps even earlier. As the tensions of our society mount, it is a pattern with ever greater attraction for readers, collectors, publishers, museum directors, and other connoisseurs of suffering who desire, rather cruelly and at a safe distance, an artist to fight the lonely battles of the individual for them. Thus they can feel in the midst of an essential fight and at the same time be removed from it. This is the psychological basis for the continuing veneration for such obvious sufferers as Kierkegaard and Nietzsche. They enable others to feel in touch momentarily with the central drama of man. Nobody wishes to suffer unless he has to. But we appreciate someone else who does it for us.

There is such a demand for this sort of thing that we are already, with our customary business acumen, producing dozens of culture-victims who carry portable aluminum crosses with them that they set up and climb onto at any hour of the day and at a moment's notice. Simony did not stop with the Middle Ages; it is a major modern business.

Jackson Pollock did not consciously choose a life of suffering and stoutheartedly stick to it. A life of suffering chose *him*, and he stayed with it as long as he could, producing his works in relatively helpless acts of desperation. Personally, he had the appeal, like many Americans, of a boy; aesthetically, he purified and extended certain homely folk styles of pioneer farmhouse decoration. He was no visionary, conscious, highly developed artificer. On the contrary, he illustrated Adler's description of genius as a compensation for a lack. He had a provincial's fear of culture, and he was far too insecure to take an interest in others that led to real relationships.

Part of his appeal to certain members of the advance guard seems to be that he helps them to believe that their own bad manners, which at times they cultivate as a defense against sterility, may be accepted as the right way for an artist to live today.

Psychoanalysis could naturally make no headway with him, even if administered by the most imaginative of analysts. It would have threatened his one claim to special consideration. He preferred to die, rather than become what he called a square; and psychiatry must tend, in any society, to produce squares. Even so cultured artists as Joyce and Kafka refused psychiatric help and for not dissimilar reasons.

As a person chosen for an involuntary heroic role, Jackson Pollock was nationally and even internationally significant. He symbolized those gifted people who have been thrown defenseless into the conditions of modern life, with none of the traditional help that old civilizations provide, or once provided, for the translation of raw experience into form. The source of the often observed American vigor in the arts is pain. In our formative years we Americans are deluged with the very best in the arts, great achievements that took centuries to perfect, the best that the world has done. Then our teachers ask us to observe the same high standards in the recreation of our own experience. We succeed most readily, therefore, when the form can bypass traditional requirements or is better off without them—as in popular music, electronic music, or abstract art. Nevertheless the responsibility put upon the individual artist is abnormally tense, and our most original style becomes a fascinating new scream of anxiety, squealed by performing guinea pigs (or scapegoats) in a vast, blind social experiment, an experiment that may provide novel excitements for the connoisseur but certainly disregards the artist. This was the kind of "vigor" that Jackson Pollock put into his work.

When Richard Wright left the United States for France, one of his publishers expressed the fear, within my hearing, that he would never write well in exile. When I asked the reason the publisher said, "Because he won't suffer so much." Similar fears have been expressed for white expatriates. The first job of the artist is to undergo a complex new torture for the rest of us, and we give up on him very fast when he ducks it.

One reason that American art is being scanned abroad with especial interest is that it was produced under inimical circumstances that may soon prevail everywhere. There are also those in Europe who are especially thrilled by it when it shows distinctly antihumane or anticultural tendencies. For reasons of their own they want to see the ancient humanities of their continent thrown overboard. Such people welcome certain kinds of American art as artillery in their own fight. They will not be interested in hearing that the circumstances that prevail in America are necessarily destructive to artists, or that our aesthetic "vigor" owes much to national fatigue.

But whatever these Europeans may think, in the United States the artist who wishes to survive is being forced to put a higher premium than ever upon a complex consciousness. Only by being internally as tough as the world around him—yet without losing the tenderness that is his *raison-d'être*—can the American artist hope to survive today.

Jackson Pollock did not even begin to acquire this kind of consciousness. He was a man to whom works of art happened. His heroism was "compulsive." There was no way out for him except disaster. He was at the mercy of a way of life that had to end as it did. Moralists who equate his kind of despair with sin, and psychologists who equate it with neurosis, may dispute his attitude, but if they are familiar with the way works of art are produced (sometimes even in the glorious past) they will respect it. Our most productive leaps into the unknown would be impossible without this kind of enforced experimentation. The essence of philistinism is to expect the present-day artist to become "mature" or "responsible" before he is well along in years—or helped by a favoring wind. His first responsibility is to his vocation. Petulant complaint against his moral failures means a much more serious moral defeat in the hidden life of the critic.

Jackson Pollock could not reasonably have been expected to break through to consciousness, to a responsible use of his will. The jump from his West Coast naïveté to his 8th Street prometheanism was too abrupt to permit any time for mere living. So, since he was handy with paint and unhandy with words, he fabricated a life on canvas—and became a legend to others who feel culturally cheated in the same way and are heartened by his unexpected victory. His cult has created a bull market for his pictures because there are so many other Americans who can all too easily identify themselves with him. He can be used by others to condone their own internal chaos. He restores hope to the self-alienated. He offers salvation by checkbook. The myth he left is gallant, and the pictures he left are good. But bull markets in art are not created by pictures but by hysteria.

Artists who have work of their own to do, and want better conditions in which to do it, will pay close attention to the bones he left prematurely in the Great American Desert. Despite the vogue of chaos, it is better to know what you are doing. Sooner or later real talent must face real consciousness.

24

The Highest Court

In Chapter 22 the psychoanalyst Franz Alexander was quoted as saying: "The naked unconscious, as it often appears in contemporary art, is not a suitable way of communication . . ." It was a typical ex-cathedra pronouncement of his science. The response of Jackson Pollock and others of the "New York School" of painting was to put more emphasis on the naked unconscious than ever before, to hunt it down, to lie in wait for it, to devote their best conscious efforts to setting traps for it. This is apparent not only in the paintings themselves but in the painters' statements about them, in films about them, and in the criticism they have provoked. *Because* they did not wait until their art emerged traditionally from the conscious ego, Harold Rosenberg suggests in *The Tradition of the New*, they produced "the most vigorous and original movement in art in the history of this nation." He also says: "The American vanguard painter took to the white expanse of the canvas as Melville's Ishmael took to the sea. On the one hand, a desperate recognition of moral and intellectual exhaustion; on the other, the exhilaration of an adventure over depths in which he might find reflected the true image of his identity."

Such an adventure was sometimes actually promoted by the head-shaking of analysts like Alexander, with the painter preferring to put his "naked" abreactions directly down on canvas rather than sketch them beforehand. This called for rare conviction and skill. To be ready to create a work of art with spontaneous mastery required a technical preparation at least as exhaustive as that of an analyst, a surer concentration, a greater triumph over self, as well as a certain amount of good fortune. The neat boundaries between ego and id are valid, in the artistic act, only for those who have strayed up high in some safe reconnaissance plane. Vanguard writers and composers, who also make conscious use of the unconscious, and the nakeder the better, bear witness to the present need for the artist to drop into the areas of his greatest anxiety if he is to bring back anything worth showing. The new abstract painting has caught the psychology-conditioned imagination to a greater extent than the new literature or the new music, because it is a more direct report on areas that philistines and dabblers stay away from, and also because of the speed of its communication. It offers fast excitement to the self-alienated. Its very style calls for at least a preliminary elimination of the conscious ego, and hence for greater aesthetic shock, as well as less prolonged audience work, than music or writing. These arts have not been able, despite some shrewd efforts, to make themselves quicker to take than TV. The new painting's current bonanza, after many lean years (during which one hero of the group advised his colleagues: "Fellows, you've just got to steel yourselves—and put your wives out to work") is well deserved, but already there are familiar signs of the hazards of success, except among the few who recognize that it never gets easy for a Remnant. To extend a Rosenberg image, the Coonskinner's cabin now has running water, but it is still way out in the desert. And it is haunted by more spooks than ever.

The genuine poet does not have to be told this; things are still going against him. His only hope, in fact, is a hard time. Then he cannot delude himself with apparent approval but sees his true dilemma, which has been described canonically by Yeats: "The intellect of man is forced to choose / Perfection of the life or of the work." If he takes the second, as he usually does, he has to realize that single-pointed concentration on his craft is seldom possible, as in the good old days, even under the best external conditions, and if it is, it can no longer guarantee perfection of the work, even if he most neurotically "rages in the dark."

Too many unknowns have entered the theorem to permit us to be sure that even incontestable genius will achieve a satisfactory conclusion. That is precisely why incontestable genius has paid close attention, as we shall see, to the psychologists, who for the most part have replaced the philosophers as guides through the underworld. We live in trickier times than ever, because external conditions are so well organized. We selfishly study the errors of Pollock and Hart Crane, to avoid the destruction that follows "not knowing what thou doest." Some may be content with the beauty wrung from shortened lives and truncated visions. It is also possible to imagine publishers, dealers, biographers and legatees who actually rejoice when works and legends are left behind without the embarrassment of their falling-down-drunk creators. But the question arises, whether this now rather repetitious pattern does not mean that a law of diminishing returns is at hand. Genius cannot stay childish forever; too much adult life escapes its attention; it may lose its authority. It is a consideration that seems to have occurred some time ago to Rimbaud, almost the prototype of the *poète maudit*, who acted to expand his vision and his experience when he turned his back on poetry and began his antipoetic wanderings.

None of the poets and novelists to be considered here—Yeats, Joyce, Kafka, Lawrence—had to turn his back on his art, but all of them found ways, and wrote their best when they did so, of replenishing themselves with nonliterary experience. Their characters and habits were formed, however, before 1914, when it was still possible to avoid the distracting new disciplines that since that disastrous date have made uninterrupted aestheticization of experience increasingly difficult or, when it has been practiced, increasingly irrelevant. While our knowledge of man has undergone revolutionary changes, the cleavage between writer and reader has intensified. We prefer the poet who is "born" to the poet who is "reborn," but we make demands upon him that have never been satisfied by a mere gift. Beauty is no longer enough; he must serve us now not only as artist but as seer—and frequently as religious sacrifice. We put him to ancient tests of spiritual leadership, and are only impressed by hemlock or the cross.

The real dilemma of the poet is whether he is to remain a talent or whether he is to satisfy these more formidable demands. Even if he is to remain a talent, says Eliot in his best-known essay, he must acquire "the historical sense, which we may call nearly indispensable to anyone who would continue to be a poet beyond his twenty-fifth year." This sense is essential to an awareness of tradition, "which cannot be inherited, and if you want it you must obtain it by great labour. . . . The historical sense compels a man to write not merely with his own generation in his bones, but with a feeling that the whole of the literature of Europe from Homer and within it the whole of the literature of his own country has a simultaneous existence and composes a simultaneous order." Hart Crane admired

Eliot's verse, but recoiled from such a prodigious dose of learning. He wrote as if Panis Angelicus meant Heavenly Pan, which makes schoolmasters laugh. More important, he dried up and killed himself, and a clue to his self-murder was his reliance on his own provincial vision. He may not have had to become erudite, but it was fatal that he did not know how to extend and surpass himself.

Pollock's death was not free from similar cultural limitations. A time arrives when the Coonskinner must come out from behind the trees and learn to live with the Palefaces as well as the Redskins. The Rousseauist myth cannot continue much longer in a land that has become a power in art as well as in economics. We are doomed to *know what we do*. Even today there is more to be learned abroad than our American teaching of history, which naturally favors Coonskinism, cares to admit. The new national complacency means occasional eruptions of individual talent, the more picturesque for their isolation, which chiefly benefit editors, curators, spouses, and that newest graverobber, the prospective Ph.D. An intelligent this-worldliness, intent upon getting as much personal fulfillment as birth in the tundra will permit, would strive in every fiber for relatedness, and relatedness not only to art, history, and other people, but to our own minds in all their complexity. All experience passes through our minds and can only be apprehended in the images that it releases there. The first step is therefore psychological. When this is speeded up or avoided, the battle is already lost. Apprenticeship to the unconscious is the longest, most necessary of all. That is the price we pay for an efficient civilization which now imposes its order on pioneers as well as dons, on Arabs no less than on the French Academy, on California equally with New York.

Ordinarily the poet has forgotten the psychologist's prescription. It was easier to take Eliot's, which made him a better reader, got him a job in a university, and so changed the fashion in verse that if he lost any vigor through his studies it escaped his students' attention. It was also pleasanter to jump over the earth-bound psychologists directly into the midst of the angelic choirs of theology. A leap from one's own ugliness to the beauty of pure mind was facilitated by the prosperity of the postwar period. Victory had encouraged the belief that "anything goes." We discovered Zen without the Zen master's rod—that is, no Zen at all.

This bypassing of the "headshrinkers," accompanied of course by downgrading them, is thrown into some relief by the respect shown them, along with some spirited opposition, by four outstanding literary artists of our century—Yeats, Joyce, Kafka, Lawrence—who seem best qualified to deliver the rebuttal of their craft. These men got everything they could from their scientific antagonists before they disagreed with them. If there is any supreme court qualified to rule on the effects of close, working proximity to the unconscious, we have at last arrived at it. We must not, however, expect unanimity even here.

A case could be established for Yeats as a man who, while not at all attuned to the scientific temper, indeed most of his life virtually unaware of it, nevertheless in his final ripeness satisfied any demand that a psychologist could reasonably make of a poet. When towards the end of his life he was a fully assembled bard, with many kinds of carefully recorded experience to season him, including the irksome trials of a "smiling public man," he had met the Freudian demands of undeceived maturity, the Adlerian demands of social interest, and demonstrated his understanding of the Jungian archetypes in poems that can bear comparison with our most revered classics. I do not believe this can be said of any other poet of our time. He suggests a norm, a level of fulfillment that the other three writers, despite their high degrees of excellence, did not reach. It is also a level which may interest those sculptors, painters, composers who do not believe in verbal culture—if any alien craft can find its way into their snug harbors.

Virginia Moore, in her book about Yeats, *The Unicorn*, suggests rather plausibly some affinities between him and Jung. His later writings make it clear that he was also familiar with Freud. On the whole he was so secure in his own rhythms that he did not feel called upon to hail or resist the new psychology, as the other writers did; he was older than they and less subject to the new pressures of cultural disintegration. His private religious drama was therefore less acute. He made the transition from talent to seer, but he did not feel called upon to take the further step of becoming a religious sacrifice—unless to become a fully ripened artist involves that, in slower motion and in less impassioned images, as much as crucifixion. Such an idea is suggested by the *Upanishads*, the ancient progenitors of modern psychology, which he took the trouble to help translate from the Sanskrit. At the very beginning of them is the significant line: "Then hope for a hundred years of life doing your duty." What else is duty, in the full, poet's sense of the word, but a daily Golgotha? Was not marriage, for him, the real *ascesis*, as well as the final fulfillment? He lived out his life with untypical steadiness of nerve—and so many stray patches of alchemy, Rosicrucianism, Celtic Twilight, Cabala, and Gnosis peeping out from under his bardic mantle that today, despite his unfailing ballast of skepticism, he would surely be denounced as at least schizoid and might be in danger of being called for by a man in white. Our fierce tough-mindedness, which conceals so much rankling frustration, so much hatred of the poet's more tolerant ways, will not soon permit such a man to appear again. Even Edmund Wilson does not conceal his dislike of Yeats's familiarity with mystical thought, and seems to wish he had read the newspapers like Shaw. We new puritans have crisp Ivy League standards: It would have been better all around if there had not been so much damn nonsense in Yeats.

Only a privileged birth in pre-Parnell Dublin, aided by upper-class shuttles to London, could have permitted such a madman to exist. He was so mystical as to believe: "Is not the poet's labour mere rejection? If he seeks purity—the ridding of his life of all but poetry—will not inspiration come?" In America today he would soon be a lily pad in Bellevue, taking the water cure until he was soggy. In Ireland then he was free to follow his fancy. But even in Ireland the glow soon departed from the Celtic twilight. Seventeen years later, a new young genius came down O'Connell Street, a dreary place but cleaner than the slum where he slept, and told Yeats what was wrong with him: he was not mad enough. ". . . He began to explain his objections to everything I had done. Why had I concerned myself with politics, with folklore, with the historical setting of events? Above all why had I written about ideas, why had I condescended to make generalizations? . . . These were all signs of the cooling of the iron, of the fading out of inspiration." Characteristically Yeats wrote down his first encounter with the twenty-year-old James Joyce as soon as it occurred.

Joyce had had none of Yeats's privileges. His once prosperous family, which lacked Sassenach steadiness, had gone to seed, and he was touchy about it, very touchy. He knew how hard his life was to be, how comparatively neurotic. When Yeats befriended him, he replied with an insult. His brother Stanislas got even worse treatment. Throughout his life his manners swung between those of a simulated prince and those of an angry pauper, but at the time he did not realize that this curse was to prove his greatest practical blessing,

which endeared him to thousands of other literate paupers, a whole
new intellectual class, who read him for his slum-scarred brilliance,
because they felt the same way.

He was under the additional strain of breaking with the Catholic
Church, which had educated him for nothing only to learn that it
had produced one of its most eloquent apostates. Actually, he only
seemed to break with it, for if he was through with it, it was far
from through with him. He was fated, in fact, to erect one of its
principal monuments in the twentieth century, a monument which
only an acute church historian would appreciate as such, but none-
theless a great edifice, truly Catholic in its realistic sacramentaliza-
tion of everyday life.

There was a time when modern psychology was credited with a
large part in freeing Joyce's mind for its immense task of secular
mythmaking. Schools debated which had had a greater effect upon
Ulysses. In the light of the latest biographical data, as collected by
Richard Ellmann, such speculation seems pointless. He did use his
psychological reading for his ever-present literary purposes, when it
fitted in with his mythological talents; but there is little evidence
that he understood it, except as it stimulated his satirical gifts. He
was so obsessed with self-vindication through his books that he did
not even come close to the human give-and-take presupposed by psychological discipline. There was none of the Yeatsian openness and
none of the Yeatsian development. He died untouched by commonly
shared experience. He was perhaps as hermetic a genius as our
century has produced in literature, and since he had the greatest
verbal talent in English letters since Milton, he produced the most
hypnotic language of our time. Scientists rarely understand it, and
men of letters sometimes overunderstand it, in their delight at its
victories of style over the banality of experience and the humiliations of fact. In that sense Joyce has been a bad influence. In another
and more important sense he was a great poet who celebrated the
sordidness and ecstasy of modern life in a rite that may have done
more for the glory of God than any number of rites chanted at dawn
by the frightened and ignorant kind of Irishman he refused to be.
The last chapter of Ulysses, for instance, to name no other part of
his amazing achievement, presents the flesh with a lyric intensity
that will eliminate all pretenders to the spirit, if they fail to respond
to it. Perhaps it was his prior understanding of this paradox that led

him to call Freud and Jung Tweedledum and Tweedledee and to expect none of his kind of intelligence from them.

He had the Catholic temperament par excellence: priestly rather than prophetic, sacramental rather than revolutionary, explicit rather than suggestive. He had also typically Catholic limitations: remote-ness from the modern experience, proneness to immersion in an historic order rather than in contemporary intellectual struggle, a preference for plain song over mere "generalizations." He turned away from Ireland, he turned away from Europe, he turned away from everything but the written page. Hence his amazing mastery, his magic power—and his dissimiliarity from the psychologists, who were mainly Jews in love with a revolutionary world which at last, after centuries of exclusion, they could hope to influence. He wanted to stay out of that world; to portray it with acidulous accuracy, but to have none of it. They wanted to get in, to play the active part in it to which they felt entitled. And Jung was a Protestant; an in-sider, a very much at home insider with whom he desired no con-nection. Joyce was a schoolman from the day of Aquinas, the victim of a mischievous bet between Yahweh and Satan who was dropped into the day of Parnell and given an enchanter's pen. Since poetry flowed from his pen, withdrawn, embittered poetry hard for anyone but "exiles" to understand, he despaired of communication with "grisly old Sykos" who talked as if the world made sense.

Franz Kafka reveals a similar seizure by religious origins—and, as might have been expected of a well-educated Jew, a more detailed encounter with psychoanalysis. If Joyce transfigured the ritualistic faith of God the Son, Kafka transfigured the earlier faith of God the Father. Yahweh was no more through with him than Aquinas was through with Joyce. (Jesus had little hold on Joyce; we have to wait until we come to the Protestant Lawrence to find enough interest in Jesus to speculate on his sexual awakening.) Kafka had experi-enced no comparable exposure to Judaism. Aside from the Cabala, his chief reading was in two Christian writers, Pascal and Kierke-gaard. He was educated by the state (Austria-Hungary), worked for the state, and attempted to fight for the state. Yet when he wrote his masterpiece *The Castle*, he described the passionate efforts of a man to reach a Count who is as inaccessible, as unpredictable, as exasperating, as awesome, as contradictorily reported as Yahweh. Out of a secularized modern mind, so neurotically disturbed by his struggles with his own oedipal problem that he wrote a book-length letter to his father, as well as his father's imaginary reply, and found it impossible to go through with a marriage that he most earnestly desired, and died young of a possibly psychosomatic disease: out of a typically modern "case history" of frustration and despair came a portrait of God the Father as intense and meaningful, for those who can live equally with ancient and contemporary interpretations, as any to be found in the Old Testament.

Kafka may have lacked the robustness of a barefoot prophet, but he had the gentleness, the subtlety, and the exactitude of a great visionary. When he dramatized the modern religious search he reinstalled a forgotten portion of it, mysterious and terrifying, that could only have reappeared to an uprooted Jew. The appositeness of his creation becomes increasingly apparent to both Jew and Gentile, as the secular disguises of religion fall away. Even so, only a few readers can be expected to appreciate what he has done.

Because of his own mental illness, he was urged by friends to be psychoanalyzed. He refused, as Joyce had also refused, but he gave more explicit reasons. Psychoanalysis, he said, avoided the real issue. To bring the origin of a neurosis to the surface, to subject the unconscious to conscious examination was not enough. Speaking presumably of faith, he wrote in *Meditations*:

You say you do not understand it. Try to understand it by calling it disease. It is one of the many symptoms of disease which psychoanalysis claims to have uncovered. I do not call it disease, and I consider the therapeutic part of psychoanalysis a helpless error. All these so-called diseases, pitiful as they look, are beliefs, the attempts of a human being in distress to cast his anchor in some mother-soil; thus what psychoanalysis finds to be the primary source of religion is none other than the source of individual "disease." Today, to be sure, there is no religious unity, the sects are numberless and mostly confined to individuals, or perhaps that is only how it seems to an eye entangled in the present. But such anchorings which find real soil are not a man's individual possession, they are preformed in his being, and afterwards continue to form his being (his body too) further in that direction. Who can hope for cure here?

Far from desiring the easy, illusionist, comfortable God denounced by Freud, Kafka saw God as indifferent and cruel—and essential. The way to God was through the most painful anxiety; and such anxiety must not be removed by rational therapy. He preferred a Kierkegaardian search, even though it meant an unhappy life and an early death. He was an unacademic existentialist, willing to be a religious sacrifice.

The Third Member of the Trinity has been revived by a Protestant, by the most characteristically Protestant poet of our century, who wrote:

> The Father had his day, and fell.
> The Son had his day, and fell.
> It is the day of the Holy Ghost.

Lawrence, as a hymn-singing, disputatious, amateur-theologian Protestant, was dedicated from birth to the Holy Ghost, which is also metaphorically the final reference of modern psychology, the mind which creates all projections, the glass that must be wiped clean if we are not to see darkly. Lawrence did not have to struggle against the mortmain of Rome, like Joyce, nor against the mortmain of the Patriarchs, like Kafka; he was a child of his own time, ready to struggle against the Zeitgeist. Ancestral ghosts did not obsess him, but present horrors did. The chief of these, he felt, was man's "mental" misuse of the "dark gods" within him. The sin against the Holy Ghost was to exploit our internal mysteries, which are the source of all wonder and the source of all corruption. Nearly everyone commits this sin, he said, and begins committing it very young. You, reader, have committed it, and there is no forgiveness for you.

Psychoanalysis will not help. Psychoanalysis is "mentally derived"; it can only assist in your radical defeat. He says this in two books, *Psychoanalysis and the Unconscious* (1921) and *Fantasia of the Unconscious* (1922) which have recently been reissued as a single paperback on the cover of which the blurb writer apologizes for them. "Their interest, perhaps, lies less in what they say about the unconscious—which sometimes seems almost whimsical today and makes very amusing reading—as (sic) in the light they shed on Lawrence himself." We observe the new conformity in a significant moment; Lawrence does not talk about the unconscious as the doctors do, so he must be saying something silly.

Nearly everyone today, says Lawrence, is infected with "idealism," which he calls "the death of all spontaneous, creative life, and the substituting of the mechanical principle." This "idealism" is responsible for all that is sick in the modern world. It dominates not only the bourgeoisie but the proletariat, not only business and politics and education, but the sciences and the arts; and it has not been touched either by the Marxist doctrine of social alienation or the existentialist doctrine of metaphysical alienation or by any churchly doctrine of fall and salvation. It arises when we refuse or fail to live from our deepest and earliest emotional centers, when we let ourselves be cut off, for one reason or another, from "the true unconscious," which is "the well-head, the fountain of real motivity." More and more people, every day, are consenting to this radical surrender, which no amount or kind of psychoanalysis can help. On the contrary, psychoanalysis abets this most disastrous of all defeats.

The Freudian unconscious is much too small and limited. It is "the cellar in which the mind keeps its own bastard spawn." It merely helps along the last stages of man's mechanization. "We must discover, if we can, the true unconscious, where our life bubbles up in us, prior to any mentality. . . . By the unconscious we do mean the soul. But the word *soul* has been vitiated by the idealistic use, until nowadays it means only that which a man conceives himself to be. And that which a man conceives himself to be is something far different from his true unconscious. So we must relinquish the ideal word soul."

The unconscious is inconceivable, but we "know it by direct experience. All the best part of knowledge is inconceivable. . . . Knowledge is always a matter of whole experience. . . .This is indeed the point of all full knowledge: that it is contained mainly within the unconscious, its mental or conscious reference being only a sort of extract or shadow."

This suggests the extent to which he disagrees with Freud, whose promise to man is "Where Id was, there shall Ego be." Freud's Id is a surfaceable submarine compared with Lawrence's unconscious, which must always and should always remain under water. We also see why Freud's ideas could be packaged for mass distribution and why Lawrence's could not. Freud's suggested adjustment and reward, Lawrence's the readiness to write an unsaleable poem about a snake that came to a water trough. Freud's discoveries are seen by implication as springing from alienation from society and self; his chilly precision of style also; his quick understanding of the typical urban psychic casualties of his day; his ability to dramatize the rise of science against the decay of the church; above all, his understanding that civilization and efficiency must be paid for with instinctual disorders, which were most readily observed and most thrillingly demonstrated in the hidden sexual life. His genius itself came out of a profound disease and profoundly diseased way of making the most of it. He represented the last stages of a sick humanity which would soon destroy itself if it did not—and there was little hope it would—discover a way "out of the ideal castle and into the flux of sap-consciousness," into what Lawrence calls a "nourishing creative flow" between itself and others. Science can help greatly, Lawrence says, but only if it "abandons its intellectualist position and embraces the old religious faculty. But it does not thereby become less scientific, it only becomes at last complete in itself."

Although Lawrence himself declares his own preference for Freud and says that "Jung dodges from his university gown into a priest's surplice till we don't know where we are," Kenneth Rexroth claims that Lawrence's writing on psychoanalysis owes much to a limited knowledge of Jung. There *are* certain similarities to Jung, most suggestively in an assertion of ageless country wisdom as opposed to modern city insight, and of unspoken religious values as opposed to overcerebral science. In a sense Lawrence contributes to Jung's dialogue with Freud. But a careful reader will know that Lawrence would have had to disagree with Freud anyway, even if he had not been aided by Jung's prior position. Freud believed he could bring the "dark gods" to the light of day without injury to man. To Lawrence this was abomination. Freud was a meddling fixer of things he did not understand—and not nearly as interesting to study, for instance, as a mother with her baby. A man who wrote novels was *ipso facto* superior to a scientist. "Being a novelist I consider myself superior to the saint, the scientist, the philosopher and the poet." This superiority was all the more true when the novelist spoke for a rootedness in self and soil that most other novelists (Joyce, for instance, whom he despised) despaired of, and when the scientist, in his ignorance, did not begin to understand such essentials and was willing, in the name of a supposed enlightenment, to help to destroy them.

In his second psychoanalytic study Lawrence summarizes the first characteristically: "As for the limited few, in whom one must perforce find an answerer, I may as well say right off that I stick to the solar plexus." In the first he had reiterated that our first center of consciousness lies in the solar plexus. "Here the child knows beyond all knowledge. It does not see with the eyes, it cannot perceive, much less conceive. Nothing can it apprehend, the eyes are a strange plasmic nascent darkness. Yet from the belly it knows, with a directness of knowledge that frightens us and may even seem abhorrent. The mother, also, from the bowels knows her child—as she can never, never know it from the head."

Lawrence is introducing subjective criteria that the scientists had carefully avoided in their quest of an objectivity that he deplores as mental and destructive. This fundamental difference is illustrated throughout his two books, which before the general acceptance of science might not have seemed as strange as they do now. "After our long training in objectivation, and our epoch of worship of the objective mode, it is perhaps difficult for us to realize the strong, blind power of the unconscious on its first plane of activity. It is something quite different from what we call *egoism*—which is really mentally derived—for the ego is merely the sum total of what we *conceive* ourselves to be. The powerful pristine subjectivity of the unconscious on its first plane is, on the other hand, the root of all our consciousness and being, darkly tenacious. Here we are grounded, say what we may. And if we break the spell of this first subjective mode, we break our own main root and live rootless, shiftless, groundless."

It is a way of life that a growing number of rebels admire—and find extreme difficulty in realizing. Lawrence is being revived because he vigorously reminds a disappointed minority, and not all of them women, of what they have not been getting from more objective modes of existence. Even among literary connoisseurs his prophetic shrillness is beginning to hold its own with the melodious priestly chant of Joyce and Eliot. This may mean that a formalist period, which gained its present ascendancy as a protest against the emotions and journalism of World War II and the preceding Depression, is losing some of its momentum. If so, the new enthusiasm for Lawrence can be profitably tempered with an appreciation of his blind spots. He was far from the relatively uncursed poet that Yeats became. Though a bitter antagonist of "intellectuality," he was himself a victim of it, as a comparison of his style with Joyce's, for instance, will at once make evident. Though he vehemently demanded self-honesty on every issue, he was not able to admit the name of the long-suffered disease that killed him at forty-five. Though an advocate of "groundedness," he travelled constantly and made only a wanderer's verbal connection with the places he saw. He was savagely intolerant of the science and business that made his travels possible. He could not forgive those unlike him—that is, nearly everyone. He disregarded the help that Freud and his followers were able to give the world's unfortunates. And when he became convinced of his undebatable rightness on every issue, and lost his original many-sidedness as a storyteller, his novels became less interesting.

Like all the others examined here, he is a single pigment to be used with discretion in our own painting. But he raised issues that from now on we shall have to face. It is possible that he took psychology further back into the personal origins of health or sickness than anyone else had taken it before. A poet has spoken words about the unconscious that no scientist can henceforth put aside.

IV

The Re-Education
of Our Leaders

25

The Remnant Is Not an Elite

This book has attempted to present a complex dispute from the standpoint of the discriminating reader most likely to be able to understand the issues at stake. The psychologists have been confronted with their most articulate opponents—thinkers and artists able to ask the best questions of them. An effort has been made to tell a confusing story as clearly and as justly as possible. Yet this book cannot pretend to be objective. It is subject to all of its author's many biases and blind spots. Unfortunately, these are such that they will increase the resistance of some readers.

If the reader is American, he will refuse to believe that the United States is in some ways already as decadent as its enemies allege, and that reassurances from our professors of American civilization are only making the ice thinner to skate on.

If the reader is Russian, he will laugh at the attention given subtleties that his country will never have to face, because great technical power will never lead to the "Americanization" of Russia, and the many dishonesties he now has to practise will of course come to an end when the revolution is global.

If he is French, he will refuse to believe that the American maladies described here can ever invade France.

If he is Moslem, he will be grateful for the immunizations of economic backwardness.

If he is Israeli, he will regard this as a discussion of fine points that must be put aside until Israel is out of danger.

If he is a Freudian, he will resent the suggestion that present-day neo-orthodoxy is really a nostalgia for the Patriarchs.

If he is a Jungian, he will feel that I have been insufficiently re-

194

spectful of the one psychologist who gives him a sense of purpose.

If he is Indian, he will feel confirmed in his conviction that the best thoughts in the West come from India, and that an Indian acquires them at birth.

If he is antifeminist, he will think I have been too kind to women.

But not all of the protests will be petty. One is this: a Remnant smacks too much of an elite. Elites go bad. What is worse, we have at present a "power elite," described by C. Wright Mills as a "system of organized irresponsibility," which is running our land and running it badly. The Remnant may be confused with our misrulers.

Actually, this confusion is not justified, since a Remnant means, both originally and in the sense in which it is used here, a group of people who have survived or can survive a great catastrophe, while an elite means a group of socially superior persons. The origin of one word is religious, of the other social. In its flowering a society may produce an elite. It is only in a time of extreme trial that it is called upon to produce a Remnant. Nearly everyone wants to belong to the elite, few to the Remnant.

There is also no connection between the Remnant and the Neo-Gnostics feared by Father White and Martin Buber. The Remnant takes no satisfaction in its relative scarcity, while the spirit of gnosticism is exclusive. Since the Remnant is created by disaster, actual or impending, its members want as many fellow-members as possible, in all walks of life. One of its worst fears is that it may fail to come sufficiently into being. It must contend with its own tendencies toward exclusiveness, neurotic withdrawal, solipsism, toploftiness, and kindred vices over which it must be victorious or fail. Its purpose is religious, in a nonecclesiastical sense of that word. It seeks not merely survival as individuals, though that must come first; but also to achieve the survival of the best characteristics of its society, the characteristics that may be called sacred. The United States, for instance, has certain qualities which no thoughtful person will want to see perpetuated. It also possesses other qualities which should and must be perpetuated. The unworthy traits will never be extinguished, but they can be made to seem shameful—through the influence of a Remnant. The Remnant is thus a practical idea, which may have a marked usefulness even in pre-disaster times. It can help to prevent hysteria or stampede when disaster strikes. Every life must encounter grave vicissitudes in time. Those who meet theirs with grace (not the same as numbness) have been preparing for the test. A Remnant reconditions a nation's reflexes.

The practical meaning of this is that the Remnant does not secede. It is committed to its social task. The United States is the center of a great revolution, which frequently looks like a great mess, where the prospective individual has as much to learn from his society as from his mind, though his prior task is psychological. He faces an extremely active life, without much fear of corruption, if he sticks to his double task. Corruption comes to those who do not break away from the mass. (The other-directed conformists.) Or who cling to a minority. (The pressure groups and cliques.) The person who tries to fulfill himself without either mass props or minority props has little chance of rotting. He also has little chance of being approved. He goes "against the weather."

We are centuries away from Gnostic refinements. We build imaginary jungles in our natural history museums with great effort—and real jungles in our cities with no effort at all. The only chance for the individual is to complete his revolution, so that he may re-join society and give it the kind of leadership it is not getting. He climbs out of the melting pot, dries off at the edge (amid the psychopomps), tours all the other kitchens, (through reading and travel) goes back to the melting pot and slips into it again—to add a new flavor to the stew.

His re-education varies, according to his work. Let us now examine his work.

26

The Guilt of Science

If he is a scientist with the sensibility required of the Remnant, he will be better aware than anyone else of the immaturity that causes some of his professional colleagues to wish to get rid of a dark "Faustian image" and to replace it with one of boyish charm. He will recognize the origin of these self-purifying ruses in a refusal to accept one's own evil—in an insipid, narcissistic philosophy of natural goodness which led inevitably, through unawareness of the real forces at work, to darkly inspired weapons that now menace all life.

Enantiodromia is a word, first used by the Greek philosopher Heraclitus, which means "a running counter to" or "a reversal into the opposite." It has been revived and extended by Jung "to describe the emergence of the unconscious opposite, with particular relation to its chronological sequence. This . . . occurs almost universally wherever an extreme one-sided tendency dominates the conscious life." The unconscious must erupt in time, and when it does the result is startling, as in the conversion of Saul into Paul—or of "innocently" overspecialized nuclear physicists into Shivas of world destruction. If we insist we are only one thing (a very good thing, of course) we are pretty sure in time to give shocking evidence of being also the exact opposite. The clergyman in *Rain* is a familiar example, though there have been others subtler and more pertinent.

When this natural phenomenon is observed in political life it helps us to understand why we Americans, who have had a consciously revolutionary and youthful "image" of ourselves for almost two centuries, are now regarded so often elsewhere as extreme reactionaries, or at best as rather arthritic Uncle Sams. Understanding suggests treatment, but the treatment is hard for the stiff-necked to take. We shall examine this political stumbling block in the next chapter. Here we must return to science and the forgotten inner life of the scientist.

Hiroshima awakened the nuclear physicists to the consequences of their ingenuity—those of them who had not already foreseen it and tried to forestall it. Surely it would not become anyone else to reproach them with a one-sidedness to which we are all subject. Theirs had more spectacular results than ours, but it has also led some of them to chastened self-revaluations such as few men ever have the courage to face. They have in fact pointed the way to a better understanding of *our* dilemma.

Our dilemma is this: are we going to continue to increase our lopsided specialization, for fear of being outdone or destroyed by others who are still more lopsided than we; or are we going to open our eyes, come out from behind our lucrative (and terrified) blind spots, and try to see ourselves and the world we live in? The second alternative is infinitely more dangerous. It runs counter to all our institutions and customs. Yet it alone can save us from destruction, on the off chance that man is at last so afraid of his ultimate weapons that he will not dare employ them. It demands harder and more unpredictable work than specialization—and the acceptance of unexpected joys. (Enough to damn it among the new puritans.) It also runs the risk of failure. Those who try to see the whole picture rarely come off as persons today. They have wandered too far from their group.

Yet when we observe the nuclear physicists we find some new and heartening responses to this dilemma. Werner Heisenberg, a Nobel prize winner for physics who did more perhaps than anyone else to prevent Hitler from getting an atom bomb, writes: "The space in which man has developed as an intellectual being has more dimensions than that of the single direction in which he has moved during the last few centuries." Wolfgang Pauli, who won the same prize for his work in the same science, writes: "Since the seventeenth century the activities of the human spirit have been strictly classified in separate compartments. But in my view the attempt to eliminate such distinctions by a combination of rational understanding and the mystical experience of unity obeys the explicit or implicit imperative of our own contemporary age."

The attitude of C. P. Snow is entirely different. As government official, physicist, and industrial magnate, as well as novelist, he would seem in his life to be opposed to overspecialization, yet when he writes of the armament race between the West and the East in his recent *Science and Government,* he says that the first concern of Britain and America must be to find a way, despite our parliamentary handicaps, of holding our own in the scientific struggle that lies ahead. He says that we must produce more and more scientists: "If we don't do it, the Communist countries will in time." We need not worry about the wider horizons advocated for the scientist by Heisenberg and Pauli. He gives no consideration at all to the present disillusionments of the scientists. The important thing is simply to produce more of them than the Russians and the Chinese can. The psychological and philosophic issues are wholly avoided.

Could it be that Snow, the able Jack of all trades, now champions the cause of specialization so vigorously because he is in the grip of an *enantiodromia?* Could Heisenberg and Pauli, who overspecialized in their youth, now champion broader dimensions and mystical experience for the same reason? If so, the tender-minded will prefer the Heisenberg-Pauli kind of *enantiodromia* to Snow's kind. Theirs seeks to correct one of the worst evils of the age, while his continues it. His can be excused on military grounds, however, since we do not wish to be inferior to our enemies in strength. That is why the tough-minded will favor Snow's position.

It is a real dilemma, with much to be said for both sides, and both sides largely determined by unconscious factors. Unconscious factors, moreover, that are quite different from our usual associations with that term. Factors conditioned less by sexual problems than by philosophic problems.

"There are many scientists who avoid having a *Weltanschauung* because this is supposed not to be scientific. But it is manifestly not clear to these people what they are really doing. For what actually happens is this: by deliberately leaving themselves in the dark as to their guiding ideas they are clinging to a deeper, more primitive level of consciousness than would correspond to their full conscious capacities." These words were written by Jung in 1927. In 1945, after Hiroshima, they constituted a remarkable prophecy of what the atom bomb taught the nuclear physicists about themselves. Today they justify Jung's preoccupation with a *rapprochement* between philosophy and psychology—and remind us of the folly of assuming that life stands still where we want it to stand. Our tidy positivism has also been a victim of *enantiodromia.*

The repressed philosophic inquiries of scientists now cry out for expression. To take a neat, pessimistic view of man is not enough, even in a time of holocausts. It is a lazy way of avoiding the real problem, which involves a patient understanding of man's capacities for progress as well as regress. To assume that the Russians and Chinese are wholly evil, besides being capable of infinite mathematical destructiveness, is a form of mental illness, especially prevalent among the fearful. Snow's educational program is a rather hysterical form of power politics which would fail of its objective, because the consciousness of young scientists is being changed by recent events. It is unrealistic to imagine that they are going to be eager to become a new kind of pawn in a new kind of chess game, or that, even if they were willing to assume such a role, they would be able to bring much inventiveness to it. The old moral dynamic of overspecialization is gone.

Its departure means that its fertility of ideas will go too, if it has not done so already. We are slowly building a new dynamic out of a larger picture of man which takes into consideration his appetite for meaning. The really important scientific discoveries of the future will come out of this dynamic, because first-rate minds are drawn to first-rate goals. Philosophic considerations such as those expressed by Heisenberg and Pauli (who could almost have been quoting from the philosopher Whitehead's *Science and the Modern World* of 1925) may complicate the scientist's task for a while, but in time they are sure to lead to more valuable and more humane discoveries than we have ever had before. We are learning that we *lose* too much when we exploit nature or other men—or ourselves.

It was their skill as weaponmakers that led "the new men"—the physicists—to melancholy reflection. The need of scientists to face up to philosophic issues was felt inevitably by them after they were forced, by their military usefulness, out of their laboratory cloisters into a full share of action and responsibility. But how does one face up to philosophic issues? Not by hiding behind "objective" standards. One cannot play safe. That is one reason why academic psychology has received no attention here; it assumes that the subjective issue can be ducked. One faces these issues by frank confrontation of oneself in action.

In other words, one explores one's emotional life. This need not lead to self-indulgence. If it is done with the thoroughness that one devotes to a test tube, it leads on the contrary to judging oneself by stricter standards than before. One is not permitted to escape into delusions of grandeur about one's usefulness or originality. (The selfless facade of many scientists permits their hidden vanity to become monstrously luxuriant, because it is supposed not to exist.) One must face up to *ancient* standards of human measurement which are still able to cut anyone down to size. Therefore a certain ancient standard is being revived today.

"The Zen approach to reality which may be defined as antescientific is sometimes antiscientific in the sense that Zen moves entirely against the direction pursued by science. This is not necessarily saying that Zen is opposed to science, but simply that to understand Zen one has to take a position which has hitherto been neglected or rather ignored by scientists as 'unscientific.'

"The sciences are uniformly centrifugal, extroverted, and they look 'objectively' toward the thing they pick up for study. The position they thus assume is to keep the thing away from them and never to strive to identify themselves with the object of their study. Even when they look within for self-inspection they are careful to project outwardly what is within, thus making themselves foreign to themselves as if what is within did not belong to them. They are utterly afraid of being 'subjective.' But we must remember that as long as we stand outside we are outsiders, that for that very reason we can never know the thing in itself, that all we can know is *about*—which means that we can never know what our real self is."

These words were delivered in 1957 to a psychoanalytic conference in Mexico by D. T. Suzuki. Most scientists will find it difficult to understand them. Fromm reports: "The conference was attended by about fifty psychiatrists and psychologists from both Mexico and the United States (the majority of them psychoanalysts)," and "that most of the people present were not just 'interested' but deeply concerned, and that they discovered that the week spent with Dr. Suzuki and his ideas had a most stimulating and refreshing influence on them to say the least."

Suzuki describes the difficulties of the person who tries to find a durable metaphysics through the study of his own mental processes. "He is now pushed to the corner where there is no way to escape. At this moment the master may say, 'It is good thus to be cornered. The time has come for you to make a complete about-face.' The master is likely to continue, 'You must not think with the head but with the abdomen, with the belly.'

"This may sound strange. According to modern science, the head is filled with masses in gray and white with cells and fibers connected this way and that. How can the Zen master ignore this fact and advise us to think with the abdomen? . . . The head symbolizes intellection. . . . But the abdominal part where the viscera are contained is controlled by the involuntary nerves and represents the most primitive stage of evolution in the structure of the human body. The abdominal parts are closer to nature, from which we all come and to which we all return. They are therefore in a more intimate contact with nature and can feel it and talk with it and hold it for 'inspection.' "

Where have we encountered a very similar description of this step toward real education? In Lawrence, who said that we can only find our roots by living through the solar plexus. "Here the child knows beyond all knowledge." And here the man who would "become as a little child," that is, learn the secrets of moral survival, must also return.

A few scientists are showing that they can learn from the philosophers (and poets) as well as from their own kind. To use the less developed parts of their own minds does not terrify them because, temporarily, it may make them seem ridiculous. They know that it is only thus that they can find the way to fuller humanity and perhaps finally to more adventurous science. Who can be sure that personal distortion is the sole key that unlocks the imagination? Is it certain that the mind-body split is required any longer, even for military defense? Out of our humiliations we are learning some new lessons and acquiring a new ideal, the ideal of conscious health. As surely as slower minds have imitated nimbler minds in the uses of self-exploitation, they will in time imitate them in being awakened to its penalties. Such an awakening will take many years, however, and meanwhile there may be bloodshed on a vast scale, out of ignorant misunderstanding. The best way to avoid the bloodshed is through a re-educational process of which only a few at present, unfortunately, seem capable. The odds are that re-education will only begin *after* a grave disaster.

This hidden drama lies at the heart of the East-West struggle. Its recognition will unite the Remnant in many lands, on both sides of the Iron Curtain.

27

The Politics of Shipwreck

Let us imagine a young and gifted President of the United States who wished to avail himself of the discoveries of psychopolitics, as far as it was practical to do so. Let us assume that he became interested in its kind of reasoning and wished to use it, in the interests of his country. What new insights might he acquire? It is a fair question. If psychopolitics is any good, it will have to demonstrate its value, though of course only hypothetically, to such an executive.

Surely the President would be struck by a remarkable circumstance. Two of his recent predecessors in office provided instances of *enantiodromia*. President Truman, who passed almost his whole life as a man of peace, whether as haberdasher or politician, was given a chance to live out previously unrealized desires for action in 1945. He was called to the White House in April, and shortly afterward he made the decision to drop the first atomic bomb. There were many other factors in his decision besides the psychological one, but that cannot be overlooked, since in 1950 he made another warlike decision—to fight in Korea—a decision it is difficult to suppose his successor would have made. In 1953 he was succeeded by a man who had been a professional soldier all his life. What did President Eisenhower do? He stopped the war in Korea as quickly as possible, and proceeded on a path of inaction so pronounced as to become a major campaign issue at the end of his administration, in 1960. He gave the impression of being in the grip of an obscure emotion, perhaps religious in origin, which bade him be personally serene even if it required the avoidance of tasks customarily performed by men in his office. And his popularity was such, among a people who shared his desire for escape from disagreeable thoughts, that he was permitted to pursue his course of inaction without reproach. If he had been eligible for re-election in 1960, professional observers agree, he could have won with ease. The nation preferred repose. It enjoyed feeling morally superior to the rest of the world, as well as the conviction that everything would come out all right.

Psychopolitics also helps us to see a little more clearly the unsuccessful landings in Cuba in April 1961 which proved such a blow to our national prestige. Surely a young President will be interested in any light he can get on the disaster at the Bay of Pigs. These landings would never have been authorized by Washington if Washington had thought with its belly. These landings originated in a belief that something could be got for nothing. Long-standing habits of easily bought success entered that decision. Salvation by checkbook lay at hand. Someone was offering to pull our chestnuts out of the fire—why not let him do it? Questions of right were ignored. Even routine tests of intelligence reports were suspended, in our greedy haste.

Psychopolitics would suggest that government by report-reading, which present-day conditions require, is apt to lead to disaster unless the report-reading is done by men with a deep subjective experience of life that is equal to the facts that have to be assimilated. Adversity seems to sharpen this experience. Some of the most successful statesmen of our time—Lenin, Churchill, de Gaulle, Mao, Nehru—became so only after years *out* of office. Prison educated some of them. Disease educated Franklin D. Roosevelt. It was fortune's darling, the handsome, lucky Eden, who made unthinking mistakes at Cyprus and Suez. That is why fortune's darling, the handsome, lucky Kennedy, must learn from the solar plexus what he has been spared by disaster.

An adult is more likely to think with the solar plexus if he faces his daily humiliations. The cause of the greedy mind-body split is the hope of escaping these humiliations. This homely truth is one of the cornerstones of psychopolitics. We can rarely expect of a statesman that he live with this truth, since as a rule he wins our vote merely because his falsehoods are slightly less distasteful than a rival's. The will to believe is strong in politics, because we want someone else to do the boring chores of administration. We also long to be identified with a group that can command our wholehearted loyalty. That is why we prefer political leaders who are adept at fixing guilt on others, preferably on others who live far away from us. In times of trouble we can always blame anything that goes wrong on someone else, and not on ourselves.

Yet a few statesmen do think with their bellies from time to time, when they have spent a long period out of office. One should not expect too much of the others. The first step toward getting good leaders is to expect a great deal of oneself. Then only can one pick the good ones from the others.

The problem of the Remnant in politics is to avoid secession. Politics has become so distasteful to sensitive minds that even today, when so many threats of totalitarian extinction surround them, they have not rallied to active participation. This is because they still hope they can be spared all the nastiness. It is not a good betting proposition. Withdrawal becomes less and less feasible. For even the most exquisite natures the present exaggerated swing away from politics and towards art will last no longer than a general avoidance of catastrophe. Freud was protected until his eighties, but then the Nazis came. Jung was confronted with the hydrogen bomb in his seventies. The pattern is now so familiar that we feel no guilt at all about our aesthetic spree. It is none the less stultifying. The present is the time when a Remnant, in an intelligent use of its anxiety, will be drawing the right conclusions from political events. It is possible of course that survival will not be won by courage or clarity, but on the other hand it will certainly not be lost by them.

The position of the Remnant has been described by Ortega y Gasset: "The man with the clear head is the man who . . . looks life in the face, realizes that everything in it is problematic, and feels himself lost. . . . Instinctively, as do the shipwrecked, he will look around for something to which to cling, and that tragic, ruthless glance, absolutely sincere, because it is a question of his salvation, will cause him to bring order into the chaos of his life. These are the only genuine ideas, the ideas of the shipwrecked."

This statement will do as a further definition of solar-plexus thinking. It is commended to our hypothetical young President, who, if he uses the eyes of the shipwrecked, will discover an important fact. (This fact has been briefly mentioned in Chapter 3.) We Americans, who seem almost the most conservative people in the world today—or at least are so described, rather vehemently, by a steadily increasing array of enemies who now number more than half the population of the earth—we Americans are actually in the midst of the most advanced revolution our century has seen. But it is also the least publicizable of revolutions, precisely because it is so advanced. It makes no impression on other peoples because they have not yet gone through it. They cannot even imagine it. Only Americans, only a few Americans can put it into words and thus enable their country once more to communicate with others. And thus also prevent their country from making further progress toward disaster. We have introduced a literal *deus ex machina* into the plot, in the hope that the very newest machine will snatch us from a tragic end.

The ironic result is the rapid emergence of a serious competitor in machine-making—and a growing belief in the audience that we shall lose out to our competitor because his revolution is less advanced than ours and can be put into a ready-made ideological language that still has meaning for the really backward areas. Our pragmatic contempt for theory has come full circle in record time. We must forge a theory and *live* it—that is, cleanse ourselves with it—or lose our present position. The odds are heavy that our pragmatic blind spot has already condemned us to a fairly colossal disaster with unimaginable consequences, but if we avoid disaster, one thing is already clear: America will be saved by a handful of "men with clear heads."

The language they speak will most likely find more deafness at home than abroad, reaching neither our people nor our universities, because it cannot contain the reassurances that the former demand, and because it will horrify the latter by its antispecialist, technically unacceptable latitude. Brief cries of "alarmism" and "incompetence" will momentarily trouble the dormitories. Then our unnoticed revolution will again be forgotten.

If however it is genuine, and not the self-congratulatory moralizing that our Commission on National Goals seems to prefer, our revolution will make itself felt by contradictory symptoms, such as a drying up of the traditional ferment of youth; premature prudence; early marriage on a large scale; youthful eagerness for the economic security of large organizations; youthful unwillingness to stick its neck out; overconcern with fashion; overconcern with things; youthful demand for group approval. These symptoms, which superficially suggest conformity and are forever being denounced by the sociologists as such, mean that we are in the midst of an anxiety-creating revolution.

Along with many similar symptoms, these are sure signs that the inner life of our young people has become too exciting. They must smother it in boredom and group approval, otherwise they could not stand it. They must refuse the symbolic life, they must plunge as soon as possible into a demanding drabness which permits no troubling vistas and no "agenbite of inwit" at all. *America is the land of the refused revolution.* The leisure offered by mechanical mastery is here. At the same time, surely not through chance, leisure becomes economically ever harder to sustain—and psychologically more terrifying. So we see without seeing, read without reading, and fall back on mythologies in which we no longer believe. The age of the Holy Ghost demands too much. Every novelty is embraced because it can keep our true situation from becoming too clear. Every *external* drama—that of a minority, or of a remote place in Africa—is welcome. Anything but *our own* drama, here and now. To be born into a minority means that we rarely recognize its *secondariness* among our real concerns. When literature is examined, it becomes a technical study of style. The history of art is absorbed in three years, so that a new collector may make as sound investments in pictures as in the copywriters employed by his firm. In short, Isaiah *is* counting famine on this lee.

These disturbing truths, if faced and told, would enable us to regain a moral dynamic. If we were to tell the world of the revolution we refused, and why we are having such a hard time in accepting it, we should win the clarity and strength that come from facing the truth in all humility. It would help us to purge ourselves of whatever exploitative or imperialistic motives we do possess. Democracy would take the initiative. Otherwise, it never will, since it is a religious idea, as much as a political one, that must lead to genuine religious action or perish.

If Europe understood why America, which once seemed to her so vigorous, so sprightly, now has lost the *mystique* of invincible, evil-destroying youth, but suffers instead from some visible middle-aged disorders, she would laugh at first and thoroughly enjoy our comedown, but after a while she would see us as more human and more interesting. It is our dazed or mendacious unrelatedness to the humbling facts of common experience that has puzzled observant Europeans. As a matter of fact, they have *already* been laughing at our comedown, which they regard as a *fait accompli,* but they do not yet understand what is behind it: the revolution that we refused and that *they* also are pretty sure to refuse when it is required of them.

The technical revolution demands in time that man be equal to

208 THE RE-EDUCATION OF OUR LEADERS

his own creations. He cannot merely run his airplane well. His consciousness must go as high as his body does. He must be not merely a flyer but a Saint-Exupéry. Otherwise he becomes a mere chauffeur. This may have been a reason why, as Lombroso suggests, the great innovators of the Renaissance called a halt to their inventions; they sensed that men would not be worthy of them. But we have gone ahead with ours, and now we must equal them or perish. A first step would be to realize how dangerous they are to mental health. One can so easily misuse them as ways of short-circuiting personal experience.

But that is hardly an idea one can expect a mechanized peasantry to understand. The lonely crowd will prefer being lonely, because it is wrapped in the latest polyester. And the vaginal images used to sell the garment will delight our Russian competitor, who considers them degenerate, next to his cult of the old-fashioned woman.

It will require real courage of our imaginary President if he is to tell the lonely crowd the truth about the lonely crowd. Yet it is the only story that will be believed. Because it is a real story, the story that all peoples, including the Russians, are going to be encountering in their own lands some day, if they have not already done so. We cannot escape the tragedy of timelag. We are doomed to be misunderstood—and outmaneuvered—until we find a moral dynamic by telling the truth. At present it is difficult to imagine any of our leaders who is capable of *seeing* the truth, let along telling it. And yet both clarity and honesty are now demanded by the facts.

If we tried to match the Russians in messianic appeal, we should not only be lying, we should be outclassed. The Russians have on their side the master messianic of them all. His name is F. M. Dostoevsky, and he has been ghostwriting the speeches of the Soviet leaders, who cut his antirevolutionary ideas but make subtle use of his Byzantine image of the Russians as a chosen people destined to regenerate the world. No American is capable of producing so powerful a myth. Our best myth-making talents, which are to be found of course among our poets (not admen or politicos, as the grossly miseducated believe) have been devoted to the destruction of falsehood, not the proclamation of faith. Falsehood, as we have seen, has become so widespread that it has to be cleared away by an honest talent, before the poet can function at all—unless he is to be merely decorative.

It is not enough to say that time is working against the Russians, that the countries near them have seen through their myth, and the more remote countries will see through it in time. It is still united to a hardheaded political program that can have a great appeal among proletarians. (Our own dishonesty about class would be purged by some truthtelling.) It is also united to a strong will to leadership. There is little evidence that our will to leadership is as strong. What we have to say is more reasonable. We are obliged to speak the unappealing plain talk that daily use of technical power bestows along with its advantages. We do not feel romantic any longer about machinery. We are further along; that is, more seriously uprooted, poorer in time-tested imagery. But we are also further along in historical development; we have lived with the new power long enough to know what it costs in continuous effort toward consciousness, unless one is to be dehumanized by it. So we—or those of us able to speak out—have a great deal more to say than the Russians. To become a true moral dynamic, however, our discoveries must be part of a profound religious experience that genuine leaders will share with our people.

The conditions for such a sharing of experience are not here. Our genuine leaders live on a level of experience which alienates them from their people, because the people are being deliberately alienated, through the mass communications, from themselves. It is therefore not enough to gloat about "the god that failed." Anticommunism soon degenerates into impotent self-righteousness. *Our job is to find the new god that is within us.* That alone will heal the breach between leaders and people, but it will require much re-education of everyone. First, a great many of us must learn not to be put off by metaphorical language which speaks of "the new god that is within us." Our mind has produced all the gods. Some day, after great travail, it will produce a new one (which may be an old one, redefined) in whom the subtlest minds of our leaders and the earthiest minds of our people can find some agreement. The best in philosophy, government, science, literature, and art is an effort in this direction. To use the language of William James, our "I" wants harmony with our neighbors, and our "me" does all it can to prevent it. One more reason why there can be no true morality without a clear understanding of the unconscious forces in our "me."

To explore the hidden emotional factors in our government suggests how unlikely it is that we shall get a really good President. To be elected he must give the impression that the dark forces discussed here do not exist. Yet, unless he has been chastened by these dark forces, genuinely chastened, he will be incapable of re-education. Our fate will then continue to be drift toward disaster. We shall go on refusing our revolution, under the spreading atom tree, amid the corruption that grows daily among the nicest, cleanest, best-willed people on earth.

At least we are about to meet Walter Rathenau's demand of us. In 1921 he told André Gide that America had no soul and did not deserve to have one, because she had not yet "deigned to plunge into the abyss of suffering and sin." Though we have not yet deigned, we are already plunging, and some day it will be apparent to everyone that we are just as deep in the abyss as anyone else.

The psychologists have pointed the way to this saving humiliation. Here lies the humanizing secret of psychopolitics. And here will begin our capacity to replace the old fake mythology of God's Country with one that the world can respect. It is a task that belongs, not to an imaginary ruler, but to a real Remnant, born of disaster.

28

The Mind of Demos

"The redirection of Madison Avenue's power needs the guidance of the new pantheon which waits unused in our minds." Thus ended Chapter 4. In the subsequent pages we have made a tour of the best insights available into the new pantheon. Now we must apply these insights to the questions raised by Madison Avenue. This means that in the end, of course, we shall still have to find the answers in our own minds.

It is a problem that is by no means restricted to our own land. Considerable light on it, in fact, is thrown by the rather familiar glow that is beginning to be visible on distant horizons. The best way I can convey an interesting new crisscross between the Old World and the New is to describe a situation that I encountered in Austria in 1959, when I wrote the following letter:

If an American wanted to get a quick, admittedly restricted, but pretty reliable impression of recent cultural developments in Europe, he could do a lot worse than come here. The excellent and much needed Salzburg Seminar in American Studies, where I am currently lecturing on our twentieth-century fiction, continues to provide the most enlightening full-scale intellectual collision that I know of between the Old World and the New. To its handsome rococo Schloss Leopoldskron, built in the eighteenth century by a Protestant-persecuting archbishop and in our time occupied successively by Max Reinhardt and the Nazi Gauleiter, have come forty-eight "fellows" from fourteen European countries—Finland, Norway, Sweden, Denmark, Great Britain, Ireland, France, Switzerland, Germany, Austria, Belgium, Holland, Italy, and Yugoslavia. This session lasts the habitual four weeks and has for its subject Literature and Mass Media. The last session was on American Foreign Policy, the next will be on Labor and Industry in the U.S.A. Each day the fellows debate the merits of Henry James and Jack

211

Kerouac, Eugene O'Neill and William Inge, D. W. Griffith and Elia Kazan, William Randolph Hearst and Henry Luce. The fellows' average age is thirty; a few of them are about to take doctorates; most of them are already embarked on careers in teaching, journalism, advertising, law, science, or television. At this moment I can hear a girl from Berlin typing a thesis on Ralph Ellison. A London circulation manager is humming "Tom Dooley." Some others have just left to examine the archaeological finds at Hallstatt. Still others are examining their skis. They will go to Berchtesgaden on Sunday, to slalom around the ghosts of Eva Braun and her sinister court.

My outstanding impression is that the so-called Americanization of Europe—really, its "technicization"—has proceeded even faster than expected, and has now already entered an unanticipated phase. It is breeding what might be called a new kind of isolationism. These people are remarkably hep to certain facts of American life. They know all about our Negro problem, our conformity problem, our Madison Avenue problem. They have, in fact, on the whole become familiar with our difficulties with lightning speed—and then congratulated themselves on their own blessed immunity: an overseas twist to the "It Can't Happen Here" myth.

Yesterday when my seminar discussed William Faulkner's long story *The Bear*, everyone agreed that Faulkner was in a way expiating the sins of his slave-owning forebears and, like so many other writers, was a kind of "guilt-bearer." Then, since European parallels are helpful in this kind of teaching, I asked if there could be similar guilt-bearers in other lands.

At first no parallels were seen. Upon questioning, however, the British contingent conceded that E. M. Forster had performed a similar task for Britain when he wrote *A Passage To India*. The French group needed more pressure, but finally admitted that Albert Camus and François Mauriac had done pretty much the same thing for French guilt in North Africa. The Italians, however, could not even remember Ethiopia, and the Germans announced complacently: "We don't have any colonies."

"What about the Jews?" I asked.

Then only did the Germans—all of whom were children or adolescents when World War II ended—recognize what was obviously one of the major guilts of our day. There was also a momentary understanding, *perhaps*, of Faulkner's heroic burden and its international relevance. The names of two young German writers and one theater man were mentioned; they were dealing in their arts with the plight of the Jews under Hitler. It was also recalled, after a question or two, that the play made from *The Diary of Anne Frank* had had a great success in Germany.

It is not always so easy to get these Europeans to realize, however briefly, their common identity with us. They are prosperous, and although a few shared problems disturb some of them—the Germans are certainly worrying about Berlin at the moment—they prefer to believe that we Americans suffer from outlandish ailments that will never trouble them. (We return the compliment: witness the moralizing tone of our foreign policy and of most of our tourists.) Their new isolationism makes them howl at the clumsiness of our Victorian melodramas, smile superiorly at our TV appetites, and read our best writers chiefly as reportage. Above all it makes them snicker at our interest in modern psychology, which you would never guess had originated in Europe and not far from here. Sometimes I wonder if the Marshall Plan has sown a continent of passive, entertainment-hungry conformists. These people know almost nothing about new painting, new music, new poetry, new architecture; and they have degrees from the very oldest universities to back up their conventional tastes. When I compare their questions with those I get from my classes at the New School in New York, I am convinced that Americans of comparable age and talent are forced by our greater tensions to live on a deeper level.

In extenuation it must be pointed out that these Europeans have been exposed more recently than we to the full lure of the mass media. Also, this particular group contains almost none of the advance-guard leaven that, when I was here four years ago, made another session more exciting. But the chief fact about them is inescapable: a new conformism is at work here, quite as much as it is at home, and it is aided materially by the new film, radio, TV, and advertising jobs that have been added to traditional school and university jobs. Also, this new conformism is more insidious because it is well-bred, well-educated, multilingual, and quite sure it does not exist.

I must add, however, that four years ago one fellow from France kept a pistol under his pillow and distressed his roommates by singing the "Horst Wessel" song every morning. Another, from Germany, got drunk one night and told us that Germany was only using the U.S.A. for the moment and would some day rise again in her full Wotanic wrath. There have been no such incidents this time—and no tendencies in that direction. I get an impression of a much soberer Europe, now reconciled lucratively to Coca-colonization but not yet aware of the after-taste. The old humanities are in flight, and a conscious resistance to mechanization of the mind has still to organize new ones. We are now in a sense the oldest nation on earth, and have something to say to our juniors.

I must add as a postscript that only a few Americans as yet have something to say to these Europeans, since only a few Americans are aware of these issues. It was experiences like this one that helped me to perceive the need for a Remnant able to speak both to Europeans and to fellow countrymen at home. Most Americans will not listen to a Remnant, however, no matter how well it masters their idiom—because it will want to stop their joy ride.

The last word is in the idiom of the nineteen twenties, and has become quaint because our motoring habits have somewhat sobered

up and it is chiefly juvenile delinquents who go joy riding now. Yet
the emotions generated by the mass media are joy rides—and they
are considerably more dangerous than drunken driving. These emotions lock the young and unwary in false attitudes—sentimentalities,
unrealistic demands, self-delusions, expectations of the stereotype—
which will in time unfit them for any showdown with their antagonists among the have-not nations. (Another omission in Snow's engineer crash program.) Who are the real betrayers of our country? Not
the Hisses and the Rosenbergs. Some of our most respected publishers and broadcasters.

This is all so familiar—and still so unfaced. The gimmick, a one-
time swindler's word that has grown respectable, is in danger of becoming our national style. Since the source of all contemporary
power lies in the mind of the man in the street, we compete in in-
genuities for estranging him still further from himself. (Meanwhile
doing the same, even more surely, to ourselves; and developing, as
we shall see, some typical gimmickeer's diseases.)

The gimmick has entered even our most serious activities. The
writing of books, for instance. "Nonbooks" and most anthologies
are an example. More insidiously, the gimmick mentality leads more
than one author to fear he is not communicating to enough people,
and so to fall back on some popular emotional appeal, couched in
language that even backward children can understand—and to lose
thereby all worthwhile readers. A variant of Gresham's Law is at
work. This horrifies the scholars, who stop trying to communicate
with anyone who is not in their own set. So the problem of true communication is made more difficult for everyone.

The belief that a gimmick can be used in our deepest concerns is
a natural consequence of our mass culture. Inevitably, clever men
who have seen great elections and mighty fortunes won by transparent falsities have pressed on to exploit every evidence of popular
passivity. This is one more cause of the decadence our non-admirers
find in us. Future historians may well decide that the chief injury
done the mind of man by technology was the assurance it gave him
that he could find a way of life in the misuse of public relations. We
continually quote Lincoln on the people's final sagacity, in the hope
that no one *can* fool all the people all the time. At the moment, con-
gratulating ourselves on Hitler's destruction and McCarthy's defeat,
we think no other demagogue will ever repeat their temporary triumphs. Meanwhile the admen sell us more goods than ever before,

by not dissimilar methods, and our book reviews usually save their best space for intellectual confidence games.

Because of the atomization and dissociation of our society, the gimmick is now an everyday part of our life. Despite its dangers, it does not do much good, however, to view it with alarm. It is more useful to try to understand it. A few examples may help.

They are not sordid, these examples. I collected them myself, among especially gifted artists who were more or less forced into them by the struggle for existence. First, there was a prominent and gifted theater man who said of a prize-winning play which he directed for "the road," that is, the theaters outside New York: "Of course the wife of the salesman wouldn't be like that in real life. She wouldn't stand up for her husband, especially since he has failed to make enough money and has been unfaithful to her. She would feel closer to her sons. Don't you get it? She has to be the kind of long-suffering good woman that women in the audience think they are. She has to be *good*. The husband slips, but not she! She's a gimmick."

Then there was the talented advance-guard painter who put aside the favored, slowly created paintings of years, on the advice of a critic who told him that a particular painting would make a more bulletlike impression on reviewers and collectors and therefore should be imitated instantly in several other pictures. In two weeks the painter painted a galleryful of remarkably similar paintings that did indeed make a bulletlike impression on reviewers and collectors, because they repeated the same abstract theme with an advertisement's insistence, and thus won for him the admiration he wanted from art magazines and museums. Like the theater man, he is now rich.

Then there were the remarkably similar images that were found again and again in a suddenly popular poet who had once put down only the words that he had to write. And finally the composer whose chamber works had been dissonant because his world was dissonant, but when he wanted to "communicate," began to write in a more dulcet style, because "modern music doesn't *have* to be painful." He also is rich.

It does no good to view these familiar instances of "slickness" with alarm. A moralizing attitude ("At least I'm not guilty of that!") merely prevents us from understanding the artist's dilemma, which is finally everybody's dilemma. It would be more to the point to try to see his alternatives, which are: (1) shall I ignore the public and just do what I feel like doing? (2) shall I shape my work to have the strongest possible effect on the public? Time and consciousness make it progressively more difficult for him to follow the first alternative in perfect innocence, much as he may prefer it. (Jackson Pollock died in the midst of this decision.) If he lives long enough he is sure to be confronted with the second alternative, which contains these subalternatives: (1) shall I try to find a not too disgraceful way to give the public what I think it wants—in my style, of course? (2) shall I try to find a way to make the public accept what I want it to have?

The playwright, the painter, the poet, the composer have taken the first subalternative. Few if any of our artists are sufficiently resolute—and resourceful—to take the second subalternative, which implies a paternal act of leadership that would almost surely be resented or ignored, unless put into the form of criticism. (We have been spoiled so long that we dislike any suggestion of paternal clarity, though we go on demanding the best in leadership.) And even then such clarity would probably be dismissed as didactic.

When people are as estranged from themselves as we Americans are, there can be no serious national art; there can be only serious minority art. And nearly always this minority art is susceptible to majority attitudes, even when it pretends to be wildly advance-guard. It wants group approval just as much as the majority does, though its group is smaller (less lucrative but more congenial). So it is not surprising that some of the cleverest minds among our artists go toward the first subalternative—that is, toward the gimmick. If therefore we ever hope to achieve a gimmick-free art, it would be only sensible to stop denouncing the gimmick and try to understand it.

The gimmick is the surest way to get the attention of a large disconnected mass. It will therefore remain a permanent temptation in our society until we are weeded out by a new but easily imagined military encounter. The gimmick follows naturally after the gadget. Having gone so far in our conquest of nature, why not go on a little further, since men's minds are still more lucrative? Faust was a sentimentalist. And most gimmickeers do not even stop to ask the question, or state the comparison; they simply grab what they can of easy money. Mass communication was made for them, and as yet, unlike the Nazis, they do not have to take on blood-guilt as well as money-guilt.

What can the Remnant do about this situation? A while back we spoke of its desire to clean the Augean mess in Madison Avenue. Will this ever be accomplished?

If our study of the mind has been competent, it has obliged us to understand that Madison Avenue—and its various counterparts—can never be essentially changed. There can be minor reforms, but human beings are such that "hidden persuaders" and other tricks of the kind will always work on a very large number of them. In the mass we are hopeless "oral types," viscerotonic, other-directed, and as predictable as Pavlov's dogs. The more dangerous of these tricks can so alarm us as to demand control, but it is a delusion to believe that mass education will ever solve this problem. There is only one kind of education that means anything, and that is the kind that gets the least attention—*your own education*. The ignorant you will always have with you, and you will be more deluded than they if you imagine their circuses will ever be a vast improvement on the Roman kind, or that you can duck out of your own obligations by daydreaming about an intelligent and rational society. It will be a sufficient achievement if you bring off one or two rational moments now and then yourself.

The Remnant is not going to find some convenient nearby stream that will handily perform this Herculean labor. It is going to have to live in these stables. Its children are going to be corrupted by them —and *perhaps* outgrow them. By force of character and intellect it may convert a small corner of them to its own purposes. It can also have Madison Avenue rezoned. Almost all of it will go into a frank new red light district, but a tiny corner will be sacred ground.

The corruption of the innocents will go on—in all but a very few cases.

29

Sensibility and Survival

If miseducation is certain, the first step toward getting rid of it is to become aware of it. Then perhaps it can be removed and replaced with the real thing. Such a replacement—or "rebirth," as it is sometimes called—occurs rarely, since it requires a change in direction as well as in character. It means breaking bad habits and forming good ones. It takes us back among formative influences that shaped us long before we could become aware of them. Now we must see them clearly—and when necessary, offset them. So radical a realignment of one's original destiny is impossible without an understanding of the mind's dynamics. Uninstructed will is not enough.

The desire for rebirth may be as common as the desire for wealth and fame. It is the shy longing and tense anxiety that one often sees in other people's eyes, if one looks closely. It is the most moving of expressions, because on its fulfillment depends a human being's happiness. Ordinarily this desire is passive: that of an Eliza Doolittle waiting for Pygmalion. Sometimes the desire for rebirth wears the mask of arrogance, or excessive hopefulness, which means merely that all real hope of its fulfillment has been lost. It is therefore still as important for a psychologist to read eyes as to interpret dreams. Eyes also lead to the unconscious—and its chances of successful emergence.

Since this sort of understanding means nothing if it is not concrete, let us attempt to consider a subtle and generally unnoticed source of present-day American miseducation.

It might be called numbness. The evidence of our literature and clinics is that almost all Americans are "frozen" emotionally, and for reasons not difficult to understand. (This applies not only to the

218

old Anglo-Saxon stock but to Negroes, Irishmen, Jews, Italians, and other relative newcomers. Their expressiveness, bounce, restlessness, and other "shouts of freedom" cover up not only a "rattle of chains" but a profound unrelatedness and a profound mistrust of genuine feeling. As is always true of the self-alienated, their emotions, when they come out, are theatrical. They show off, they express more than they really feel—to conceal a lack of connection. Our cult of the cowboy, for instance, in ballet and film, is a nostalgic substitute for real masculinity of purpose directed at present concerns. Its hoe-downs are cute rather than robust. *Oklahoma!* is a masterly example of Fake Folk. There is no way back to Rousseauist harmony with the people. Thomas Jefferson and Abraham Lincoln can make bad heroes who actually lessen one's chances of survival. Emerson, Thoreau, and Whitman can be almost equally injurious. Romanticism rots the brain, and the right replacement for it is not Eliot's antiquarian classicism but the habit of facing one's daily humiliations—or, as Suzuki would put it, a deliberate policy of getting into outrageous corners that make one think with one's belly. The psychopomps, even when composed polyphonically, will not suffice. The theologians, the mystics, the poets are also inadequate when taken by themselves. We are most complexly threatened with extinction. One is either aroused to action or one waits numbly for the end—humming, "Oh what a beautiful morning!"

Numbness is so much part of us that only the half-thawed will know what I mean. Most likely our numbness got its start in early Pilgrim days when any strong inclination to enjoyment was considered retrograde. Today it is an analgesic against the harrowing sense that one is trapped in a senseless experiment. People do not dare to have genuine emotions, which would soon lead to a glimpse of their real plight. So we demand of popular art that it give us false emotions. But they must not be transparently false emotions. They must seem real long enough to divert our attention from what on a deeper level we are concerned with: our appetite for meaning. That is why there is a rapid turnover in the cowboy myths, and why the cowboy myths have been extended to the most advanced abstract painting, as in the case of Pollock, or to the most expert fiction, as in the case of Hemingway. A child is satisfied by TV, but an adult demands more and more elaborate forms of self-deception.

The cynicism behind the gimmick also fosters numbness. If you are doing something slick, you cannot admit what you are doing. And this attitude is passed on to your children, who are taught by their teachers to be almost immoderately idealistic—and by you to be like you. The real miseducation is always transmitted unconsciously. Children then repress their true feelings, which would make them look naïve, and win applause by the expert delivery of theatrical— that is, false, group-approved—emotions. We are then dominated morally by our children, who give all the right answers in piping voices and inspired timing. Their motive is to extract prestige and presents, which they obtain in such abundance that they become bored with everything except knowledge that can be used as a step toward still more power. Thus the mind-body split begins early, the exploitative mentality is off to a head start. Sterility and impotence lie ahead for bright youngsters who prematurely need psychiatric guidance. The guidance they get can almost never afford to look into the real trouble, which would constitute an attack on their parents' way of life.

The child who remains naïve is considered backward or mentally retarded. The only way this child can find playmates is through accepting the shrewd mixture of numbness and falsity indoctrinated by "peer groups" of semisavage, unmastered children who want power more than the artless joys of childhood. This is the new categorical imperative in a miniature world which imitates know-it-all stage children: act as if you knew every minute what the point is. If you do not, pretend you do. Don't ever let out your real feelings, they might make someone laugh at you. Unless you know how to dominate a situation, keep your mouth shut and communicate silently that anyone who takes it seriously is a dope. In time you will learn what people want you to say, and then you can rattle it off perfectly. But until then, until your lines are fed you, not a word!

No independence of mind, no powers of creation, will ever grow out of this extremely prevalent, though unofficial, kind of education. Historically it seems to be an other-directed extension of puritanism. Until recently it has had the sanction of success. When our emotional tundra became the most prosperous land of all, our numbness seemed to be justified. When the application of puritan maxims to our great natural resources (and Europe's scientific discoveries) made us the unchallenged masters of the material world, the prestige of numbness redoubled. We rejoiced in our efficiency. A few grumblers among us said that it meant we were only half alive, but the great majority among us believed—and still believes—that we had become strong through our ability to get along on a spartan diet which did not permit emotional satisfaction. Numbness paid.

The prestige of numbness has lately dropped, for a discerning few, with astonishing speed. These few have seen that it can only perform engineering tasks. It does not produce ideas, and these heathen adornments, to the increasing surprise of the majority, are needed urgently for survival. As a nation we are still in the early morning hours of reappraisal. Yet even the majority seems to be waking up to the suspicion that we have been on the wrong path for some time, and that we have no clear idea of what the right one would be.

If there is any common characteristic of the members of the Remnant, I believe it is their instinct for the right path. They know that the first enemy is the numbness they were bullied into when they were young and defenseless. They must remove the false education that seeks to deaden them. The first thing they do, then, is to thaw out. Hence the bohemianism of artists and scientists. It is a risky action, because it violates a strong tabu. Nothing is more harmful to a professional career, for example, than *not* to do as the new puritans do. A career requires constant attention, and it cannot get this from a man who is intent on discovering the delights of the world, rather than its profits. As a matter of fact, there is considerable danger that he will be lost irremediably in his enjoyment of unsuspected pleasures. It may take years to pass beyond these. But in time it can be done, and when it is done he will have a ripe personality to draw upon, rather than the meagerness and slickness that our present methods favor.

30

Cultural Leap

Another source of miseducation might be called cultural leap. This is an undiscussed side of the land of opportunity. Millions of people have been called from rural or semirural backgrounds to complex city tasks that make excessive demands on their psychic resources. They have not been ancestrally conditioned to the technical expertness that their jobs require, and when they succeed in achieving it they have little desire left for mere living. Behind their bleached oak desks sit the bleached experts, while their womenfolk weep at home for lack of love and their children talk like quiz kids. Some essential sap has been drained out of such people. They look like "American Gothics" who wear city clothes. Portrait painters, if they are to catch a flattering likeness, must fall back on morticians' prettifications. No candid, challenging personality has been left. Other-directedness has been at work.

Leslie Fiedler says that Jewish writers are "skillful at creating myths of urban alienation and terror" because they have had previous conditioning in exile and urbanization. "What they in their exile and urbanization have long been, Western man in general is becoming." This suggests that Jews do not lose as much from cultural leap as Gentiles, because they have been better prepared for our day. As a rule, Gentiles either falter in urban competition because they are still under the spell of the past, or they succeed by personal desiccation. Only a few of them are psychically ready for life as it is lived today.

On the other hand, there is no evidence that cultural leap helps anyone's health, whatever his origins. Its body blows are repaired by our new discoveries in antibiotics, tranquillizers, vitamins, hor-

222

mones, and enzymes, but few patients can take advantage of them who do not make a real break with the social values that accompany them. Our new way of life made these new medical discoveries necessary and possible. Usually, it also turns them into mere temporary emollients. Cultural leap leads to conformity in all but a few cases, and conformity makes us ill. This implication of psychosomatic medicine has been appreciated by the English physician Arthur Guirdham: "All diseases, like duodenal ulcer, with an obsessional foundation, are submissions if not to the power of the herd at least to its potential menace." And: "To rise above one's fellows is, in terms of psychology . . . to submit to their dictation. One is driven to rise because one cannot accept a comparison." An obsession with social approval thus leads to many stress diseases. (Guirdham includes hypertension, diabetes, hyperthyroidism, rheumatoid arthritis, coronary disease; others have included cancer.) He says more than once that the only way to avoid or cure these stress diseases is to bring about a complete change of philosophic values. Under the new conditions that prevail in technicized societies, he concludes, there can be no health, except among those who do what they believe in doing. The implications for a Remnant are obvious. Unless you remove your false education and put a real one in its place, you will not "remain."

Another casualty of cultural leap is the art of love. This was a major item on Lawrence's denunciation: that modern industrial society, into which so many of us have leapt from humbler origins, requires a divorce from erotic sensibility. We have lost touch with feeling. We pursue the one green thing obsessively—and inhumanely.

Lawrence was appalled by psychoanalysis. He hated its vulgarizing effect. Only those who insist on a life of delicate feeling will know what he means. Most of us do not even notice the pedantic boorishness coiled in the single psychoanalytic word "forepleasure." The frozen millions have to be told that sexual intercourse is best preceded by some minimal consideration for "the sexual object." There are still a few, however, who whatever their original selfishness, cannot treat anyone as a sexual object. The cultural leap from the rocks and rills to the bedroom is great, and the road is now lined with loathsome books on How to Do It. But there are still a few who do not need them. To the uncivilized, as our films make clear, these few represent effeteness; they are not "regular guys." To the civilized they mean hope.

Alfred Stieglitz used to tell a story about the newly married couple who had grown up in a slum but spent their honeymoon in a de luxe hotel. They ordered eggs for their first breakfast together, and they were served fresh eggs. They did not like them and sent them back. Through their rough speech some alert person in the kitchen understood what was wrong. He sent them up cold storage eggs, and they loved them.

31

Women Need a Favoring Wind

When the gentler emotions have been taken over by the cliché masters of the media, when a people's gifts of tenderness are astutely exploited by salesmen, there is an outbreak of vulgarity which paradoxically is most noticeable among the most sensitive. Poets who write exquisite verses about love also write frightening novels about social decay which contain shocking four-letter words. The most famous example is James Joyce, whose brilliant coarseness in *Ulysses*, for those who understand him, is only the other side of his extreme delicacy in *Chamber Music*. If he had not been so sensitive, so startled and so offended by the gross cynicism of the admen of his day, he would not have responded with so indecent an attack on their hypocritical gentility.

Sensibility that is horrified by the copywriter's daily misuse of love can appear to be mere vulgarity—and to end in a total rejection of love. Tenderness can express itself with a satirical violence that utterly mystifies the naïve. And this confusing state of affairs is considerably worse today than it was at the turn of the century, when Joyce was young and the art of emotional merchandising in its infancy. This confusing state of affairs is one of the principal causes of the current literary stalemate. Today a sensitive writer finds it still more difficult to express his tenderness *directly*—unless he is to address himself solely to a small group of his own kind. The age of electronics, which promised better communication than ever, has greatly widened the gap between reader and writer. And yet, since the oblique, minority expression of sensibility through filth has been overworked, there is a great hunger in both readers and writers for direct expressions of love. It is rarely satisfied.

225

To speak up for sensibility in cynical times makes one ridiculous. Even women, who stand to lose most through coarseness, find it difficult to express their finer emotions. They have to contend with the sexual callousness that has been promoted, among other things, by contraceptives and antibiotics. They too are susceptible to the roughness of mind that usually accompanies our new control of nature. They are also subject to the temptations of exploiting their own femininity. Prostitution of the crude sort seems to be statistically on the decline, but as might have been expected by those disabused of romantic expectations, prostitution has taken new forms. Women sell their bodies less often now than they "sell" their personalities. Such a "sale" meets with full public approval in offices, stores, politics, airplanes, and institutions of higher learning. For it they get fairly well paid—and patted on the decent part of the back. In most cases this kind of exploitation of self seems harmless enough, though it may have something to do with the increase of neurosis among women. Women are expected to be *the* other-directed members of our society, always on the lookout for the feelings of others, and finally more dependent than anyone else on the good opinion of others. It is a definition of insecurity to depend on someone else's approval. This may contribute to the fact that most psychiatric patients are women.

It is even harder for women than for men to complete their private revolutions and become self-reliant. The very possession of a womb makes them subject to far more social pressure. Graceful femininity means acceptance of biological dependence as natural and beautiful. Exceptional women often do not realize their full individuality until after the climacteric. All women suffer seriously when social pressures insist that they be eternally young.

Women need a favoring wind. The masculine cult of efficiency gives them less cultural assistance than it seems to. It tries to bribe them with presents. It denies them the life of sensibility that would make them happier than the best appointed kitchen. When all women have good kitchens, and something to cook in them, a few women will know better what they really want. The emancipation of woman has barely begun.

32

The Only Riches

In some ways a Remnant would correspond to the shamans, or medicine men, who provided the spiritual leadership of primitive tribes. A Remnant could gain no authority today, however, through magic. Its initiation would have to be self-imposed, and not only a toughening but a suppling. Instead of the capacity to dry wet sheets with psychically generated body heat, it would develop the capacity to pick a sound path between mechanism and vitalism. Instead of being able to put its hands unharmed into fire, it would have to match Freud in skepticism and Yeats in fantasy.

A Remnant's initiation, though self-imposed, would have to meet severe traditional requirements. As Mircea Eliade says, while relating ancient preparatory rites to modern times in *Birth and Rebirth*: "initiation lies at the core of any genuine life. And this is true for two reasons. The first is that any genuine human life implies profound crises, ordeals, suffering, loss and reconquest of self, 'death and resurrection.' The second is that, whatever the degree of fulfillment that it may have brought him, at a certain moment every man sees his life as a failure. This vision does not arise from a moral judgment made on his past, but from an obscure feeling that he has missed his vocation; that he has betrayed the best that was in him. In such moments of total crisis, only one hope seems to offer any issue—the hope of beginning all over again."

These words might serve as a definition of the vulnerability required of the Remnant—and the hope it creates from its suffering. But that hope, as we have seen so many times, proves illusory unless it is united with an accurate—that is, a Freudianly skeptical—attitude toward one's fabulous gifts for error. Hence the emphasis here has been on the psychologists *before* the philosophers and *before* the poets. We need a philosopher's steadiness and a poet's freedom, but the best road to such rare equilibrium, for the uprooted man of today, is by way of the psychologists. An attempt to bypass their sharp-eyed critique, however brilliant, means a stunted personality. Our present interregnum is dominated by such stunted personalities, because they make up in intensity what they lack in clarity or honesty. They have given us exciting short-term myths, but now both society and individuals need durable myths that can stand up under the assaults of time and criticism. There is no escape from self-knowledge. As Emerson said, "You are known." If we are ever to find a solid faith again, it must be based on a solid knowledge of man.

Since all experience passes through the psyche, the psychologists remain our best mediators between the new disciplines that we must master and the regenerative power that lies within the unconscious. Some time ago Jung found that "in the American a distance separates the conscious from the unconscious that is not found in Europeans. It is a tension between a high level of culture in the conscious, and an unmediated unconscious primitivity. But this tension provides a psychic potential that endows the American with an indomitable spirit of enterprise and an enviable enthusiasm which we in Europe do not know." Those words were published in 1927. Since then we have shown more "enviable enthusiasm" than power to channel it imaginatively, and we have also been called to a position of world leadership. There is not much evidence as yet that we possess the will or the gift for that leadership, except in technical skills that can be mastered and matched by other nations somewhat faster than we imagined possible. We have put our money on a horse that is a sprinter, and the race is a long one.

Thus the pressure on the Remnant is greater than ever before. Its members probably take longer to mature than anyone else, but they alone can breed a horse that is good for distance.

The Remnant might be described as those people, necessarily few, who retain a sure sense of "the best that is in them." They outwit the subtlest efforts to miseducate them. They acquire *mana*, or a personal power that is more than equal to external pressures. They are *not* crushed by their environment. On the contrary, they come as close as man can come to defeating an ever hostile environment. Their victory is symbolic, however, and can only be appreciated by a few. They are the "saving" Remnant in the sense that, if they become conscious and numerous enough, they save others from being overwhelmed by brute nature. They are rarely thanked for it. But no one else, finally, wins as much respect or wields as much influence.

The Remnant itself is a myth, but the kind of myth that meets the pragmatic test. Its power is real, scientifically demonstrable.

There is only one kind of durable myth, the myth that a person has retrieved from the unconscious, that possesses him with a strong need to express it. The myth that has crowded him out of his own skin. The myth that he shares with his people. This is the kind of myth that people listen to, in time, because it tells them what they knew all along but could not heed or express.

In the presence of this kind of myth, art ceases to be "a thing of no consequence." Science ceases to be a sedative. The antagonisms between science and art and religion and politics are temporarily reconciled. The possessed one, made ready for his task by dispossessing himself of older myths, can meet the demands of his people upon him.

In this sense, a durable myth is simply another name for a tested, empiric truth that enables you to cope with reality, instead of leaving you defenseless before it. Science no longer blocks you, but ignites your mythopoeic spontaneity. The sterner its discoveries, the more intense your aesthetic satisfactions. You detest illusions, except as stage sets, children's games. Existence grows none the less hard, but it has verifiable meaning in mental fertility and bodily health. However painful, your yoke feels mild. Death becomes a constant friendly companion, and you demand nothing after it. Experience will still surprise, terrify, brutalize you—but not for long. Your anxieties provide your fuel, and your humiliations your light.

Lawrence ended his book on America (1924) with a very short paragraph:

The only riches, the great souls.

At the time it seemed flamboyantly romantic. Now it reads like a sober estimate of the requirements of survival. To be able to keep alive today—morally and perhaps physically as well—demands that we first get rid of a systematic, group-approved miseducation which neglects any mention of "great souls," or what they mean or how they are acquired. And then we must re-educate ourselves from solar plexus to the bodily extremities, *one* of which is the head. Magnanimity, or the possession of a great soul, has become a condition of survival. It is also democracy's hope.

The future does not terrify the man who knows he can cope with its worst trials. The tragic sense is the beginning of enjoyment. The eyes of "the shipwrecked" are eyes that light up. When a few people find a way—*after* catastrophe—the others will find a way too.

Notes

Foreword

PAGE x: The author of *The Hollow Men* is T. S. Eliot. PAGE xi: Arnold's use of "remnant" is to be found in his *Discourses in America*, New York, 1907, p. 68. Yeats uses it in his *Autobiography*, New York, 1938, p. 398. The word occurs frequently in the Old Testament—Isa. 1:9; 37:32; Neh. 1:3; Mic. 5:3. Arnold describes Plato's use of the word.

Chapter 1   Faust Is a Boy

PAGE 2: The philosopher is A. N. Whitehead, *Science and the Modern World*, New York, 1925—paperback edition, 1948, p. 200. PAGE 3: The historian is José Ortega y Gasset, *The Revolt of the Masses*, New York, 1932—paperback edition, 1950, p. 116. The journalist is Robert Jungk, *Brighter than a Thousand Suns*, translated by James Cleugh, New York, 1958, p. 327. The psychologist is C. G. Jung, *The Undiscovered Self*, Boston, 1957, p. 99. PAGE 4: Roderick Seidenberg, *Post-Historic Man*, Chapel Hill, North Carolina, 1950, to which my attention was called by Waldo Frank, *The Rediscovery of Man*, New York, 1958, p. 225.

Chapter 2   The Price of Technology

PAGE 6: Herbert Read, *The Innocent Eye*, New York, 1947. PAGE 7: The poet is T. S. Eliot, *For Lancelot Andrews*, London, 1928. The line inverts St. Paul's "The letter killeth, but the spirit giveth life" (II Cor. 3:6). PAGE 7: "another poet" is D. H. Lawrence, *Lady Chatterley's Lover*, Florence, 1928, p. 1. PAGE 11: Gabriel Marcel, *The Decline of Wisdom*, translated by Manya Harari, London, 1954, p. 37. PAGE 10: Boris Pasternak, *Doctor Zhivago*, translated by Max Hayward and Manya Harari, New York, 1958. PAGE 11: Freud is quoted in Hanns Sachs, *Freud, Master and Friend*, Cambridge, Mass., 1944, p. 68.

Chapter 3   Serpent Wisdom for Modern Doves

PAGE 18: Freud, *Civilization and Its Discontents*, translated by Joan Riviere, New York, 1958, p. 61. Jung, *Essays on Contemporary Events*, translated by Barbara Hannah, London, 1947, p. 6. Adler, *Social Interest*, translated by John Linton and Richard Vaughan, London, 1938, p. 73. Adler, *What Life Should Mean to You*, New York, 1937, p. 8. PAGE 19: Fromm, *Escape from Freedom*, New York, 1941. PAGE 20: William Sheldon, *The Varieties of Temperament*, New York, 1942, and *Varieties of Delinquent Youth*, New York, 1949, p. 23. PAGE 20: The caustic Frenchman is said to have been Georges Clemenceau, who lived for a while in the United States, but I cannot find it in his works. The statement has also been attributed to André Malraux. I have heard its equivalent often in conversations in France.

Chapter 4   The Source of Contemporary Power

PAGE 22: David Riesman with Nathan Glazer and Reuel Denney, *The Lonely Crowd*, New Haven, 1953, paperback edition, New York, p. 349. PAGES 23–24: Herbert Marshall McLuhan, *The Mechanical Bride*, New York, 1951, pp. 98, 75. PAGE 26: Luigi Pirandello, *Naked Masks*, New York, 1952—*Henry IV*, translated by Edward Storer.

Chapter 5   The Uproar in Acheron

PAGE 28: Freud, *Basic Works*, translated by A. A. Brill, New York, 1938, pp. 179, 966. Kazin in *Freud and the 20th Century*, edited by Benjamin Nelson, New York, 1957, p. 21. PAGE 31: William Blake, *Poetical Works*, New York, 1941. Walt Whitman, *Leaves of Grass*, New York, 1891, p. 77. William James, *Varieties of Religious Experience*, New York, 1902, Lectures IV and V. Philip Rahv, *Image and Idea*, New York, 1949, p. 1. PAGE 33: Ps. 137.

Chapter 6   Science and Emotion

PAGE 40: Freud, *The Future of an Illusion*, translated by W. D. Robson-Scott, New York, 1928, p. 98. See also Freud's letter to James Jackson Putnam, quoted by Robert Waelder, *The Living Thoughts of Freud*, Philadelphia, 1941, p. 17. Freud's debt to Havelock Ellis is described in *A General Selection from the Works of Sigmund Freud*, edited by John Rickman, New York, 1957, p. 104. For the super-ego see Freud, *The Ego and the Id*, 1923. For the death-instinct see *Beyond the Pleasure Principle*, 1920—both available in paperbacks. PAGE 41: Dante, *Paradiso*, III, 85, Matthew Arnold's translation. Jung, *Psychology and Religion*, New Haven, 1938, p. 114.

Chapter 7   Reinitiation

PAGE 46: "Psychopomp" derives from Hermes Psychopompos, the mythical Greek guide to Hades.

Chapter 8   The Novels of Sigmund Freud

PAGE 53: In contrast to Freud's desire to explain man scientifically, see his words to Albert Einstein, "Doesn't every science come in the end to a kind of mythology?"—*Collected Papers*, London, 1949, V, p. 283. PAGE 54: Ernest Jones, *The Life and Work of Sigmund Freud*, Vol. 1, New York, 1953, p. 317. PAGE 57: Hyman, in *Freud and the 20th Century*, p. 167. The words "nasty, brutish and short" come from Thomas Hobbes, *Leviathan*, Chap. XIII.

Chapter 9   Adler and Women

PAGE 59: Freud, *New Introductory Lectures on Psychoanalysis*, translated by W. J. H. Sprott, New York, 1933, p. 192. PAGE 60: Adler, *Social Interest*, p. 36. PAGE 61: See Joseph Wortis, *Soviet Psychiatry*, Baltimore, 1950, p. 119. Phyllis Bottome, *Alfred Adler, a Biography*, New York, 1939, p. xii.

Chapter 10   Jung and Comedy

PAGE 64: Jung, *Psychology and Religion*, p. 114. PAGE 65: Adler, *What Life Should Mean to You*, p. 8. PAGE 66: Jung, *Modern Man in Search of a Soul*, translated by W. S. Dell and Cary F. Baynes, New York, 1933, p. 70. PAGE 68:

Jung, *The Integration of the Personality*, translated by Stanley M. Dell, London, 1940, p. 305. PAGE 68: Campbell, *The Hero with a Thousand Faces*, New York, 1949, pp. 27 f. PAGE 70: See Freud's letter to his fiancée, Jones, *op. cit.*, p. 190. See also Freud, *Group Psychology and the Analysis of the Ego*, translated by James Strachey, London, 1921. Jung, *Psychology and Alchemy*, translated by R. F. C. Hull, New York, 1953, p. 461. Jung, *Psychological Types*, translated by H. G. Baynes, London, 1923, p. 616. PAGE 71: Freud, *Basic Works*, p. 977. Jung, *Contributions to Analytical Psychology*, translated by H. G. and Cary F. Baynes, 1928, p. 140. PAGE 73: Jung, *Symbols of Transformation*, translated by R. F. C. Hull, New York, 1956, p. 226. PAGE 74: Jung, *Two Essays on Analytical Psychology*, translated by R. F. C. Hull, New York, 1953, p. 223. David Riesman, *Individualism Reconsidered*, Glencoe, Illinois, 1954, p. 100.

Chapter 11   Otto Rank: The Laocoön of Ideology

PAGE 75: Rank, *Will Therapy and Truth and Reality*, translated by Jessie Taft, New York, 1947, p. 250. PAGE 76: Rank, *ibid.*, pp. 213, 233. Rank, *Beyond Psychology*, New York, 1958, p. 170. For Freud's "crapule" see Helen Walker Puner, *Freud*, New York, 1947, p. 109. PAGE 78: Rank, *Will Therapy*, p. 96. PAGE 79: Rank, *Psychology and the Soul*, Philadelphia, 1950, pp. 192 f. PAGE 79: *Beyond Psychology*, p. 12. See also Ira Progoff, *The Death and Rebirth of Psychology*, New York, 1956.

Chapter 12   A French Intruder

PAGE 80: For Janet-Freud controversy see Lewis Way, *Alfred Adler*, London, 1956, p. 25. See also Janet, *Principles of Psychotherapy*, London, 1925, and Jones, *op. cit.*, p. 59. Lionel Trilling, *The Liberal Imagination*, New York, 1950, p. 34. PAGE 81: George Santayana, *Egotism in German Philosophy*, 1940, p. 168, which quotes Montaigne. PAGE 83: D. T. Suzuki, *Introduction to Zen Buddhism*, New York, 1949, foreword by Jung, p 24. PAGE 83: Benoit, *The Supreme Doctrine*, New York, 1955, pp. 114 f. PAGE 84: Huxley's translation appears in *Vedanta for Modern Man*, edited by Christopher Isherwood, New York, 1951, p. 387. The related idea of Yeats is quoted below, p. 183. PAGE 85: *Supreme Doctrine*, pp. 240 f, 106, 109.

Chapter 13   The Americanization of Erich Fromm

PAGE 89: Fromm in *The Family: Its Function and Destiny*, edited by Ruth Nanda Anshen, New York, 1949, p. 358. Riesman, *Lonely Crowd*, p. 349. PAGE 90: Fromm, *Psychoanalysis and Religion*, New Haven, 1959, p. 77 *et seq.* PAGE 91: Fromm, *Sigmund Freud's Mission*, London, 1959, *passim*. PAGE 92: Bettelheim's opinion appeared in the New Leader, Winter Book Number, 1957.

Chapter 14   Karen Horney: A Lost Cause

PAGE 95: Horney, *New Ways in Psychoanalysis*, New York, 1939, pp. 7, 101–103. PAGE 96: *ibid.*, p. 108. Her phrase "womb-envy" was heard by me in a lecture at the New School, *circa* 1947. PAGE 98: Horney, *ibid.*, p. 125 *et seq.* PAGE 102: For debate on American "matriarchy" see Philip Wylie, *Generation of Vipers*, New York, 1942, and J. B. Priestley and Jacquetta Hawkes, *Journey down a Rainbow*, New York, 1955, p. 32.

Chapter 15   Harry Stack Sullivan and the Human Pyramid

PAGE 103: Fromm, *op. cit.*, New York, 1958, p. 93. PAGE 104: Miller, *The Air-Conditioned Nightmare*, New York, 1945, p. 60. Sullivan, *The Interpersonal*

Theory of Psychiatry, New York, 1953, p. 374. PAGE 105: *ibid.*, p. 334. PAGE 106: Sullivan, *ibid.*, p. 74. PAGE 107: Riesman, *ibid.*, p. 47 n. See also Patrick Mullahy, *Oedipus Myth and Complex*, New York, 1948.

Chapter 16   William Sheldon and the Human Physique

PAGE 110: Peter Viereck, *Conservatism Revisited*, London, 1950. PAGE 111: Sheldon, *Psychology and the Promethean Will*, New York, 1936. PAGE 112: Sheldon, *Varieties of Temperament*, pp. 257, 260, 65, 255. Huxley, *The Perennial Philosophy*, New York, 1942, p. 147. PAGE 113: Huxley, "Who Are You?" *Harper's Magazine*, 1944, p. 522. PAGE 115: Sheldon, *Varieties of Delinquent Youth*, p. 800 *et seq.*

Chapter 17   The Existentialists

PAGES 118–119: May, *op. cit.*, p. 11 *et seq.* PAGE 120: Jung, *Modern Man* etc., p. 129. PAGE 120: May, *ibid.*, p. 70. PAGES 122–123: Snow, *op. cit.*, Cambridge, 1959, pp. 2, 35, 51, 12. PAGES 123–125: Sartre, *Being and Nothingness*, translated by Hazel E. Barnes, New York, 1956, p. 557 *et seq.*, and p. 626. Barrett, *Irrational Man*, New York, 1958, p. 222. PAGES 135–136: Frankl, *The Doctor and the Soul*, translated by Richard and Clara Winston, New York, 1955, p. 113. See also Frankl, *From Death-Camp to Existentialism*, translated by Ilse Lasch, Boston, 1959.

Chapter 18   Summation for the Founder

PAGE 127: Reich, *Character Analysis*, New York, 1945; *The Function of the Orgasm*, New York, 1942. George Groddeck, *The World of Man*, translated by M. Collins, London, 1934; *The Book of the It*, translated by V. M. Collins, London, 1950. PAGES 130–131: Jung, *Modern Man* etc., p. 132. For a different opinion see Edward Glover, *Freud or Jung?* New York, 1956. PAGES 131–132: Freud, *Basic Works*, p. 966 *et seq.*, p. 617 n. PAGE 133: Bruner, *Freud and the 20th Century*, p. 258. PAGES 134–135: *The Basic Writings of C. G. Jung*, edited by Violet Staub de Laszlo, New York, 1959, p. 149. PAGES 135–137: Freud, *On Creativity and the Unconscious*, selected by Benjamin Nelson, New York, 1958, p. 226. PAGES 135–137: Freud, *ibid.*, p. 235. See also E. H. Erikson, *Childhood and Society*, New York, 1950; Otto Fenichel, *The Psychoanalytic Theory of Neurosis*, New York, 1945; Karl Abraham, *Selected Papers on Psychoanalysis*, London, 1927; Franz Alexander, *Psychoanalytic Therapy*, New York, 1946; Abram Kardiner, *The Individual and His Society*, New York, 1939; Theodore Reik, *From Thirty Years with Freud*, New York, 1940; Sandor Ferenczi, *Sex in Psychoanalysis*, New York, 1950; Gardner Murphy, *Personality*, New York, 1947; Lionel Trilling, *Freud and the Crisis of Our Culture*, Boston, 1955; Norman O. Brown, *Life against Death*, Middletown, Conn., 1959; Freud, *Collected Papers*, 1950.

Chapter 19   Isaiah Counting Famine

PAGE 142: Crane, *Collected Poems*, edited by Waldo Frank, New York, 1933, p. 7. Kazin, *op. cit.*, p. 21. PAGE 143: Ralph Waldo Emerson, *English Traits*, Boston, 1856.

Chapter 20   The Oldest View

PAGE 144: The information about Columbia University was given me by Professor Steven Marcus. Zilboorg, *Mind, Medicine and Man*, New York, 1951, p. 326.

PAGES 145–147: White, *God and the Unconscious*, Chicago, 1953, p. 41 and *passim*. See also White, *Soul and Psyche*, New York, 1960. PAGES 147–148: Maritain, *Freud and the 20th Century*, p. 230. PAGES 149–150: Tillich, *The Protestant Era*, Chicago, 1948, pp. 228, 148. Tillich, *The Courage to Be*, New Haven, 1952, p. 186. Niebuhr, *Freud and the 20th Century*, p. 259. See also Chad Walsh, *Early Christians of the 21st Century*, New York, 1950, p. 65. PAGE 152: Buber, *Hasidism*, New York, 1948, p. 54. See also Buber, *Eclipse of God*, p. 78; *At the Turning Point*, p. 44. See also *The World of Martin Buber*, edited by Will Herberg, New York, 1956, pp. 20, 31, 61. PAGES 153–154: *Vedanta for the Western World*, edited by Christopher Isherwood, Hollywood, 1946, pp. 53–55. PAGES 154–155: Huxley, *op. cit.*, pp. vii, 114.

Chapter 21   Sex and Philosophy

PAGES 157–158: Kaplan, *Freud and the 20th Century*, pp. 219–228. PAGES 160–161: Jung, *Modern Man* etc., p. 140; *Symbols of Transformation*, p. 222; *The Integration of the Personality*, pp. 293, 61; *Psychology and Religion*, p. 58. PAGE 162: Mann, *Freud, Goethe, Wagner*, translated by H. T. Lowe-Porter, New York, 1937, p. 23. PAGES 163–164: Campbell, *The Masks of God: Primitive Mythology*, New York, 1959, p. 471.

Chapter 22   The Revolt of the Writers

PAGE 165: *Art and Psychoanalysis*, New York, 1957; Trilling, p. 518; Phillips, p. xxiv. Rank, *op. cit.*, p. 430, pp. 427–428. Freud in *Art and Psychoanalysis*, p. 3; Alexander in same, 346; Fiedler, p. 454; Hyman, p. 473. PAGE 167: Jung, *Modern Man* etc., p. 175. The description of Mann as "senatorially robust" is from Trilling.

Chapter 23   On Knowing What You Do

PAGE 170: Charles Williams, *op. cit.*, p. 6. PAGE 171: Phrases from Crane, *The Bridge*. PAGE 174: See Arthur Mizener, *The Far Side of Paradise*, A Biography of F. Scott Fitzgerald, Boston, 1951.

Chapter 24   The Highest Court

PAGES 179–180: Rosenberg, *op. cit.*, New York, 1959, p. 31. Yeats, *Collected Poems*, 1934, p. 284. Eliot, "Tradition and the Individual Talent," *The Sacred Wood*, New York, 1921, pp. 43–44. PAGE 182: *The Ten Principal Upanishads*, translated by Shree Purohit Swami and W. B. Yeats, London, 1937, p. 15. PAGE 183: Yeats, *Autobiography*, p. 318. Ellmann, *James Joyce*, New York, 1959, p. 87. Stanislaus Joyce, *My Brother's Keeper*, New York, 1958. PAGE 185: "grisly old Sykos" comes from *Finnegans Wake*, New York, 1939, p. 115. PAGE 186: *A Franz Kafka Miscellany*, New York, 1946, p. 74, translated by Sophie Prombaum. See also Frederick J. Hoffman, *Freudianism and the Literary Mind*, New York, 1957, p. 194. PAGE 187: Lawrence, *Studies in Classic American Literature*, reprinted in *The Shock of Recognition*, edited by Edmund Wilson, New York, 1943, p. 1010. PAGES 187–190: Lawrence, *op. cit.*, New York, 1960, pp. 11, 9, 13, 15, 18, 53, 21, 27. Kenneth Rexroth, introduction to Lawrence, *Selected Poems*, New York, 1947, p. 8. Lawrence's pride in his status as a novelist is quoted in *The Portable D. H. Lawrence*, edited by Diana Trilling, New York, 1947, p. 308.

Chapter 25   The Remnant Is Not an Elite

PAGE 195: Mills, *The Power Elite*, New York, 1957, p. 361.

Chapter 26   The Guilt of Science

PAGE 197: Jung, *Psychological Types*, p. 541. PAGE 198: Jungk, *op. cit.*, pp. 340–341. See also Pauli, *The Interpretation of Nature and the Psyche*, translated by Priscilla Silz, New York, 1955, p. 149. PAGE 199: Snow, *Science and Government*, New York, 1961. Jung, *Contributions*, etc., p. 145, quoted by Jolan Jacobi, *Psychological Reflections*, An Anthology from the Writings of Jung, New York, 1953, p. 253. PAGE 200: *The New Men*, title of novel about physicists by Snow, New York, 1954. PAGES 201–202: Suzuki, Fromm and Richard de Martino, *Zen Buddhism and Psychoanalysis*, New York, 1960, pp. 24, vii, 52.

Chapter 27   The Politics of Shipwreck

PAGE 205: Ortega y Gasset, *op. cit.*, p. 115. PAGE 210: André Gide, *Journals*, translated by Justin O'Brien, New York 1956, Vol. 1, p. 314.

Chapter 29   Sensibility and Survival

PAGE 219: Phrases quoted from Lawrence, *op. cit.*, p. 913.

Chapter 30   Cultural Leap

PAGE 222: Fiedler, *Love and Death in the American Novel*, New York, 1960, p. 463. PAGE 223: Guirdham, *A Theory of Disease*, London, 1957, p. 136. PAGE 224: The story told by Alfred Stieglitz is from my own recollection. See also Dorothy Norman, *Alfred Stieglitz*, New York, 1960.

Chapter 31   Women Need a Favoring Wind

See also Erich Neumann, *The Great Mother*, translated by Ralph Manheim, New York, 1955; Margaret Mead, *Male and Female*, New York, 1949; Helene Deutsch, *Psychology of Women*, Philadelphia, 1944; Ruth L. Munroe, *Schools of Psychoanalytic Thought*, New York, 1955; M. Esther Harding, *The Way of All Women*, New York, 1932; Theodor Reik, *Of Love and Lust*, New York, 1957; Florida Scott-Maxwell, *Women and Sometimes Men*, New York, 1957.

Chapter 32   The Only Riches

PAGE 227: Eliade, *op. cit.*, translated by Willard R. Trask, New York, 1958, p. 135. PAGE 228: Jung, *Contributions*, etc., p. 140. PAGE 229: "Art a Thing of No Consequence" appears in Ortega y Gasset, *The Dehumanization of Art*, New York, 1956, p. 45. PAGE 229: Lawrence's short paragraph ends his *Studies in Classic American Literature*.

Acknowledgments

Grateful acknowledgment is made to the following publications, where some parts of this book first appeared in considerably different form: *Harper's Magazine*, *The Nation*, *The New Leader*, *The New York Times Book Review*, *Perspectives USA*, *Aujourd'hui*. Other parts were given as talks on the BBC Third Programme.

Index

* References to p. 231 designate bibliographical citations covered in the Notes beginning on that page.